SAINT LEONARD OF PORT MAURICE

THE LIFE
OF
SAINT LEONARD
OF PORT MAURICE

By

Giuseppe Maria of Masserano

Translated by the Oratorian Fathers
of the Brompton Oratory

Gaude Maria Virgo, cunctas haereses
sola interemisti in universe mundo.
–Antiph, Ecclesiae

MEDIATRIX PRESS
MMXXIII

APPROBATION

We hereby approve and sanction the Series of Lives of the Canonized and Beatified Saints, the Servants of God declared Venerable, and others commonly reputed to have died in the odor of sanctity, now in course of publication by the Congregation of the Oratory of St. Philip Neri, and we cordially recommend it to the Faithful, as calculated to promote the glory of God and of His Saints, the increase of devotion, and the spread of our holy Religion.

Given at Westminster, the Feast of the Nativity of our B. Lady, A. D. 1851.

To the regular clergy
Of the catholic church in England, the children of St. Benedict
and St. Bernard, St. Dominic and St. Francis, and the sons.
Of the holy Ignatius, the great master of the spiritual life, and
the nursing-father of saints and martyrs, who, in the
straightness and neglect
Of their unhonored cloisters, or the cheerless solitude
Of their hired lodging, have joyfully embraced the poverty of
Jesus, and earned by loving zeal
The crown of martyrdom, and who, through scenes of awful
sacrilege, and times of bitter persecution, through the long and
weary visitation of active malice or of cold contempt, have
perpetuated, amongst their unworthy countrymen, the blessed
lineage of their holy founders.

ST. WILFRID'S,
FEAST OF ST. BERNARD, MDCCCXLVII

ISBN: 978-1-957066-37-0

Cover art: *Leonardo da Porto Maurizio.*
—Francsco Antionio Vanzo (1754-1836)

Mediatrix Press
607 E 6th Ave
Post Falls, ID 83854
www.mediatrixpress.com

PREFACE

THE following Life is a translation from the Italian of Father Giuseppe Maria, of Masserano, Postulator of the cause. The translation is free, and in some parts slightly abridged; nothing, however, of importance has been omitted. It was published at Rome in years 1796.

CONTENTS

THE LIFE
OF
ST. LEONARD OF PORT MAURICE

PART I

EFFIGIES BEATI LEONAR
ARM. MISS. AP. 1845.

CHAPTER I

The Birth, Country, and Parentage of Blessed Leonard, with the History of His Childhood.

E are told by the Holy Spirit, in the Book of Proverbs, that the "Path of the just is as a shining light, which goeth forwards and increaseth even into perfect day." Such was precisely the career of the just man whom I am about to describe, I mean the Life of Blessed Leonard, who, as soon as he came into the world, and from his earliest years, gave evident signs of that perfect holiness which he continually attained. At a very early age he proved that he had the grace and blessing of Almighty God, and was by Him chosen to accomplish great things, and ever to increase in virtue; during his childhood there shone around him those bright rays of innocence and virtue, which gave a sure hope that he would attain in the end the highest degree of perfection.

In order to gain some useful lessons from this history, I shall divide it into two parts; the first will contain the relation of his admirable works, and also the history of his whole life. The second part will treat of his virtues, which, as they dwelt in his heart, frequently breathed through his lips; and also of those gifts with which the Almighty had so richly endowed him.

Blessed Leonard was born on the 20th of December, 1676, in Port Maurice, at that time a ducal city of the kingdom of Genoa, and in the diocese of Albenga, and on the same day received the sacrament of baptism, with names of Paul Jerome, in the church of the famous college of S. Maurizio. His parents were Dominic Casanuovo, and Anna Maria Berga, honest people, possessing ample means of subsistence, and virtuous, living in the fear and love of God, especially the father, who, in order to preserve his chastity from danger, made a vow when he first commanded a

1

vessel, never to admit a woman amongst his passengers. He kept this vow so strictly, that on one occasion, being obliged for some reason to take one on board at Genoa, he immediately left the vessel to the care of the sailors, and returned by land to his native place, eighty miles distant from Genoa, in the depth of winter, over hills and roads almost impassable. On the death of his first wife, the mother of Blessed Leonard, which occurred when the latter was only two years old, he formed a second marriage with Maria Riolfi, a native of Artallo, by whom he had four children, three sons and a daughter; the eldest of them, after having studied medicine for a while, determined to follow the example of Blessed Leonard, at that time a monk in the retreat of S. Buonaventura in Rome, and took the name of Father Antonio in the same convent, where he became a priest, and died at an advanced age, having led a most exemplary life. The second son remained in the world, and the youngest assumed the habit of the Minori Riformati in Florence, and afterwards that of San Francesco del Palce, near Prato, of which his blessed brother was afterwards superior. The daughter also renounced the world, and became a nun of the Dominican order, in the convent of S. Catherine of Sienna in Taggia, where she took the name of Sister Mary Magdalene. These were the five blessed fruits which Almighty God vouchsafed to grant to the two marriages of the good Dominic Casanuovo. This worthy man, who, by his kind and winning manner, made everyone in his employ obedient to the will of God and lead Christian lives, passed into a better world on the 18th of March, 1721, with the praise and blessing of all good Christians, for his many works of mercy, and the great care he had taken of his children, especially Paul Jerome, in whom he had discovered an early promise of holiness and virtue, and pleased himself with the conviction that the child so dear to him was created for Paradise.

Much delighted was Dominic in observing the dispositions of his beloved son, so spiritual and full of devotion, and desired to educate him entirely without assistance; but on considering how frequently his profession obliged him to leave home, he thought it better to consign him to the care of John Paul Casanuovo, his father, and the grandfather of his children, a man of perfect integrity, devout and well mannered, who instructed him in everything worth acquiring, and led him on in the love and fear of God. From his earliest years Blessed Leonard showed no inclination for the amusements and games of children; the only thing which gave him delight was that of raising little altars, and forming religious processions, to which he invited his companions; then they said prayers, sang hymns, and often preached short sermons, to the great edification of all present. It was wonderful to see a child of his tender years every morning and evening saying the Rosary and other prayers with the greatest devotion, so entirely giving himself to God and his blessed Mother. The love and respect he bore towards his stepmother was so great, that he always spoke of her as his "Mamma," saying, that Almighty God having taken his own mother had given him her instead. In speaking of his father he used to say, that if he had not given him a good education he should have been worthless, and always thanked God for giving him so excellent and kind a parent. He was beloved by all who knew him, especially his father and stepmother, to whom he endeared himself by his perfect obedience, piety, and devotion. From his earliest years he manifested a most tender devotion to the Blessed Virgin Mary, which increased wonderfully as he grew in years.

He raised a little altar to her in his own room, and besides his many prayers and devotions performed at home, he would often walk barefoot to the church of the Madonna dei Piani, two miles distant from Port Maurice. Here he poured forth his pious prayers; and on one occasion in particular, when Naples had suffered from an earthquake, he prayed fervently to the Mother of God, that by her intercessions the country might not be again visited by so severe a calamity. In company of his chosen companions he also visited other churches, where, after having prayed with them, he gave them instructions in his simple childish way in all the Christian doctrines, and the means of avoiding sin.

One day on returning from Oneglia by the seashore, they were met by a sailor, who stopped blessed Leonard, who was then about ten years old, and his companions, and beginning with caressing and giving them presents, he ended by endeavoring to lead them into sin. The innocent children were astonished and frightened at this, and finding themselves like young lambs in the fangs of a wolf, in a solitary place, with no human aid, they prayed to God for assistance, and took to flight as fast as they could, the most certain means of escaping similar dangers. The first to run away was our Blessed Leonard, who was quickly followed by the rest. The wicked man, seeing himself thus foiled, was enraged, and pursued them sword in hand, but he did not succeed in overtaking them, and they arrived safe at Port Maurice, and visited the nearest church to return thanks to God for having so mercifully delivered them from the danger of temptation. He was, in short, from his very childhood entirely given up to religious duties, and was always held up as a bright example to his companions; his only care was to keep from sin, and preserve his innocence. The first years of his life were occupied solely in religious exercises, but he afterwards applied himself at the public school, where he was placed to every branch of learning suited to the age and his station in life, with so much diligence and profit, as to gain the praises and good opinion of all the masters. Thus his early piety, together with his literary acquirements, clearly proved to all interested in him, that he was destined in after years for great things, and that in time he would attain an eminent degree of perfection. It became generally believed and understood that Almighty God had filled the soul of His servant with special

Divine graces from his birth; and the dutiful obedience and attention to his studies gained him the esteem and love of those who had the care of his education, and all who knew him in Port Maurice.

CHAPTER II

Blessed Leonard Goes to Rome;
His Life as a Secular in That City.

BLESSED LEONARD had reached the age of twelve years, when the fame of his spotless purity, devotion, and extraordinary talents became known to Agostino Casanuovo, his paternal uncle, who was living in Rome, in easy circumstances, who sent for him, in order to have him instructed in Christian knowledge, and the general literature, which he did most conscientiously and thoroughly, giving him a master well qualified for the task of instructing youth, and a pious confessor, Father Grifonelli, of the Chiesa-Nuova, and in a very short time he increased so much in virtue and learning, as to entirely gain the affections of his uncle. In fact, he could not help observing how very superior he was to his two sons, in good manners, love of learning, seriousness, modesty, humility, and devotion, and for this reason treated him with greater affection. Blessed Leonard well repaid his uncle's love, and obeyed him in all things, for he soon perceived how profitable to him were the counsels of this good man.

After remaining three years at a private school, Agostino Casanuovo thought proper to send him to the Roman college, where he would have for a master one famed for virtue and learning, Father Tolommei, a Jesuit, who, for his great merits, afterwards became cardinal. He remained for some time under the tuition of this gifted man, and others of the same establishment, who reported so favorably of him, that he was considered competent to teach in the Church. He was about the age of sixteen when he was sent from the private school of Don Francesco Santoleri, where he had learnt grammar, to the Roman College, where, for two years, he studied humanity and rhetoric.

St. Leonard of Port Maurice

From thence he was sent to the Minerva, to learn elocution, and afterwards returned to the Roman College, where he went through the whole course of philosophy, under the direction of Father Tolommei. During the time he was studying logic, he began to attend the oratory of Father Caravita, into which he was afterwards admitted, and reckoned amongst the twelve members of that community, who, for their devotion and zeal in the salvation of souls, give instructions in the church, and lead those who on feast days had been in the habit of idling in the streets, to the missions and sermons, and are called the twelve Apostles. It was at this time that he gave himself in an especial manner to a devout and spiritual life, approaching the sacraments on all feast days, and recommending his soul to God every morning and evening, as if he were about to die. He was very modest, humble, devout, studious, and diligent, and was never heard to say or to do anything that could give scandal; on the contrary, all his words and actions were admirable. In conversing with his companions, it was always on the subject of religion, or study, so that he became a model of perfection, and a bright example to all in the college. From his love of solitude and retirement, he had few companions, but these were worthy of him; he carefully avoided those who were leading sinful lives, and in this he succeeded so well, that in after life he used to say, that through the grace of God, during the time he passed at school and college, he always found his masters and companions endowed with virtue and holiness. One of his school companions was Luigi Foggia, afterwards a gilder by profession, whom he held in high esteem. He used to say, that he possessed a friend from whose lips he had never heard anything but heavenly doctrine, and from whom he had learned that great maxim, that he who would keep from falling into sin must always remember that he is in the presence of God. He related of this same friend, that he one day asked him to go and hear a sermon, and conducted him to the gallows, on which a criminal who had just been executed was still hanging. "Behold the preacher," said he, "the man who leads a sinful life must sooner or later be brought before the judgment seat of God, for he who does not fear God is capable of committing any kind of iniquity; this fearful spectacle must excite compunction, and give us a greater horror of sin."

Pietro Miré, of the same college, who, for his good qualities, became the friend of blessed Leonard, relates of him amongst many written testimonials in his favor, that during one vacation, when he accompanied him to his uncle's country house, he proposed that on the journey they should say the Rosary, and so commence their holiday with devotion. During an uninterrupted friendly intercourse of five years, from the time blessed Leonard became a member of the oratory of Father Caravita, he edified all his companions with his perfect humility, going to them for instructions in the observance of the rules of the congregation, all of which he kept to the letter, at the time when all looked on him as their example. In order to exercise himself in all the offices of that congregation, he went out early on feast days into the squares and public places in Rome, to exhort the people to attend the sermons, or retreats, which at that time the Fathers of the Society of Jesus were giving in certain churches. He was only seventeen when he was received into this community, but he took upon himself the work of an Apostle with so much humility and discretion, as well as zeal, that he succeeded wonderfully, leading many into the Church, and never ceasing in his holy work, or seeming the least disturbed, however he might be ill-treated by the idle and vicious, and loaded with contempt and injuries. He was not satisfied with the great devotion, and the many religious exercises which were practiced, and by him in particular, in the oratory of Father Caravita, but he joined that of S. Philip Neri, where, as I have already mentioned, he had for his confessor, Father Grifonelli. Besides this, intent on practicing every virtue, and the studies suitable to his years, he read many spiritual books, particularly "The Devout Life," by Francis of Sales, which he always carried with him wherever he went, having a great devotion for that saint. He constantly frequented the sacraments, and found his greatest delight in visiting churches and hearing sermons, a great portion of which he remembered, and afterwards repeated to the servants, who esteemed him as a youth of steadfast piety and great virtue. Amongst the many mortifications he practiced, he related of himself, that when he was a scholar, in making his general confession to Father Grifonelli in the private chapel which had once belonged to S. Philip Neri, Almighty God vouchsafed to give him much contrition, which soon changed into another feeling, an increase of the love of mortification and penance; he added with perfect humility that the fervor of contrition instantly left him. He preached in Rome in 1749, and in exhorting the people to preserve the grace of God, he advised them, besides other means, to join some confraternity, assuring them that he spoke from experience, and attributed the little good he had in him, and the evil he had avoided, to the society and prayers of the young men of the oratory of Father Caravita, and that of S. Philip.

In this mode of life he became so inflamed with divine love, and the desire of suffering, and mortification of the flesh, that when he returned to his uncle's house, he could speak of nothing but spiritual things, the Lives of the Saints, or the lectures and sermons he had heard in the oratory and churches.

At his meals even he could not refrain from speaking of spiritual things; sometimes he forgot to eat, and his uncle, seeing supper over before he had eaten a morsel, was obliged to check his ardent spirit, by telling him to eat his supper, that he had said enough to induce all present to imitate the saints of whom he had been speaking. However, some amongst them said within themselves, "That young man will one day be a famous preacher;" others discovered that it was for a mortification he passed suppertime discoursing in this way, as in the meantime everything on the table would become quite cold, and not so pleasant to the taste. In the same way he most studiously concealed other penances which he imposed on himself to mortify the flesh and subject it to the spirit, but, notwithstanding his care, many in the house were aware that in the night he left his bed, and slept on the bare cold pavement of his room, resting his head on a stone which be concealed in his room, in which he kept also several instruments of penance, a discipline, hair shirts, etc., of which it was evident he made use. Such, in short, was his mode of life. His uncle, seeing him given up to severe mortifications, so retired, always shut up in his room, began to fear his health would be injured, and wrote to his father on the subject. So innocent, exemplary, and mortified was his life, that he edified all in the house. Most wonderful did they think his virtue and the inclination he manifested for the apostolic ministry, predicting future greatness, and that he would be a saint.

CHAPTER III

*Blessed Leonard Manifests a Vocation to the
Religious Life. The Difficulties He Had to
Encounter in Carrying it into Effect.*

E had for some time past, as I have already said, felt almost certain of a vocation to the religious life, without, however, having determined what order he would join, but, with fervent prayer, added to severe penances, in order to discover the will of God, he experienced an increasing desire in his heart, and in the nineteenth year of his age it was proved most decidedly. He very soon communicated the fact to his confessor, Father Grifonelli, who, knowing so well the holiness and virtue of his penitent, made up his mind that it was from God; still, however, he determined to prove it in various ways, exercising him in every virtue, to which he showed the most perfect obedience. On one occasion he sent him to a library in Rome to buy a book of engravings bound together with the fables of Esop, Bertoldo, and Bertolini. Although Blessed Leonard saw in an instant the impossibility of finding such a book, and the contempt and ridicule he should bring on himself by asking for it, he went as he was desired, and returned to Chiesa Nuova, quite joyful for having patiently endured the scorn and derision, saying to Father Grifonelli, that he had not succeeded in finding the book he wanted, but that he was willing to return and make a more diligent search. The only reply Father Grifonelli made, was to tell him he must be very foolish indeed not to have found a book so common and well known, to which he said not a word in defense. Whilst the wise and cautious director in this way made sure of the vocation of blessed Leonard, he continued to exhort him to pray for a clearer manifestation of the Divine Will, which he did, and redoubled his penances and mortifications. One day, when he was passing by the Gesú, his thoughts occupied with the order he was to choose, he saw two monks poorly clad, and very humble and recollected in appearance; he was struck by their deportment, and as he himself afterwards said, in speaking of his vocation, they seemed to him like two angels from heaven, and he was instantly seized with a desire to join their order, but not knowing to which order they belonged or what monastery they inhabited, he followed them in order to discover, and saw them enter the convent or retreat of S. Buonaventura, then inhabited by the Minori Riformati of Francis. He entered the church at the most favorable time, just when they had begun Compline, and these words were intoned, "Converte nos Deus salutaris noster," and he felt a deep impression made in his heart; enlightened by the Holy Spirit, he determined at once to join this order, saying within himself, "Haec est requies mea." He returned to Father Grifonelli, and after having related what had occurred, he turned to him, expecting to be told plainly whether it was the will of God he should take this step. The prudent father, who had never given a decided answer to the repeated questions regarding his vocation, remained silent, reflecting on what he had heard a little while, and then told him that he had a true vocation, and also assured him that he believed it to be the will of God he should enter the convent of S. Buonaventura, with which Father Grifonelli was well acquainted, and of which he knew exactly the mode of life. All these particulars have been mentioned by those who gave their evidence in the process of beatification, and were made known by blessed Leonard, who added, that Father Grifonelli, after having assured him of his vocation, in order to give him courage and time for preparation, often sent him to the convent of S. Buonaventura, and ordered him to lay open his conscience to certain learned and pious persons, in order to avoid the possibility of error.

He placed himself under the most entire obedience to three

religious, who at that time were highly esteemed in Rome, Father Baldigiani, a Jesuit, Father Pio di S. Columba, superior that year of the retreat of S. Buonaventura, and a Dominican father who lived in S. Sabina, but whose name is not recorded. To them he made known the desire of his heart, and having the assurance of all three that his vocation came from God, and that it was His blessed will that he should become a Franciscan, he determined to follow it in spite of all the opposition and obstacles he knew he would have to encounter. He met with violent opposition from his uncle, who, when he heard of it, was very indignant, reproved him severely, and tried to prevent him executing his design, telling him that his father would be greatly displeased, for he had sent him to Rome to study physic, and destined him for that profession; he placed before him the severity of the rule, and when he found he could not succeed, he treated him with harshness, contempt, and disdain; and at last, finding him firm and resolute, he turned him out of his house, and he was forced to seek a home with Leonardo Ponzetti, another relative, whom he intreated to intercede for him with his uncle to obtain that which he so ardently desired, but he refused to see him or even give him the small sum of money requisite for his clothing; he was obliged to beg it of his other relations in Rome. Far different, however, did his good father Dominic Casanuovo act. On reading his son's letter, intimating his intentions, he was struck to the heart, and wept bitterly, and thought only of the separation from a child he so tenderly loved, and in whom his highest hopes were centered. Yet with the letter in his hand he went into the church, and prostrating himself before the altar, offered him as a sacrifice to God; and very soon after sent his reply and consent, saying, that by doing so he fulfilled the will of Him whose servant he was. His father, acting in this heroic manner, gave him great satisfaction, but the continued opposition of his uncle was a severe trial to him; he was at last obliged to leave his house and take up his abode in that of Leonardo Ponzetti, paternal grandfather of Don Giacinto Ponzetti, the private chaplain of his holiness Pope Pius VI, where he was kindly received. He entreated his host to assist him in his resolution to embrace the religious life, which he did so well, that when at last he attained the end he so ardently desired, he took the name of Leonardo, as a memento of the services rendered him. Another obstacle was raised at this time; his companions, by whom he was much beloved, represented to him his delicate constitution, and reminded him how frequently during his life as a secular, when well fed and clothed, he was sick, and that his strength would certainly give way in the religious life, when he would be obliged to conform to a severe rule. This reasoning caused him much grief, and he began to fear that after having assumed the habit, he would be forced to lay it aside and be dismissed from the novitiate; however, he said one day to his friend Pietro Mir, that if it was decided that he had not strength for the rule of the order, he would retire into the country, to his native place to instruct in piety and learning the children of the poor. They also reminded him, that if he joined the retreat of S. Buonaventura, he who was so zealous for the salvation of souls could not be employed in so meritorious a work, because there they attended only to their own sanctification, for the first of the order who ever applied himself to the apostolic ministry was Blessed Leonard.

In the midst of all these difficulties and objections, he turned to God alone in the firm belief that it was His holy will that he should embrace the religious life, and prayed without ceasing. To inure himself to the rigorous rule, he began to practice self-denial in everything, fervently praying for strength to follow out his pious design. Almighty God vouchsafed to hear him, and inspired him to leave off his penances for some time. When in a few days his health was quite established, and he felt more than ever thankful and grateful to the Giver of all good, Who never fails to help those who trust in Him. Having at length overcome every obstacle, he went to the retreat of Buenaventura, and presented himself to the superior, Father Pio di Columba, an excellent man, who afterwards founded the retreat in Florence and died there; he threw himself at his feet, and humbly besought him to admit him into his order. The father Guardian did not for a moment hesitate to grant his request, for he perceived at once his heavenly dispositions, from his humble and sensible way of speaking, his sincerity and openness of heart, and felt sure that he was fitted for that sacred place, into which, in the next reception of novices, he promised he should be admitted, provided he remained steadfast in his resolution, and continued in prayer to God. As soon as he had received this reply, so consoling to him, he went to Chiesa-Nuovo, to inform his confessor of the gracious manner in which his request had been received, and the hope given him of being received into the Franciscan order. Having with great fervor sought the Divine assistance for the favorable issue of this his most ardent desire, in September, 1649, the time fixed by the Fathers of the Minori Riformati for the reception of novices, he was admitted into the monastery of S. Francesco a Ripa, as one of the elected for the retreat of S. Buonaventura. He was then in the twentieth year of his age, endowed with every virtue requisite for the religious life, calm and cheerful, and entirely detached from the world, his friends, and relatives. In leaving Rome for the convent of Santa Maria di Ponticelli, the novitiate for the retreat, the only thing about which be concerned himself was to consign to the care of his best friend, Pietro Mire, his youngest brother; he gave him at the same time his writings, desiring him to give them to his brother when he was old enough to appreciate them. This brother, after having studied medicine in Rome for some time, also became a monk in the retreat of S. Buonaventura, and took the name of Father Antonio.

Blessed Leonard arrived at the convent of Santa Maria delle grazie, and was received by the father guardian with affection and true charity. When he had ended the spiritual exercises, he was clothed on the 2nd of October, 1697, when he changed his name of Paul Jerome for that of Leonard, for the reason mentioned above.

CHAPTER IV

The Conduct of Blessed Leonard During His Novitiate and Studies, until He Became a Lecturer on Philosophy.

THE zealous and ardent youth being admitted to the Franciscan order, in the convent of Santa Maria delle grazie in Ponticelli, began the year of his novitiate under the direction of Father Bernard of Calenzana, a man famed for his zeal and austerity for six months, and after that he was subject to the changes which usually occur in monasteries. Father Cristino of Oneglia succeeded Father Bernard as his director, and by these two excellent men was Blessed Leonard instructed in the observance of the rule, and all which regarded the religious life and his spiritual well-being; he was also tried in many of those mortifications customary in the retreat, especially with the novices, in order to discover if they have a real vocation. However, in consequence of the death of those who were his masters or companions, little is known of him and the virtues he practiced, excepting that he began, and continued his novitiate with much fervor, and was most zealous in the exact observance of the rule and constitutions of the retreat, and by his modesty, good behavior, and the practice of every virtue, he distinguished himself even amongst the most fervent of his companions, and became the admiration and example of all the community many of whom predicted his future greatness and sanctity. He himself, after he had been many years in the order, in speaking of his novitiate, used to call the day on which he was clothed in the religious habit the day of his conversion, and the year, the holy year, lamenting with great humility that he had lost much of the fervor he then possessed, and had gone back instead of advancing in the way of virtue. He was admitted into the order on the 2nd of October, 1698, in the convent of Santa Maria delle grazie, and consecrated forever to God with the three vows.

He had at this time formed a rule for the employment of his time in the study of religious perfection, spiritual reading, prayer, and attention to all which his state required, and also determined to keep the vows he had made to the very letter, and was most particular in the exact fulfilment of them, not only in things of importance, but also in minor matters. When he had finished his novitiate and went to Rome to go through the ordinary courses of philosophy and theology, he was most diligent and attentive in keeping the promises he had made, and was most earnest in exhorting his friends and companions to be faithful to God even in small things, and exact in every ordinance of religion, telling them that they should never consider anything unimportant which is pleasing or displeasing to God; he would say, "If now, when we are young, we make light of small things, when we shall be old and have more liberty, we shall fail in greater and weightier matters of the law." He often spoke in this way, and very wonderful did it seem to the community, when they beheld this youth so fervent in the practice of every virtue, and leading others to the same degree of perfection. At the time of recreation, when they were walking in the garden, he endeavored to animate every one present with the same degree of fervor, and would often say to his companions, "Let us hope in God, and with His grace, which never fails to assist those who ask for it in faith and humility, we may not only become good men, but even may be saints."

He persuaded his companions to choose every week one virtue in particular to practice, and gave them advice as to the manner of performing it. In the conferences they held amongst themselves, he induced those who had fallen into sin to kneel before one of his companions, and beg him, in charity, to warn him of his failing, and promise, with the Divine aid, to amend. With this holy zeal he gained much for himself as well as his friends, and by degrees converted the recreation into a school of perfection. Very often he spoke with great delight of the desire he had of going amongst the heathen to convert souls to Christ, to shed his blood and sacrifice his life, if called on to do so. So strong in him was this desire that he was constantly fancying himself amongst a barbarous people, what he would say, and what means he would use to induce them to hear the Gospel, how he would behave if he were taken and imprisoned, what kind of martyrdom he would suffer, and what prayers and acts he would make when he was about to die for the love of God. It happened about this time that Monsignor di Tournon, afterwards a cardinal of Holy Church, was preparing to go on a mission to China, and wished to take with him some zealous and fervent laborers in the Lord's vineyard, capable of succeeding in so arduous and difficult an undertaking. Blessed Leonard, on hearing this, determined to offer himself for the great work, and after some deliberation with the superior and cardinal, it was decided that he, with Father Pietro da Vicovaro, should go to China. This determination, however, was not carried into effect, in consequence of some difficulties which arose, to the great regret of the servant of God, who, in speaking of it, used to say that he was not worthy to give his life for the love of Jesus, and when he heard that the Christians had suffered persecution in China, he would raise his eyes to heaven, and exclaim, "I ought to have been there, and should have been there, but for my sins." Thus did he see extinguished the desire he had so long cherished, to promulgate and even die for the true faith.

Having abandoned the hope of going to China, he desired to go on the mission of the Vale of Lucerne, but by the advice of Cardinal Colleredo he gave it up, being assured that it was not the will of God he should convert heretics, but that he was destined for a missioner in Italy. We shall presently see that the cardinal was inspired to give this advice, and so it was felt by Blessed Leonard, who never again desired to be sent to distant lands, but applied himself to the study of theology in the retreat of S. Buonaventura, and was afterwards sent to give missions in different parts of Italy. The father superior of the retreat sent a request to Father Pio di San Columba, to appoint one of the monks preacher during Lent in the Conservatorio of S. John Lateran, in which three hundred girls were then assembled, and whose confession were heard by the FF. of S. Buonaventura. Blessed Leonard was chosen for this office, although he was then only a student and in deacon's orders, for in several discourses given by him in the refectory he had displayed much talent and ability in preaching.

He received the order, bowed his head in obedience, disposed himself to set about it, and in a few days left the convent of S. Buonaventura for the Conservatorio, undertook and finished the Lenten duties with so much edification, that for a long time after they never ceased speaking of the fruits of his preaching. The spiritual director of the girls was much edified and pleased in hearing him, and seeing the compunction caused by the efficacy of his words, and the truly apostolic spirit by which he was moved, full of admiration and wonder, exclaimed: "This young man will be a sounding trumpet of the Gospel, and lead many into the way of salvation." Soon after this he was ordained priest in Rome, and from that time began a course of life even more perfect than his former one; he went to confession every morning before he said mass, and frequently confessed both morning and evening, in order to render himself more pure and spotless before celebrating the holy sacrifice, which he always performed in the most perfect manner with all the ceremonies appointed by the Church. To the disciplines, fasts, and other mortifications prescribed by the severe rule of the retreat, he added many more, and besides the exact fulfilment of his profession, he practiced many virtuous and meritorious works, which excited the wonder and admiration of the whole community, who never, on any occasion, discovered anything in his actions or words which did not tend to edification. Meanwhile the course of study required was ended, but he still continued to apply himself in teaching others; and in the many discourses he held on the subject he exhorted all to the practice of virtue and spiritual perfection; and often advised them never to cease from application to study, for without it the knowledge of the glory of God and the salvation of souls could not be acquired, and he would add, "that in all his studies the glory of God was his sole aim and end;" during the whole course of his life he had always united the study of holiness with that of science.

CHAPTER V

Blessed Leonard Is Appointed Professor of Philosophy. Is Taken Ill and Sent to Naples, and from Thence to Port Maurice, for the Restoration of His Health.

THE superiors felt so sure of the talent and virtue of blessed Leonard, that they had no hesitation in appointing him philosophical lecturer in the retreat of S. Buonaventura. He accepted the office, and everyone hoped he would have great success in teaching in the schools; however Almighty God, in His adorable providence, disposed it otherwise; he was destined to give instructions from the pulpit instead of the chair of the lecturer, and before the expiration of the year he was obliged to resign the office. His constitution was naturally weak, and in consequence of his intense study and severe penances, he had quite lost his strength, and was obliged to go to the infirmary, where every means was used to restore his health. The fathers discovered to their great sorrow that his malady was rapidly increasing, and that he was beginning to spit blood; the physicians pronounced him to be consumptive, and considered his case hopeless; he was ordered to Naples, where he remained some months, but as he became worse there, the father guardian wrote to desire him to return to Rome which order he immediately obeyed. From thence he was sent to Vallecorsa, the climate being considered most salubrious, and with the permission of the superior he remained there some months, without however deriving any benefit. But for all this, weak and ill as he was, not liking to be entirely unemployed, he used to go on feast days to preach in the oratory of S. Antonio; and as they were then employed in building the church and the convent for the Minori Riformati, he exhorted the people, after the sermon was ended, to assist in good works by carrying stones, and to encourage them, he loaded himself with the first stones and led the way, when all followed him in procession with the utmost eagerness. Finding the air of Rome did him no good, he was advised to return to the Infirmary of the retreat, but here he became worse, notwithstanding the care and remedies used. The doctors, not knowing what further means to use, suggested that he should try the effect of his native air; consequently, the father guardian obtained permission for him to go to Port Maurice. He accordingly left Rome in the year 1704, and on arriving at his native place he was received into the monastery of the Annunziata of the Minori Osservanti, where he was most carefully attended to. Having availed himself of every earthly assistance, he turned with trust and confidence to the Blessed Virgin, beseeching her to intercede with her Divine Son that his health might be restored, and promised if she obtained this blessing, that he would henceforth give himself up entirely, with the help of God, to the mission for the conversion of sinners. His prayer was granted, and in a very short time he recovered entirely from that disorder from which he had suffered for five years, and was quite able to undertake the laborious duties of which we shall speak in the course of the present history. As he had not received permission from the superior to begin a regular course of sermons, he preached in the meantime several discourses in praise of some of the Saints, when he gave a proof of his eloquence, although some time after, in speaking of it, he said he had injured his health and done no good. He gave at this time some meditations on the Passion of our Lord, to which he had a great devotion; and in order to excite it in the people, he introduced the pious exercise of the "Way of the Cross," which he practiced as long as he lived, showing great devotion to it, and representing the infinite treasure of indulgences which those who joined in the devotion would gain. When he went to live in the convent of the Minori Osservanti, he placed the stations in fourteen chapels which were built in the square by the benefactors of the convent, and under the pictures painted by himself, he wrote with his own hand verses on the different stages of the Passion, and also suitable meditations. When the chapels were quite finished, he devoted himself to this holy exercise, which he celebrated processionally with a priest, in a cope, and ended with benediction of the blessed Sacrament, and a most fervent discourse; he also placed the stations in the garden of the convent.

In the thirtieth year of his age blessed Leonard was approved of by Monsignor Giorgio Spinola, bishop of Albenga, to hear confessions, and as he was so well aware of his zeal for the salvation of souls, he gave him full faculties for this important duty throughout his diocese, consequently he began to attend in the confessionals and preach with so much fervor that the fruits were most abundant. In 1708 he began his first mission in Artallo, a town two miles distant from Port Maurice; he went there every morning and returned in the evening when the mission was ended; the fatigue was very great, for as he had no one to assist him in preaching, giving instructions, and hearing confession, he took upon himself alone the laborious office of missionary. Although it was winter, he walked there and back barefoot; but be was amply repaid for the fatigue, for the mission for which he had prepared with so many prayers ended so happily, that he gained courage and strength to continue his apostolic ministry to the greater glory of God, and he was sent to give another in the church of the "Madonna dei Piani," which was also most successful.

One evening when he was returning as usual to the convent, he perceived a man following him, who seemed in great distress; the servant of God stopped and began to speak to him, and inquired what had happened, for he was ready to give him assistance. The poor man fell on knees, and replied, weeping, "Father, you see at your feet the greatest sinner on earth!" Blessed Leonard was touched by this reply, and said, "And you,

my son, have found one who will be to you a loving father." He
then encouraged him to be reconciled to God, conducting him to
the convent, and having heard his confession, sent him home
quite joyful, released of a heavy load of sins, which for some time
past had burdened his conscience. He was invited to preach at
Caramagna, on the feast of S. Bartholomew. On his way there,
being informed of the manner in which that day was spent, in
dancing and other amusements, he strongly deprecated and
preached against such abuses and disorder, telling them that it
was at balls the devil always gained so many souls;
notwithstanding this, a great many who had heard him, the
moment they came out of the church wont as usual to the dance.
Seeing this, he took a crucifix in his hand, and accompanied by
two men with lighted torches, repaired to the place of meeting.
At his appearance the musicians and all assembled were
beginning to take flight, but he exhorted them to stay, when he
preached with so much fervor and zeal that they burst into tears,
and the scene of festivity and amusement was very soon
converted into one of lamentations and penance. It happened
that whilst he was preaching an arm of the crucifix detached
itself from the cross. As soon as the people perceived it, they
uttered a loud cry, calling on God for mercy; he availed himself
of this circumstance to inveigh more strongly against the sin of
abusing and profaning the feasts of the saints, and added, that
perhaps it was the will of God to give them this sign, and that He
would visit them in His anger if they did not promise never more
to desecrate the holy days. The people were struck with terror,
and promised to keep the feasts of the church with due reverence
for the future. The good missionary, seeing the Lord so blessed
his labors, took courage in fulfilling the promise made to Him, to
promote, by his preaching and instructions, the spiritual good of
his fellow men.

Not content with this but bearing in mind the strictness of
the life in the Retreat, he determined ever to correspond fully to

his vocation, considering the circumstance of Father Tommaso being elected minister of the Minori Osservanti, of the province of Genoa, a man well known for his talent and virtues, then professor of theology there, and who had also been so in the convent of S. Buonaventura when the Blessed Leonard was there, he, after much deliberation, decided that Almighty God had in His just designs opened a way for him to institute in this province a retreat for those who desired to lead a more retired and devout life. He mentioned this to the new provincial, who willingly gave it his approval, and offered him any convent he thought suitable for the purpose. Blessed Leonard was rejoiced at having succeeded in his project and having found some zealous religious to join him, he chose the convent of Bernadino, which being a mile distant from the town of Albenga, seemed most suitable for the solitary life they were to lead.

He retired to his convent in the year 1708, in company with several others animated with the same spirit, and led so exemplary a life, that the people in the neighborhood were greatly edified by their holy life, and the great benefit gained by the preaching of the divine law, and the assistance given in the confessionals. The bishop was much consoled, and rejoiced to see the happy change in his flock, in consequence of the unceasing labors of these good men, and looked upon the convent of Albenga as the sanctuary and jewel of his diocese, and called our Blessed Leonard to preach on every occasion, and give spiritual exercises, and assist him in every work of mercy.

During the summer of this year the weather became very hot, and in consequence of the low unhealthy situation of the convent, and the mortified life they led, they all fell sick, with the exception of blessed Leonard and two clerics, who were obliged to overexert themselves in reciting the divine office, in the choir, hearing confessions, and visiting the sick night and day. The heat having abated, health was restored amongst them, and they resumed their former rigorous way of living during Advent, their only food being herbs and chestnuts. But this restoration to health was only of short duration, they were all taken ill again, and as they could have no doubt that it was owing to the malaria, they requested the father provincial to give them a monastery in a more healthy situation. The change was willingly agreed to, and the convent of Port Maurice was fixed on, where Blessed Leonard had lived for four or five years, and had labored so much for the good of souls. However, this project was not carried into effect, for the devil having begun to experience the loss which the earnest labors of Blessed Leonard had caused him; and foreseeing still greater losses if they were firmly established, instigated the people, and even some of the higher class, to rise up and prevent the foundation of the retreat. The revolt of these disobedient people got to such a height, that on the first of January, 1709, two of the religious sent by Blessed Leonard from Albenga to Port Maurice to take possession of the convent, were driven away with violence, and even he himself met with the same treatment sortie days after, when he went there. He, however, adoring the inscrutable designs of Providence, without being disheartened, or losing courage, went on with his ministrations in the diocese of Albenga until the following May, giving, by order of the bishop, missions in Ortovero, Rezzo, and other places, where the memory of Blessed Leonard is still held in reverence and affection. It was he who induced the people to walk barefoot to the church of the Madonna, a mile distant from the town; which devotion was kept up for many years. The bishop was most unwilling that he should leave his diocese, and appointed him to preach in three different places during the autumn, but his superior obliged him to go elsewhere, as we shall see.

CHAPTER VI

Blessed Leonard Goes from Port Maurice to Florence, Where, after Having Employed Himself in Many Good Works, He Is Appointed to Give Retreats in Different Places in Tuscany.

HE Grand Duke, Cosmo III, having heard of the holy lives led by the monks of S. Buonaventura, and the great good they did amongst the people, obtained permission from his holiness. Clement XI, that a retreat should be instituted in Florence on the same plan, and offered for that purpose the convent of S. Francesco al Monte, of the Minori Osservanti. Accordingly, the superior of that in Rome sent four of the priests whom he considered most capable of undertaking the office, and one of these was Blessed Leonard, whose fame for wisdom and zeal was known everywhere. They received faculties from the minister-general on the 8th of September, 1709, and departed for Tuscany, where Almighty God, in establishing that retreat, had prepared a vast harvest for them to gather, and where abundant fruits of penance would be brought forth by the multitude. But as every good work generally meets with opposition and obstacles, so it happened in founding the new retreat; notwithstanding the monks who were sent to establish it were most affectionately received by the prince who had invited them, they were, for various earthly reasons, regarded with suspicion by the nobility, and even some of those about the court. Besides the jesting and ridicule to which they were constantly exposed, when they went to collect alms, the door was shut in their faces, and they were so grossly insulted, that it required all their patience and meekness to bear with it.

Their enemies were so much displeased to find that the grand duke continued to love and protect the new religious, that, in order to lessen his love for them, and to make him cease to afford them protection, they spread a report through the town that they intended to destroy the stations of the "Way of the Cross," which for a long time had hung in the way which leads from Florence to the convent of San Francesco, and which were much visited by the Florentines, especially during Lent. The report having reached the ears of the Grand Duke, he went in person to the convent, and related what he had heard, when he not only satisfied himself it was false, but, on the contrary, found that the good monks had established the pious exercise of the Via Crucis with even greater solemnity, in procession, concluding the devotion with a sermon, the preaching of which Blessed Leonard had undertaken. The Grand Duke was quite satisfied, and desired they would endeavor to excite the people to still greater fervor in this devotion, which they readily promised; however, they told him that it was necessary he should co-operate with them in making this devotion more profitable, by abolishing many abuses and disorders which had been permitted for some time, particularly on the Fridays in March, when the people were assembled in greater numbers. The good prince promised to do all in his power to assist them, and having heard that on those days booths were opened, where eating and drinking was carried on to excess, breaking the Lenten fast, and sinning against temperance, he issued an edict, in which were prohibited all assemblies, and selling wine or food, under a heavy penalty, on the days appointed for the devotion of the Via Crucis. The same edict prohibited women of ill fame to show themselves in that part of the town leading to the convent of S. Francesco, for they were as snares of the devil, and caused great scandal to those who came to assist at the devotion. Blessed Leonard continued to preach in several of the churches in Florence, and in the diocese of Fiesole, in so perfectly apostolic a manner, that the Grand Duke had reason to rejoice in the reformation of his people, and often came to visit him, and consulted him about his private affairs, and also those of the state.

Monsignor Panciatici, bishop of Fiesole, held Blessed Leonard in such high esteem, that on the days set apart for the devotion of the "Way of the Cross," he went attended by many others to the convent of S. Francesco al Monte barefoot, carrying a cross on his shoulders, to the great edification of all present, and on the Fridays in March he remained to converse with the servant of God, and partook of their simple fare, bread and water in the refectory.

One day when Father Segneri, the younger, was giving the retreat in the piazza of Santa Croce, in Florence, he beheld Blessed Leonard amongst the crowd, when he said that he need not come to hear others, for he was capable to teach any person how to give missions.

The bishop employed him in preaching and giving spiritual exercises in the monasteries; many of which he reformed, and also in giving instructions to the converts in the Conservatorio di Porta a Pinti, and in other places and churches in the town and neighborhood. The Grand Duke rejoiced in having introduced into his state laborers so zealous and useful. Besides the convent of S. Francesco al Monte, he gave them in 1712 that of S. Francesco del Palco, which belonged to the Minori Osservanti, about a mile distant from Prato. The monks went in August to take possession of it, and soon converted it into a retreat; but they met with so much opposition from the inhabitants of Prato, that the Grand Duke thought it might have a good effect, and remove their prejudices, if Blessed Leonard gave a mission there, which he did the following year.

In the year 1710, Blessed Leonard preached his first sermon in Tuscany, in the convent of S. Francesco al Monte, with so much fervor that his fame was spread through Florence, so that in a very short time the multitude who flocked to hear him so increased, that the church, which was very spacious, could not contain half of them. The Grand Duke seeing this, and the wonderful fruits of his labors, ordered him to give two retreats of eight days, one in the church of S. Lorenzo, and the other in that of S. Felicita, at which he, with his family and court, assisted.

The good prince, seeing the great advantage and eternal welfare of souls gained by the zeal of Blessed Leonard, entreated him to give missions throughout the grand duchy, and offered every assistance, even to support the whole congregation. He thanked him for his liberal offer, but added, that although he willingly undertook the mission, he could not accept the assistance offered for his maintenance, for he had a Patron richer and higher than his highness, who had provided for him during his life, and upon whom alone he depended for the future. The Grand Duke inquired who this Patron was; he replied, it was God, on whose Providence he relied, and that he wished to live by asking alms, feeling sure that the same merciful power would provide for him as long as he was laboring for His greater glory. The good prince was silent, and greatly edified when he found that this resolution of living by alms was made after many fervent prayers, established as a rule, and strictly observed during the missions by Blessed Leonard and his fellow-laborers as long as they lived.

From this time he began an open war against the powers of hell, and gave his first mission in Tuscany, at Pitigliano, in the diocese of Sorano, the native place of the holy pontiff Gregory VII, with so much benefit to souls, that the person whom the Grand Duke sent to supply what was necessary for the mission, wrote thus to his brother in Florence: "I cannot do less than inform you how much we have benefitted in Pitigliano by the teaching of a most holy servant of God, who having ended the mission, has now gone to Sorano, to reform that place. I speak of Father Leonard, who, with his sweet persuasive manner wins even the most hardened and stubborn. I was commissioned by the Grand Duke to supply him with all things necessary, but it is little they require; we had prepared for them a room containing five dormitories, with beds and mattresses, and everything to make them comfortable; but as soon as they arrived, all were removed, and bare boards were placed for them to sleep on. I really believe they are kept alive miraculously, for it is not possible for them to exist, undergoing so many penances and such fatigues, without the especial assistance of God."

In 1713 the murrain caused a great mortality amongst the cattle in the neighboring provinces of the grand duchy, and it was feared the continued drought would cause a famine; in consequence of this, the Grand Duke requested Blessed Leonard to give a triduo in the metropolitan church of Florence, which was very well attended by the people, and during the three days the confessionals were crowded.

The plague was stayed, and the Grand Duke, grateful for the intercessions of Holy Mary, to whom many prayers had been offered, entreated Blessed Leonard, by way of a thank-offering, to give another solemn triduo in the parish church of Impruneta, five miles distant from Florence, where there was a very ancient miraculous picture of the Blessed Virgin, which was always exposed on the feast of the Nativity, and on the Octave day carried in procession to the neighboring mount of Santa Maria. The Grand Duke exhorted all his people to attend the sacred function, and the church was crowded to excess. The procession having reached the mount Blessed Leonard gave a most fervent discourse, which was heard distinctly even by those who, owing to the greatness of the crowd, were a mile distant. After the sermon, benediction was given, and the guns which were placed on every eminence were fired, so that everyone throughout Tuscany should know the time, and prostrate themselves on the ground to receive it, wherever they might be. Many were the tears shed, and great the compunction of the people. The ceremonies ended by carrying the holy picture back to the church of Impruneta.

CHAPTER VII

Blessed Leonard Gives Missions in Different Places in Tuscany, and Is Chosen Guardian of the Monastery of S. Francis.

HE Grand Duke, in order to soften the citizens of Prato, who were so irritated against the monks of S. Francis, requested Blessed Leonard to give them a retreat, feeling sure that his eloquent preaching and example would gain their hearts, and, in May 1713, he began his labors in the town of Prato, after Vespers on Sunday the 21st; he was received by all the clergy, and by Monsignor Cortigiani, the vicar-general, of the bishop of Pistoia and Prato. The vicar presented the crucifix to Blessed Leonard, and gave a short discourse from the Epistle appointed for the day, on the words, "Dearly beloved, be ye doers of the word, and not hearers only, deceiving your own selves." The zealous missionary replied, declaring that he only intended to preach Jesus Christ and Him crucified, and they went in procession to the church. The first sermon caused so great a commotion amongst the people, who uttered loud cries, calling on God for mercy, that the holy man could scarcely finish the service, it was so often interrupted by the groans and tears of the congregation.

Almighty God blessed abundantly these holy exercises; they produced much fruit, and the town was soon converted into a garden of virtue, and those who were at first opposed to the retreat, became most zealous supporters of it, regarding the new monks as men sent from God to lead them into the way of salvation. The fame of the good missionary was spread throughout Tuscany, and many bishops desired his valuable services in their dioceses; he accepted all their invitations, having nothing at heart but the greater glory of God and the spiritual good of his fellow men. He went through the dioceses of Massa,

St. Leonard of Port Maurice

Arezzo, and Volterra, converting many souls to God; and all beheld with wonder, not only the zeal and energy with which he spoke, but his austere and exemplary way of living. The most hardened were moved by his preaching, and, animated by the example of his holy life, received grace to repent and be converted. It was not only the learned missionary they admired, but the holy and perfect monk, who observed during the time of the retreat so rigorous a mode of life, joined to the practice of every virtue. In 1714 he went to preach in the dioceses of Pescia, of Chiusi, Colle, S. Miniato, and Pistoia, the result of which is related in a letter from the bishop of Miniato to the father guardian of Francesco al Monte, dated September, 1714, and also in one from the parish priest of S. Rocco, about a mile distant from Pistoia, addressed to the same father in June, 1715. The bishop in thanking the superior, for having sent, for the good of his flock, so zealous and vigilant a shepherd, expresses himself thus: "Father Leonard will return to his holy retreat with every blessing and reward, for he has labored indefatigably fifteen days, and I may even say fifteen nights, for the salvation of my beloved people, and, I am willing to hope, with the greatest benefit; he is surely filled with Divine grace, for without the especial aid of the Almighty he never could have accomplished so much."

The priest of Rocco, in Pistoia, writes in the following terms: "Blessed be the day on which it occurred to you to send Blessed Leonard here. What great things has Almighty God done for us by means of His servant! All venerate him as a most holy man, learned preacher, and most fervent missionary; every soul is enchained and captivated by his discourses, even the most fastidious; all who came to hear him have been converted. The number of attendants was very great; in the second procession of penitents we had about fifteen thousand, and at the papal benediction twenty thousand. The confessors throughout the city have had much to do, and have found in all great anxiety for the salvation of their souls. The good father went away regretted by everyone, as might be seen by the tears and lamentations of the people, who all expressed desire to see him again. The nobility, and ladies and gentlemen, came at an early hour most inconvenient to them, braving the cold, which was extreme, to make their confessions to him. Blessed be God for visiting His Church, and sending such a teacher. The fruits of the mission were seen in the manner in which the devotions of the Via Crucis were attended; the nobles of Pistoia, who previously had seemed ashamed of any external demonstration of religion, came to it with great fervor and recollection, even kissing the ground, and they continued to do this after the mission was ended."

In 1715 he was chosen superior and director of the convent of S. Francis in Florence; the electors felt sure that his zeal, worth, and exemplary life would be most advantageous to that sanctuary. He, however, was most unwilling to accept the appointment, for he well knew the dangers and difficulties he would have to encounter, and also, because it would prevent him giving missions, which he had hoped would be his employment till the end of his life; he only consented to the honor conferred on him, because he believed it to be the will of God. Having accepted it, he was most earnest in endeavoring to fulfil the trust to the utmost of his powers, to induce those under his care to strive for religious perfection; he had the rule and constitutions printed exactly like those in Rome, and added some points for the better regulation of time, so that each one should know what he had to do during the day. These rules were so excellent, that not only did the superior-general approve of them, and authorize the printing, but also the holy pontiff Clement XI, who desired Cardinal Paolucci to write a letter expressive of his pleasure, and how greatly he was edified. The progress in perfection by the whole community was quite wonderful, with so excellent a guide to the practice of every virtue, and following exactly the rules prescribed by him. Every Sunday evening he gave a lecture in the refectory on the observance of the rules, and the obligation of everyone to seek after perfection; he spoke with so much energy and fervor, that everyone who heard him felt themselves incited to lead better and more holy lives. Religious even from other convents used to come to hear him, standing behind the door of the refectory, that they might not be seen; they were astonished at his wonderful powers of mind, and still more by the impression left on their own minds, and went away much edified and full of reverence for the man of God. Blessed Leonard not only observed the rules he had drawn up with the greatest exactness, but also added other penances and austerities; he took his brief repose on a bare board, with a log of wood for his pillow, and only one meal during the day, consisting of herbs; he always walked barefoot, even in the coldest weather, dressed in a ragged and patched habit.

During this year it was reported in Florence that God had revealed to a pious soul that He would visit the city with a dreadful scourge; in consequence of which the Grand Duke, Cosmo III, ordered that seven missions should be given in seven different places, leaving it to Blessed Leonard to choose any church in the city he pleased. He accordingly chose that of S. Niccolo, situated in a remote corner of Florence, and frequented by the poorest people, and gave the first mission in January, after having preached during the novena, before Christmas, to the confraternity of Ricoboli.

CHAPTER VIII

*Blessed Leonard Founds the Hermitage of
Santa Maria Dell' Incontro.*

THIS holy man of God was not satisfied with the rigorous observances which he practiced in common and privately in his retreat, but desired to follow the example of his seraphic father S. Francis, who frequently retired to some solitary place where he could give himself entirely to God and his salvation, and gain strength and courage to attend to the affairs of his soul and the attainment of perfection. For this he prayed earnestly, and his prayer was soon granted, for in the year 1715, a most suitable place for the purpose was offered to him. The hermitage of Santa Maria dell' Incontro, which was situated on a mountain seven miles distant from Florence, already sanctified as the dwelling-place of the Blessed Gerard, one of the first of the third order of Franciscans. Blessed Leonard went to see it, and being perfectly satisfied with the situation, conferred with the superior of the order, to found there a place of retirement for those of his retreat who wished to be at times quite alone.

About this time he finished the drawing up of the constitutions, which in 1716 were printed in Florence, after having been inspected by both monasteries, and unanimously accepted on the 28th of November, and in the following year on the 29th of June, were approved of by Father Giacomo de Verruchio, at that time commissioner general of the order of Minori Riformati. The bishop of Fiesole, having received the requisite sanction and power, gave possession of the hermitage to the monastery of S. Francesco al Monte, on the feast of the Annunciation. The superior and all the community had made a vow, whenever they retired there, to walk barefoot, even if the ground were covered with snow, singing psalms and praises to the Lord. The holy sacrifice was celebrated, and then, with the charitable offering of a pious Florentine, the building of that hermitage was begun, and it was occupied for the first time on the 23rd of May, 1717. Blessed Leonard superintended the building, and was most desirous that all about it should be according to the strict rules of poverty; that the eight cells for the solitaries, and four for the superior and occasional guests, should be only eight spans long, five wide, and nine high, so that standing in the middle one might easily touch the wall on either side, and in the same manner the roof, which was thatched with rushes; the walls were not plastered, in fact, all was done to inspire poverty and a mortified life. The doors were only two spans wide, and six spans high, the windows one span wide, and one span and a half high; the offices were all equally narrow and poor. As for their meals, they never ate meat, or any food made with milk, or fish, and those who wished to keep the nine Lents in imitation of their holy father S. Francis, observed a most rigid fast, eating in the morning only herbs and vegetables, and in the evening the collation allowed by the church on fasting days. It was also an established rule that they should sleep on the floor, and inflict upon themselves many other mortifications, which was done with much joy and gladness, with holy emulation, exciting each other to still greater devotion. As Blessed Leonard established the hermitage, he was the first to retire there, and followed to the letter all the prescribed rules, and even exceeded them, as the desire of mortification and the fervency of his spirit suggested. He afterwards went there frequently, not merely twice in the year, but whenever any great solemnity was approaching, to prepare for it, and when he returned from the missions which he was ordered by the pope Clement XI to give during the time he was superior of the monastery. The rest and repose he took after his apostolical labors, was retiring to this secluded place, to lead the most penitent, austere, and mortified life.

He observed also the silence ordered, and assisted night and day at the vocal and mental prayers of the community, practicing that retirement prescribed by the rule, which was so stringent that none but the Guardian could administer the holy sacraments, write, or receive a letter except from his superior. He used the discipline every night after matins, and every day after vespers he went with the others to manual labor, and always looked happy and cheerful; he used to call this solitude the place of delight, the novitiate of paradise, his consolation, and said that he wished never to leave it, but to die there. Nothing but obedience could induce him to leave it. It was here that in 1717 he wrote those sixty-five resolutions, which he often read over to see if he followed them punctually. They serve as a mirror to reflect his mode of life, his great sanctity, and the high degree of perfection he had attained. The fame of this sanctuary was very soon spread abroad, many regulars of different monastic establishments requested to be admitted for the spiritual exercises, and after staying some days, left it much edified. Many in the world even, desirous of amending their lives, made the same petition, esteeming it a great favor to be allowed to pass some weeks among these solitaries, and not only did they join in all the devotions night and day, but also put on the rough coarse habit of the order, and always left it with tears of regret, declaring it to be a terrestrial paradise. Many people of distinction, both ecclesiastics and seculars, visited the holy place, and praised God, Who never fails to send faithful servants into His Church. The Grand Duke Cosmo III, having heard the hermitage much spoken of, went with his whole court to see it, minutely examined everything, and afterwards brought his daughter, the Princess Electoress, with the Count of Gherardesca, archbishop of Florence, all of whom were filled with wonder and fear at the wild loneliness of the place, and great admiration of the sanctity of the inmates. The holy pontiff Clement XI, in reading what was there observed according to the constitutions, was so much affected that he wept, declaring that they were truly servants of God. Amongst the many instances of extraordinary mortification practiced by Blessed Leonard at this time, I shall mention one. When he was appointed superior of the monastery of S. Francesco al Monte, he determined to retire for some time to the hermitage. The evening before his departure he prostrated himself in the middle of the refectory with a stone tied to his neck, and accused himself of tepidity and negligence, asked pardon of the community, and entreated them to pray that he might receive the grace of God.

CHAPTER IX

Blessed Leonard Sets at Liberty a Woman under Sentence of Death. Gives a Mission in the Diocese of Pisa, and Is Re-elected Father Guardian.

T happened on one occasion when Blessed Leonard was about to retire to his solitude after having ended the missions, he heard that a young woman having been found guilty of infanticide, was in prison, under sentence of death, near the monastery. The case was much spoken of in Florence, for it was said the crime was not clearly proved, and the unhappy creature ought not to be executed. Although many felt and spoke thus, no one was found to defend her, the sentence was given, and the execution to take place in two days. However, one of the first Counselors of the town was at last moved to compassion, and knowing the high esteem in which Blessed Leonard was held by the Grand Duke, and the influence he had with him, went to the monastery and made the case known to him, and entreated he would endeavor to persuade his highness to suspend the execution of the sentence, and have the criminal tried again, offering to defend the cause himself.

On hearing this, Blessed Leonard went immediately to the court, where he was most graciously received by the Grand Duke, who, in reply to his request, told him that the sentence had gone forth, was to be executed in two days, and could not be annulled. The good father meekly replied, that he had not come to ask him to prevent the course of justice, but only to look over the trial, and see if some mistake had not been made, for so it was spoken of in the town. At these words the just and pious Cosmo III raised his eyes to heaven, and said, after a short silence, "It is not impossible that there has been something wrong in the evidence; the trial must come on again." This was done, and the innocence of the condemned person clearly proved, and she was set at liberty, to the great joy of all interested in her, who at the same time lauded the charity of Blessed Leonard, who became every day more endeared to the inhabitants of Florence.

About this time he went to give missions in the diocese of Pisa, where he converted many, who brought forth plentiful fruits of penance. On one occasion when he was preaching on scandals, and scourging himself so severely with the discipline, that the people were moved to tears, the parish priest rushed forwards, and taking the instrument of torture from the hand of the missionary, confessed in a loud tone, that it was he who caused scandal, cast off his cotta, and having laid bare his shoulders, began to scourge them in the most severe manner. The people were even more affected at seeing their own pastor, a holy and excellent priest, giving such public manifestations of his great humility. Monsignor Frosini, archbishop of Pisa, hearing of the wonders done by this zealous laborer in his diocese, desired to hear him preach. Accordingly he went to Pontedera, six miles distant from Pisa, where the man of God, who was then employed in saving souls, and listening to the cries of the people, who wept with compunction, calling on God for mercy, so that he was frequently obliged to pause, and exhort them to be silent; he declared that he had never, on any occasion, seen so many tears shed, or such signs of penitence. The archbishop requested Blessed Leonard to preach in the Pisa, and accordingly he gave the first mission in the church of Agostino, which Cosmo III with his court attended; and as this church, spacious as it was, was not large enough to contain the great multitude which flocked to hear him, he was obliged to preach in the cathedral, which, although very large, could not hold them, so that many were obliged to kneel outside, and nothing was heard but lamentations and cries for mercy. Having ended the mission, he gave the spiritual exercises to the students in the university, upon whom he made so deep an impression of the importance of spiritual things and eternal salvation, that from that time they gave themselves more to the study of Christian virtues than of science. Soon after this the Grand Duke sent for him to Leghorn, where, as it is well known, there are many Jews, who enjoy much liberty, and the wealthy merchants among them are allowed to make use of Christians for their servants, and even to have the women as nurses for their children; this was the cause of many disorders, as may easily be imagined. Added to this, vessels belonging to the Turks and heretics were constantly coming into the port, and the free intercourse with the people was the cause of much vice and immorality. Many who desired to correct this great evil, rejoiced at the coming of so good a laborer into this uncultivated vineyard. Blessed Leonard arrived at the most opportune time, that of the carnival, and the mission was begun, and carried on with so much zeal, that contrition was universal, and such public and manifest signs of repentance, that Leghorn seemed another Nineveh converted. The Carnival was not thought of, although every preparation had been made at a great expense, masks were prohibited, and the theaters closed. The multitude of reformed and penitent people who crowded to the feet of the priests night and day to make their confessions was so great, that they were obliged to place a guard before the confessionals, to prevent confusion and disorders which so great a crowd might cause.

Amongst many conversions, none were so wonderful as those of some women of lost character, who hearing of the great things done by these good missionaries, excited only by curiosity, went to hear them. Forty of them went together, and although it was far from their intention to change their lives, and be converted, yet, at the powerful and persuasive voice of Blessed Leonard, who so loudly inveighed against the vice to which they were addicted, they very soon felt a horror of their iniquity and a great fear of eternal punishment, and began to weep and cry aloud for mercy and pardon of Almighty God, and forgiveness of all to whom they had given scandal. The sudden and unexpected conversion of these women excited much wonder and admiration; they were sent by the pious missionary to a private house near the church, from whence they came every day during the retreat to hear the sermons, dressed like penitents, having not only their faces covered, but enveloped from head to foot in long cloaks. The people seeing them walk thus habited in procession to the church, were greatly edified and affected, and praised God for having, by means of His servant, converted these women, who for so long a time had been a scandal to the town. Still more did the wonder increase, when it was known that three of them, four days after their conversion, passed into eternity, with every sign of true contrition, praising and magnifying the divine mercy for giving them grace to forsake their evil ways, and blessing him whom God bad sent to convert and save them.

Blessed Leonard was unwilling to leave Leghorn without making sure of these poor but now fortunate women; and finding that want and necessity had driven them to their late miserable course, recommended that a collection should be made for them, which was so abundant as to provide them with the means of living honestly, and from that time they lived in the path of virtue.

Very great was the reward of Blessed Leonard for his labors in Leghorn; he returned to his monastery of Francesco al Monte, and soon after retired to his beloved solitude Maria dell' Incontro. About this time he was elected for the second time father guardian and director, in which office he was so exact in enforcing the observance of the rule, that all subject to him declared he was the model of a superior, the teacher of every virtue, and, after Almighty God, their chief support He was the first at all community acts; and not content with his labors in the confessional, he frequently went to various convents of nuns to confess them, and animate them to fervor and advancement in the spiritual life.

The Grand Duke, who had been ill for some time, was more than ever desirous that Christian piety should flourish in his dominions, and on the occasion of Blessed Leonard going to visit him, he desired that missions should be given in Florence, one in the church of S. Fridiano, and the other in that of S. Catterina delle Ruote, from which, as usual, a plentiful harvest was reaped in the conversion of souls. The Grand Duke died soon after this, and was succeeded by his son, Gian Gastone, who, following the good example of his father, held Blessed Leonard in high esteem, and invited him to preach repentance throughout the grand duchy. Amongst the many acts recorded of him at this time, in the observance of the rule, and the manner in which he used to correct those who failed in their duty, I shall satisfy my readers by relating one only. On the occasion of the canonization of S. Giacomo della Marca and Francesco Solano, celebrated in 1726 in the monastery of S. Francis, two octaves were to be kept, one in the church of S. Francesco al Monte in Florence. Blessed Leonard being obliged to go on a mission, gave a general order that they should celebrate the octave with the greatest solemnity, but strictly prohibited three things, to hang the church with silk, to have fireworks, and to ring a double chime of bells, because, according to the rules of the retreat, one only was to be rung. Having given these orders, he set off, and finding on his return they had not been obeyed, he used every means to discover the delinquents, but in vain. He determined, however, not to allow disobedience to go unpunished, and one evening when all were assembled in the refectory, he thus addressed them: " My brethren, our laws have been transgressed, the sin of disobedience has been committed, and the sinner is not discovered, therefore it is left for me to do penance." Having said this, he commanded that no one should move from his place; he walked into the middle of the refectory, and scourged himself with the discipline during the time in which he said the Psalm "Miserere" thrice in a loud voice.

All present wept and lamented, for they knew he was doing penance for the sin of others, and entreated him to desist, but in vain. Having finished the Psalms and the scourging, he returned to his place, and gave them a most impressive discourse on the importance of obedience, especially for religious, and reminded them that every sin, whether mortal or venial, must be punished. It pleased the Almighty to prove the truth of this by punishing one of the disobedient monks when he was in the very act of ringing the double chime which had been forbidden; he received a violent blow on the forehead, which left a scar as a sign of his disobedience. From this and many similar acts, it may be imagined how full of zeal Blessed Leonard was as father superior of the monastery of the retreat, and how strict in the observance of the rule.

CHAPTER X

Blessed Leonard Gives Missions in Lucca and Rome, from Whence He Returns to Florence.

THE authorities of Lucca, many of whom had heard of the preaching of our holy father in their neighborhood, were most desirous that he should give missions in that city, and to accomplish this they sent Canon Zucchesini to negotiate with him. He had, amongst many other good resolutions, formed that of never refusing to labor for the good of souls whenever he might be required; therefore, he accepted the invitation, and went immediately to Lucca. Of this place he often spoke with the greatest interest, praising the docility and tractability of the people, and blessing God for the rich harvest he had gathered, in gaining souls for heaven. As soon as he arrived he began the mission in the church of S. Fridiano, which although very spacious, was so crowded with people from the country, as well as the town, that it was feared many would be trampled on, and killed; it was therefore thought expedient to close the doors when the church was quite filled. It was on this occasion that a criminal under sentence of death sent for him, and entreated that he would attend his dying moments. He naturally felt a great repugnance to witness such a spectacle, yet charity induced him to conquer it, and taking courage, he accompanied the unfortunate man to the place of execution, and supported him to the last; and as an immense concourse of people were assembled, he remained on the scaffold, and gave them so impressive and edifying a sermon, that with one voice they called on God for pardon. From Lucca he proceeded to other places, and one day, when they were on a journey, they came near a village situated on the side of a hill; pointing to it, he said to his companions, that he was seized with a sudden inspiration to go there, but as they knew not to what diocese it belonged, he sent to inquire if he might be permitted to preach there. They had an interview with the parish priest, and found that he and his flock were quite disposed to receive the missionaries, and would procure a license from the bishop. The mission was begun, and from the following fact it was evident that his desire to go there was an inspiration from heaven. On the first day, a woman came and fell at the feet of Blessed Leonard, saying, "Father, Almighty God has ordered this mission for me." She then went on to tell him that when she was a child she had committed a mortal sin, which she had been ashamed to confess, for in that remote district there were few priests, and those either relations or friends ; she also added, that for thirty years she had been guilty of the sin of sacrilege in approaching the sacraments, but with great remorse of conscience that by many prayers and penances she had recommended herself to the holy Virgin, who had appeared to her, and promised that in four days she would obtain for her that a priest should be sent, to whom she was to make her confession, and he would give her absolution, and restore her peace. The good father was much affected on hearing this, and having encouraged the poor woman, she made a general confession, to which he listened with great patience and charity, and left her full of joy and peace. He was much consoled by this occurrence, and used to say in speaking of it, that Divine Providence sent him to a place to save one soul, and that missionaries should be satisfied, and consider themselves amply rewarded for their labors, if they never gained more than this.

Blessed Leonard had thus labored for twenty-two years in the apostolical ministry, enlightening all Tuscany with his missions, when it pleased the Lord, in the following manner, to send him to preach repentance in Rome. Cardinal Barberini, knowing the zeal and virtue of Blessed Leonard, wrote a letter, which the servant of God received when he was in the island of Gorgona, in the diocese of Pisa, giving him the requisite faculties, and desiring him to come to Rome to give instructions, which were much required, and also a mission in the town of Velletri. From Gorgona, therefore, he went to Florence, and taking leave of the Grand Duke, Giovan Gastone, and the princess Violante, of Bavaria, who gave him letters for the Pope Clement XII, on the 7th of September, 1730, he set off for Rome. On the journey, which, as usual, he made barefooted, he visited the sanctuaries of Assisi, Monteluco, and Valle di Rieti, and on the 25th of the same month, arrived at the monastery of Santa Maria delle Grazie, where, thirty-three years before, he had been clothed with the religious habit, and had made his novitiate and profession. He remained here some days, and then proceeded on his way to Rome, where he went directly to kiss the hand of the superior of the order, by whom he was affectionately received, and on the 4th of October he cast himself at the feet of the pope, and presented the letters from the princess Violante, which contained an account of the Retreat he had founded. The holy father was much pleased to learn the good he had done in Tuscany, and promising him every assistance, gave him his blessing, and sent him much consoled to his convent of S. Buonaventura.

Finding that Cardinal Barberini was not in Rome at this time, Blessed Leonard began instructing the poor in the hospital of S. Galla, and although at first he met with opposition, excited by the devil to prevent the good work, he very soon overcame all obstacles, and began his ministrations on the 28th of October, 1730. He was then in the fifty-fourth year of his age, and continued these missions in Rome with so much fervor and zeal, that his fame was soon spread abroad, and many came to hear him of all classes, even the ecclesiastics and nobility. The church of S. Galla could not contain them, and he was obliged to preach in the courtyard of the hospital, which, although very spacious, was not sufficient, and many were forced to stand at the windows and in the galleries. He astonished and edified all by the independent, unflinching manner in which he reproved vice, exhibiting it in all its deformity, and showing how greatly it was to be abhorred and detested, by frequently, during his discourse, striking his bare shoulders with the discipline, until the blood flowed. They were all much edified by seeing this holy man so poorly clad, and barefoot; and together with the efficacy of his words, and the example of his ascetic life, the impression made on his hearers was so great, that during every sermon his voice was almost lost amid the cries and lamentations of the penitents; nothing was spoken of in Rome but his preaching.

The pope issued an order, that as soon as he had finished this mission, he should preach in the churches of S. Giovanni dei Fiorentini, S. Carlo al Corso, S. Pietro, in Vincoli, and S. Maria, in Trastevere, which he joyfully obeyed, preaching in each of these churches in succession with so much effect, that the conversions were most numerous.

One day, during the time he was giving a mission in the church of S. Carlo, a young woman, who from her dress and manner appeared to be a person of high rank, went there, and asked one of the companions of Blessed Leonard to procure her an interview with him, at the same time telling him plainly that she was an abandoned character. As soon as the mass he was celebrating was ended, the message was brought to him, and he desired her to come to the confessional, when he heard her confession, she returned home humbled and changed, adopted a modest and simple style of dress, and regularly attended the mission, and although she was frequently tempted by flattery, and even menaces, from her former associates, she remained firm and constant to her resolutions, and afterwards, with a portion of five hundred crowns, which the pious missionary procured for her, she entered a convent, and remained there till her death. On another occasion, when he was preaching against impurity, a girl of lost character came to him, and expressed great contrition and sorrow for her sin, and weeping bitterly, promised never again to fall back into her former evil ways. A dissolute man, who had never failed in his designs to lead her astray, placed himself opposite the house, with a gun in his hand, and threatened to shoot her if she did not yield; he remained there until she happened to approach the window, when the desperate man fired, and killed her on the spot; her death was considered glorious in Rome, since she had preferred death to sin.

In giving these missions, Blessed Leonard often preached on purgatory, and collected alms for the suffrages of those holy souls who were detained there; on one occasion, when he saw a multitude of people assembled, belonging to every rank, grade, and condition, he determined to impress upon them the importance of this duty. The whole congregation were so much affected, and moved with compassion, that the first collection amounted to seven hundred Roman crowns, and many gave their ornaments and rings from their fingers, and swords from their sides, all of which he gave to be distributed in different churches in Rome, in order that masses might be said for the faithful departed.

The pope having heard of the great things done by the holy missionary, and the wonderful effects of his preaching, sent Father Barberini, then preacher at the palace, afterwards bishop of Ferrara, to hear him, and give him a faithful report. Father Barberini accordingly went to hear him, and in giving an account of his zeal and fervor, said, that he could only assure his holiness, that even he, who had grown old in the ministry, could not refrain from tears. From S. Carlo al Corso Blessed Leonard went to S. Pietro, in Vincoli, and as amongst the many conversions there were many profligate women, the Cardinal-Vicar desired a subscription to be made for them, the sum collected was four hundred crowns, which was sufficient to insure the safety and maintenance of all the poor creatures. Many other great things might be told of these missions and the number of distinguished ecclesiastics who attended them, but I shall only mention Father Galuzzi, a Jesuit, and well known for his piety, who not only went regularly himself, but desired his penitents not to be absent from one sermon, telling them that Blessed Leonard was truly the apostle of the times. In the meantime, Cardinal Barberini, who had sent for him from Florence to give a mission in Velletri, returned to Rome, and at his entreaty he set off for that city, and commenced a course of sermons, in which, above all things, he exhorted the people to abstain from blasphemy, if they wished for happiness and prosperity, and recommended them to place over the doors of their bouses the monogram of the holy name of Jesus, designed by S. Bernadino of Sienna, so that everyone might behold and honor it, and blasphemers conceive a horror of their sins. To avoid the crowd of people who had resolved to accompany him, he started one morning at daybreak, having effected a complete reformation amongst them, and returned to Rome, to renew his ministrations in the church of Santa Maria in Trastevero. Although the church was very spacious, it could not contain the multitude assembled, and he was obliged to preach in the square, which was crowded to excess, the streets leading to it were filled, and even the roofs of the houses.

The Grand Duke of Tuscany and the Princess Violante, being much displeased with the long absence of Blessed Leonard, sent to request his return; therefore, having received the papal benediction, and leave from his superiors, he again turned towards Tuscany. On his arrival in Florence he was received by the sovereign and people with the greatest joy; and having informed the Princess of the result of his missions in Rome, he retired to his hermitage, in order to gain more courage and strength, and from thence he went to Camajore, in the diocese of Lucca. When he was giving the missions in this place he found a most hardened sinner, who obstinately refused to repent and amend his life. The earnest appeals of Blessed Leonard were vain; and one day finding every argument lost on him, he prayed

56

to Almighty God to send a thunderbolt to break his stubborn will. Scarcely had he uttered the words when the heavens, which a moment before were clear and serene, darkened, and a loud clap of thunder was heard, and flashes of lightning were seen through the church, to the terror of the congregation, who, although they escaped unhurt, were touched and wounded in the soul, especially the man for whom the prayer was offered. Everyone present was wonderfully impressed by this manifest sign that God was with His servant to aid him in the work of their conversion. Indeed, all his missions were blessed, and brought forth abundant fruits of penance.

CHAPTER XI

Blessed Leonard Gives Missions in Rome and Vicinity, from Whence He Returns to Florence, and after That Is Sent to Viterbo, and Preaches in Several Other Places in the Papal Dominions.

HILST the servant of God was thus employed in Tuscany, some of the bishops, who from the time he had first preached in Rome had determined to invite him to give missions in their respective dioceses, induced the superior of the order to call him back to the capital. He received an order to return there in November, 1731, and set off from Lucca. After a most disastrous journey, in consequence of the inclemency of the season, he arrived in Rome on the 29th of the same month, and from thence, a few days afterwards, he was sent to exercise his apostolic ministry in the dioceses of Albano, Palestrina, Velletri, Sezze, Piperno, Segni, Ferentino, Alatri, and in some places in Sabina, gathering everywhere abundant fruits of penance. After spending some months in giving these missions, he obtained leave to retire to the monastery of S. Angelo di Montorio Romano in Sabina, a sanctuary most dear to the holy servant of God, and in which he would most willingly have passed the rest of his life. This monastery is more than three miles from any habitation, situated under a rock, halfway up a high mountain, and formerly the dwelling place of Blessed Amadeo, who was favored by Almighty God with many graces there.

This second John the Baptist came forth from his solitude preaching penance, and began teaching in the dioceses before mentioned with so much force and zeal, that the people, as soon as they saw him ascend the pulpit, felt great compunction, and began to weep and pray to God for pardon. During the mission in Sezze, where the people were much given to the sin of blasphemy, he was inveighing strongly against it, when a horrible accident happened, which proved a salutary lesson to all who witnessed it. A most licentious young man, and blasphemer, who had frequently ridiculed the threats of Blessed Leonard, was one day riding through the town just at the time he was preaching; he stopped, and began blaspheming, when he suddenly fell to the ground, his tongue hanging out of his mouth, as black as a firebrand; he had not the power to draw it in again, and thus died in great agony. This fearful death was regarded by everyone as a just chastisement of God, and caused many to stand in fear of the Divine Justice, and begin to amend their lives. Many were punished for not attending to the warning voice of Blessed Leonard. On one occasion, when he was giving a mission in a town in the diocese of Velletri, during the carnival of 1732, he in the most impressive manner exhorted the people to abstain from the usual amusements. It happened that some of the families had come from a neighboring town to attend the services, and when they returned from the church, went to a ball, regardless of the exhortations of the missionary; but soon their gaiety was changed into tears and lamentations, for in the midst of the dancing the roof of the house fell in, crushing all present beneath it; all of them received some injury, and the promoters of the feast were killed on the spot. For a penance, as soon as they were sufficiently recovered, they all walked in procession to the church where the mission was given. When engaged in preaching at Nettuno, he was returning home one evening much fatigued, when he was stopped by a man who threw himself at his feet, weeping bitterly, and intreating him to hear his confession there on the high road. One of the companions of Blessed Leonard endeavored to pacify the poor penitent, and told him at the same time, that this was not the time or place to trouble the good missionary, that he was suffering much from fatigue, and standing in the cold at so late an hour might cause a serious illness, and advised him to come to confession the following day. However Blessed Leonard, with his usual charity, interposed, raised the poor man from the ground, took him home, and the same evening heard his confession, thus proving the important duty of receiving sinners without delay, and reconciling them to God.

Having ended the missions in Sezze and Piperno, he proceeded to a town in the diocese of Sabina, where, in consequence of the fair, which was to be held on the 1st of May, he found the people much indisposed to attend a mission; however, he endeavored to convince them, that, instead of losing by it, they would gain much, by the numbers who would come from a distance to hear his sermons, and told them also, that as he had had orders from the bishop to give the mission, he could not disobey him. When he gave these reasons, those who opposed it were silent; he began his apostolical labors, and the sermons were well attended for two or three days, but soon there was a falling off, and they thought of nothing but the amusements and games going on in the front of the palace of the prince, to the great sorrow of the holy man, who was lodged near it. Many, however, came from a distance to hear Blessed Leonard, and in his concluding discourse, he severely reproved the people of the town for having neglected the means appointed by God for their eternal welfare, and ended by telling them that they would surely be punished; which prediction was fulfilled, for a few days after there was a dreadful hailstorm, which caused great destruction of property. Very different was the reception of our good father by the Romans; they ardently desired to hear him again, and when they heard that the pope had ordered him to return to Rome, they rejoiced exceedingly. The church appointed for the mission was the Basilica of S. Maria ad Martyres, commonly called the Rotunda, and that spacious temple was every day filled by people of every grade in the city. Besides the fruits of his preaching, which as usual were most abundant, he confirmed the members of the congregation for the perpetual adoration of the Blessed Sacrament, publishing the indulgences granted by the pope for this devotion, to such as are ascribed and undertake to adore once in each year, for the space of an hour, the most Blessed Sacrament of the Eucharist. He always assisted at this devotion with great fervor, and before his death had succeeded in introducing it into one hundred and thirty different places. When he had ended these missions, as Lent was near, and he was unwilling to interfere with the appointed preachers, he retired to the convent of S. Angelo di Montorio Romano, and refused to give any more missions during the season, and after a time returned to Rome, to give the spiritual exercises in the house of Prince Rospigliosi. These exercises, which were public, were not less useful than the missions, for the discourses and meditations for every morning and evening contained matter sufficient to instill into the minds of all maxims of perfection and eternal truths.

Although Blessed Leonard was laboring in this way to save souls, he did not forget his retreat in Florence; and to prevent the confusion which might occur in the election of the superior, he was desirous to be there in person; and having received the papal benediction, and leave from the head of the order, he departed for Tuscany. When he arrived at Campagnano, twenty miles from Rome, he was seized with sudden sickness and violent pain, which was supposed to be caused by eating some green herbs the day before, which they conjectured were poisonous. For all this he wished to proceed on his journey, but was obliged to stop at Viterbo for a day and take some medicine, which, however, failed in giving him relief. Thus suffering he went on his way, and when they were approaching Salci they lost their way, and night coming on, after wandering through woods and fields, at length found themselves in a morass. Blessed Leonard was so overcome by the fatigue of walking such a distance barefoot, and the malady increased so rapidly, that his companions feared he would die, and began to weep bitterly. At length, having extricated themselves from the morass, they sought shelter in a shed, and having gathered some sticks, lighted a fire, resolving to make the best of it, and pass the night there. But the owners of the shed perceiving the light, thought they were attacked by robbers, and assembling the neighbors, took arms, and went to put them to flight, but they stopped in surprise and confusion when they recognized Blessed Leonard, worn and ragged as he appeared, warming himself at the fire; they asked his pardon, and conducted him to the nearest house, where they used every remedy they possessed to restore him. The following morning he was carried to the convent of the Riformati at Cetona, where he was obliged to remain eight days, and when he was sufficiently recovered he pursued his journey to Florence, and having arranged the affairs of the retreat, he went to give missions in Viterbo.

The people who came in a large body from different parts of the country, entreated him to come into their towns and villages, and give them at least one sermon, and full of charity he willingly granted the request. At Montefiascone by the request of the Princess Piombino he stayed to give a triduo for fair weather, for in consequence of the incessant rains the country was quite inundated. From thence he went to Viterbo, where he was received with such demonstrations of respect, that in one procession they carried before and around the crucifix ten thousand lighted tapers. I cannot pass over in silence two occurrences in this mission. There were many Jews at this time living in Viterbo, and one amongst them, a young woman, went to hear Blessed Leonard preach on Eternity, when her heart was so touched with Divine grace, that she resolved to become a Christian as soon as she returned to Rome. With this determination she left the church, and some business requiring her to go to Montefiascone, she set off to walk there, but very soon she felt herself drawn back by some invisible means. Astonished at this, she made another effort to advance, but in vain; as this happened two or three times, she felt obliged to stand still, and presently she had not the power to move a step, and felt that her sight was failing. She turned back, went to Blessed Leonard, and related all that had happened to her, and asked him to give her the Sacrament of Baptism. On the same day he began to give her instructions, and she was baptized in the cathedral, to the great joy of the good father. The zealous missionary, having inveighed strongly in his sermons against those who dared to work on Sundays and feast days, threatened the most severe chastisement on all who transgressed this divine precept. On the feast of the Nativity of S. John the Baptist, a young girl, not caring for the solemn words of Blessed Leonard, went, contrary to the wish of her mother, with two companions, whom she had led astray, to gather flax in a field. Whilst she was at work, she suddenly felt a violent burning pain in her bowels, like an internal fire, and cried out several times: "I am burning, I am burning." The two other girls raised her in their arms and placed her under a tree, where they left her for a few moments to look for something they had left in the field, and returning to see how she was, they found her lying on the ground scorched as black as a firebrand, and quite dead. When this fact was made known, all believed it to be a just punishment sent from God, and it had due effect on the minds of the people, for they held Blessed Leonard in higher esteem, and practiced more faithfully what he taught them. After this he went through the diocese of Orté, of which Monsignor Tendirini was bishop, and his virtue and holiness was tested by the pious prelate in the following way. When he had finished his first sermon he was conducted along with his companions to the Episcopal Palace, appointed for their lodging; and on entering it they found in the hall a seat prepared, and a vessel of water ornamented with flowers, and all that was required for the washing of feet. Blessed Leonard wondered what this preparation could be for, and was much confused and humbled when he heard the good bishop desire him to seat himself in the chair, for he intended to wash his feet. The bishop, seeing that he could not induce him to accede to his wish in any other way, commanded him, in obedience, to consent to have his feet washed by him. At the word obedience he made no more resistance, placed himself, full of confusion, in the chair, when the devout and humble-minded Monsignor Tendirini falling on his knees, performed the pious function, washing first the feet of Blessed Leonard, and then those of his companions. This act made a deep impression on the minds of the people, and they esteemed more highly than ever their good bishop, and it aided to prepare their minds for the good seed about to be sown, and which produced most abundant fruit.

At Vicovaro, in the diocese of Tivoli, where Blessed Leonard was giving a mission, the Countess Flavia Bolognetti presented to him a valuable frame for the picture of the Blessed Virgin Mary, which he carried with him wherever he went, but he refused to accept it, saying that it was inconsistent with the vow of holy poverty he had made and strictly observed, and he returned it to the pious lady, thanking her for her generous charity. After this he preached in many towns in Tuscany, walking barefoot as usual in all seasons, poorly clad. It was the marvel of everyone how he was able to endure so fatiguing and laborious a life. In February, 1735, he traveled with great difficulty from the diocese of Jesi to Rome, and from thence, having first kissed the feet of the holy Pontiff, he returned to his beloved convent of Montorio Romano, where he stayed during Lent, employed in good works and spiritual exercises. One of the religious of the retreat of S. Buonaventura wrote to ask him if he would come to Rome after Easter; and he replied in these words: "I have many reasons for not going to Rome, but two especially; first, the flattery of the world, which over-estimates me, a miserable sinner, and causes me thereby much distress. Secondly, the loss of time, and dissipation of spirit. I desire to renounce the world, why then should I spend my time in it? Since I am crucified to the world, and forsake it, I wish to be forgotten by the world. My vocation is the giving of missions, and solitude. The missions, in which I am ever employed for the love of God, and solitude, in which I am ever occupied with God; all else is vanity." After Easter he was recommended by Cardinal Corradini to give missions in the diocese of Frascati. Satan tried every means in his power to prevent these missions, but all obstacles were overcome, and they were given in every town in that diocese. Cardinals Corradini and Guadagni, with many other illustrious persons, came to hear him. In Rocca di Papa, a place from its situation most inaccessible, materials were required for the building of a church, therefore, in his first discourse, he represented with great fervor how much it would tend to the glory of God if they exerted themselves to finish it; and after he had ended his sermon, he went directly with his companions to a place at some distance where there was a stone quarry. The congregation seeing this followed him, and all began to carry stones, in imitation of the good missionary, who, tired as he was with the labors of the day, was the first to load himself. From that time they continued to carry stones every day, so that very soon the church was finished. From this place the holy man went to Frascati, and on Cardinal Corradini telling him that he required rest after such fatiguing duties, he replied, "I wish not for rest on earth, but in Paradise." The cardinal, however, commanded him to rest at least one day, and he felt obliged to obey, and on this occasion he thus wrote to a friend: "I must stop for one day in Frascati, and this is to me a greater mortification than the discipline of a whole year, but God's will be done, I must suffer this short purgatory." Thus showing how he loved to labor and suffer continually for the glory of God and the salvation of souls.

CHAPTER XII

Blessed Leonard Goes Twice to Florence, and from Thence Returns to Give Missions in Different Places near Rome.

N the year 1735 a dispute having arisen amongst the monks of the retreat in Florence respecting some points in the institution, Blessed Leonard, who loved peace and order, went there to re-establish it. On this occasion he proved his prudence and virtue; he met with opposition, and even affronts, but he endured all with patience and admirable courage. To fortify himself for this, he retired for some days to his solitude dell' Incontro, to pray to God for light and assistance, and then having arranged the affairs of the retreat, he departed in October to preach penance in Orvieto. Being informed that in this diocese the people were much addicted to the vice of gambling, he inveighed most earnestly against it, threatening the gamblers with the severe chastisement of God if they did not forsake their evil ways, the cause of so much sin and disorder. Warned by the voice of the zealous preacher, they all ceased to play cards during the mission, with the *exception* of one man, who, regardless of the prayers and entreaties of his wife, who reminded him of the words of Blessed Leonard, still continued his vicious course, and only replied, "The missionary may say what he pleases; I am not to be frightened with his threats." Scarcely had he uttered the words when he fell to the ground, remained speechless for a few minutes, and then died.

From the diocese of Orvieto, he passed to Civita Vecchia, where he labored indefatigably in preaching to the galley slaves, and others on board the vessels in that port, and gave them a mission, which lasted twenty days. So abundant was the fruit which this zealous minister produced by preaching to slaves, soldiers, sailors, and many others, that where formerly nothing was heard but blasphemy and obscene language, now was seen compunction, tears, and humility; and not only the whole day, but the greatest part of the night was employed in hearing confessions. The galley slaves had permission to go to confession at the hospital of the Chaplins of the Galleys, where the missionaries lodged. At the concluding sermon, when Blessed Leonard was to give his blessing, all the inhabitants of Civita Vecchia attended, amongst others, three cardinals, and many of the nobles. He then returned to Rome, and employed himself during Lent in giving spiritual exercises, and in other good works for the benefit of souls. At Easter he was sent by the pope to give a mission in Perugia.

The devil being much disconcerted at losing so many souls who had been ensnared by him in sin, which would certainly be the case if Blessed Leonard went to Perugia, raised every obstacle in his power to prevent the mission. The first day he ascended the pulpit, there was heard a murmuring and whispering amongst the people, concerning the maxim and proposition given them. "Either penance, or hell." They said that it was sufficient for one who had committed mortal sin to confess, and to receive absolution for the remission of his sins, and thus be delivered from eternal punishment, penance was therefore not necessary. This they declared without reflecting that the penance of which the holy father spoke was that sincere contrition and conversion to God, with a thorough detestation of past transgressions, which is the beginning of a new life, conformed to the precepts and maxims of the Gospel, and without which it is impossible to be saved. Those who opposed the mission were very soon discovered, and defeated in their ignorant and ill-conceived design, but they endeavored to prevent another object which he had recommended in one of his sermons. He had succeeded in persuading the people to place over the doors of their houses the monogram of the most holy name of Jesus, which had been suggested by Bernadino of Sienna. One night this sacred monogram was most impiously defaced, to the great horror of all who, in the morning, beheld the sad spectacle, but no one could tell who had committed the sacrilege. All these diabolical efforts, however, instead of diminishing, stimulated the zeal of Blessed Leonard, and towards the end of the retreat he had the consolation of seeing these misguided people so changed and contrite, that the church could not contain the number of his hearers, and he was obliged to preach in the piazza; many conversions took place. I shall mention two of the most remarkable.

To the great scandal of Perugia, a person well known, and of high rank, had for many years lived in open concubinage with a woman, and no one had the power to prevent it. However, one day the unfortunate woman was induced to attend the mission, and was so struck with the words spoken by Blessed Leonard, that she remained in the church waiting until she saw him leave the pulpit; she then came forward, threw herself at his feet, weeping bitterly, and entreated him to hear her confession, declaring that she was ready to forsake her sinful life to begin a new one, and make amends for former scandals by sincere repentance. The good missionary heard her confession, and the penitent was so firmly resolved to carry into effect her design, that in order to be free from temptation, for she was young and beautiful, she decided to leave Perugia, and to go to Rome to take the habit in the strict convent of the Convertite di San Giacomo. The gentleman finding that she had left him, was first enraged, and made an attempt to follow her, but soon it pleased God to touch his heart also through the means of a sermon; he was conscience-stricken, and throwing himself at the feet of Blessed Leonard, confessed, among many other sins, that of joining in the opposition to the mission, for which he asked pardon of Almighty God, with a promise of an entire change of life, to the great joy of all the town, who thanked God for having, by His grace, converted these two persons, who had caused so much scandal. When the mission was ended, the people came and made great demonstrations of gratitude to Blessed Leonard, and he departed for Foligno, having first venerated the ring of the Blessed Virgin Mary, when it was solemnly exposed in the cathedral where it is kept. The inhabitants of Perugia, who attended the missions with great diligence, wished to possess something he had used as a relic, or memorial of him. Well knowing his holy poverty, and that he had not even a picture or image to give away, and that he was very careful in preventing anyone taking the things he had used, saying always that the world was wrong in supposing him to be a holy man, they resolved to possess themselves of the banner which he carried about with him in his missions, on which was embroidered the most sacred names of Jesus and Mary. To effect this, they had one made exactly like it, and carried it in procession to Spello, where he was preaching; they entered the church, and in the presence of all, even the good missionary, who was too much astonished to remonstrate, they left the new banner and carried away the old one. The procession of the Blessed Virgin Mary, which took place on this occasion at Spello, was numerously attended, almost all of the inhabitants of Foligno assembled, besides the people from other towns in the vicinity, with the greatest devotion. From Spello Blessed Leonard went to preach in the dioceses of Citta della Pieve, Albano, Tivoli, Velletri, and Palestrina, and in October, at the request of Cardinal Aldovrandi, he went to Montefiascone. The cardinal wished to maintain the mission at his own expense, and provide for all the wants of Blessed Leonard and his companions; but the servant of God, steadfast to the vow of holy poverty, begged they might be allowed, as usual, to subsist by asking alms. The cardinal attended morning and evening at the sacred functions, and severely reproved the canons of the cathedral for not attending the instructions on the first day. After Blessed Leonard had preached the sermon on the devotion to our Blessed Lady, on which occasion he always kissed the feet of all the priests present, the bishop was so much affected, that he went the following morning into the sacristy, and waited there until the missionary, who was celebrating the holy sacrifice, left the altar, and as soon as he made his appearance, he knelt down to kiss his feet; the holy man fell on his knees in great confusion to prevent such an act, but the cardinal reminded him of obedience, and Blessed Leonard was obliged to give way, and permit a dignitary of the church, clad in purple, to kiss his feet, to the great edification of all present. The inhabitants of several places in this diocese desired to hear him, but the Florentines having entreated him to give them another mission, he felt obliged to go there in December.

Great was the inconvenience he endured in consequence of the snow and rain, which fell in torrents; added to which he never carried any provisions with him in traveling, but always set off fasting in the morning, trusting in Divine Providence. For two days on this journey they were in extreme want. Whenever they asked alms of anyone, even when exhausted with hunger and fatigue, they were repulsed, all declaring they had nothing to give them. In this the holy man rejoiced, and he called on his companions to return thanks with him to God for having made them taste the fruits of poverty.

He reached Florence almost worn out and exhausted; however, he gave the mission in December, in the church of S. Niccolo, whilst it lasted, in order that the country people, and those who lived without the city gates, might attend. The Prince of Creon, who was then governor, ordered the two gates nearest the church of Niccolo to be opened before break of day. After this mission he gave one in the church of S. Lorenzo, which, spacious as it is, could not contain the multitude. The crowd was so great that they were obliged to have a guard of soldiers at the doors, and in the square. It happened during this mission that one day when he was preaching on obstinate sinners, all present burst into most excessive grief, weeping, and calling on God for mercy. The holy man, as his voice could no longer be heard for the greatness of the noise, took his crucifix in his hand, and held it up; at this the lamentations increased. It pleased the Almighty, in order to give efficacy to the voice of His servant, to cause globes of fire to appear in the church, which frightened and touched with compunction the most hardened sinner. The priests were obliged to go into the confessional that evening, and remain there the greater part of the night to hear the confessions of numbers who were afraid to leave the church as they had entered it, with their consciences burdened with sin. After he had ended this mission he retired to the retreat of S. Maria dell' Incontro, to go through his spiritual exercises, acquire renewed fervor, and gain strength; and from thence he went to preach in Pesaro Fano, Fossombroni, Camerino, and other places. In Camerino there had been for some time much enmity and discord amongst the people, but Blessed Leonard succeeded in restoring peace and unity, and left them all reconciled and in peace one with another. From this place he went to give a mission in the cathedral of Assisi with great pleasure and satisfaction, as it was the birthplace of the seraphic S. Francis, and also because the people were most eager to hear him, standing at the doors of the church all night, although it was November, waiting until they were opened, to secure places. From Assisi he went to Rieti, where a proud lady lived, who on hearing that he was coming, determined not to attend the mission, and retired with a companion to her country house. The same evening that the mission was begun the house took fire, and was burnt to the ground; she only escaped with her life, and returned to Rieti. On being informed that the missionary had induced the people not to celebrate the carnival that year, without heeding the remonstrances of her friends, who reminded her of the danger she had just escaped, she set off for Rome, to enjoy the amusement of the carnival there. Almighty God, however, willed that the exhortations of His servant should be heard; and as the first warning was disregarded, it was decreed she should suddenly be deprived of life. One evening when she was at a ball, gaily attired, she was suddenly seized with spasms, and died in a moment, in the presence of her mother, whose vanity and folly even exceeded that of the daughter. Amongst many conversions in this place, the most wonderful was that of Ginevra Leone, who had been dissuaded by her mother from embracing the religious life, and at the age of sixteen was married to a lawyer, very unequal in age and disposition, for she was lively, joyous, and fond of amusement, and he grave, austere, and melancholy, which gave rise to disunion and quarrels; she had parties at her house constantly, although discountenanced by her husband, who resented her conduct severely. This state of affairs went on for five years, when Blessed Leonard came to Rieti to preach penance. The evening before the mission was begun Ginevra had a party at home, and the conversation turned on that subject. One of the visitors said that Blessed Leonard had with his threats turned the brain of more than one woman, and advised all present not to attend the mission. Another said she wondered what had brought him there, for the missions were intended for remote places, and not for large towns, where everything was known necessary for salvation. Notwithstanding all this bad advice, Ginevra made up her mind to hear the man of God; but when she was preparing to go out in the morning it began to rain, and she to hesitate, when a friend ventured to remind her that the rain never prevented her going to balls and the theater, therefore a slight shower of rain ought not to deter her attending the mission, on which perhaps her eternal salvation depended. She went, and continued to attend all the remaining days. One evening the sermon was on death, and the missionary described in the most impressive manner the state of a dying man; he carried his hearers in imagination to a deathbed scene where the dying man was lying with the crucifix clasped in his hands, the tapers burning, the priest by his side, and the devil hovering near, and all his sins in array before him. Ginevra instantly felt an inward conviction of all her transgressions, and resolved from that moment to change her mode of life. Returning home she began the work of reformation, and her husband dying soon after this, she assumed the habit of the third order of S. Francis, in which, after leading a most exemplary and austere life, she passed to a better world, in 1749.

From Rieti Blessed Leonard proceeded to give missions in Corneto and Toscanella. At the last sermon he preached in Corneto, he fainted in the pulpit from exhaustion; he was carried into the air, and having rallied again, resumed, and finished his sermon with his usual fervor and eloquence, to the astonishment of the congregation, who thought him dead. The next place in which he preached was Ascoli, and one day when he was preaching on the holy name of Jesus, a dove was seen flying about and over his head the whole time, and disappeared as soon as the sermon was ended, and it was generally believed that the Holy Spirit, in that form, had made it manifest that He assisted the man of God, and gave force and efficacy to his words. When he was preaching in the Piazza, three marble pillars in front of the church, beneath which a number of people were standing, slipped from the capitals, and if they had fallen, would have caused many deaths, but, to the astonishment of all, they remained suspended in air, and no one was injured. From Ascoli he went through various dioceses in the Marca, amongst others, Marcerata, Osimo, and Ancona, and in the last mentioned town, the image of the Blessed Virgin, which he always carried with him on his missions, was exposed, with a hundred and thirty candles burning before it, and although they were lighted many times during the day, they diminished so little, that only the weight of six pounds of wax was consumed, which was what had been given us as alms by a benefactor.

CHAPTER XIII

HILST this indefatigable laborer in the Lord's vineyard was toiling for the salvation of souls in various dioceses in the Marca of Ancona, he received an order to go and preach in the neighborhood of Rome, which he hastened to obey. He went through the dioceses of Tivoli, Veroli, and Fondi, preaching with wonderful force and zeal; he destroyed vice, and turned many sinners from the way of perdition to that of salvation. From Fondi he was sent to San Germano, a town subject to the abbot of Monte Casino; he went there most willingly, fully persuaded of the spiritual wants of the people, and with a strong desire to improve them. He arrived there in January, 1740, and would have begun the mission the same day, if the abbot, who saw how exhausted and weary he was with his journey, had not desired him to rest for two days; he obeyed, and after that began the mission with his accustomed fervor and zeal, by means of which he effected much spiritual benefit for the people, who were at first much opposed to him, as will be shown by the following fact.

Amongst the many ingenious ways which Blessed Leonard made use of to rouse sinners from the lethargy of sin, and bring them to penance, was that of causing the great bell of the church to be rung during the mission, at one hour after the evening Ave, in order that the people might say three Pater Nosters, and three Aves, and to make them reflect that this bell was rung for them, to touch their hearts, and convert them to God. In San Germano, where the custom was established, there were many, who, from their station in life, ought to have promoted the mission, were quite opposed to it, and spoke against the good missionary, saying that he intended to frighten them with the sound of a bell. But the Almighty, who on so many other occasions had mercifully defended His minister and faithful servant, came to his aid in the present instance. The sacristan of the cathedral was not able to ring the bell without assistance, and had, at the appointed hour, brought some men to assist him; but when they entered the belfry, they discovered that the rope was shortened, so that they could not reach it, but, at the same time, heard the bell ringing loudly. They could only conjecture that some person was in the belfry, and had drawn the rope up, but they knew the church doors were locked, and wondered how anyone could have entered. The bell still continued ringing, and they began to call out that that was enough, the bell would be broken, but as it still went on, the sacristan lighted a candle, and with his companions, went up into the belfry, when, to their utter amazement, they discovered that no one was there, and the bell was ringing of itself, or rather, was moved by an invisible, supernatural power. They gazed in fear and astonishment for some time, and at length tried to stop it, they did this with great difficulty, for the rope had slipped away, so that they were unable to reach it, and without it they could hardly move the bell, it was so large and heavy. A clear statement of this was given in writing, and duly attested, and was sent to be the means of reforming those who had opposed the mission, and cause them to return thanks to God for sending them so zealous a missionary.

From S. Germano he passed to Nocera, from thence to Gubbio, where the bishop, not being able to conduct the solemn procession of the Feast of Corpus Domini, desired Blessed Leonard to undertake it. He at first refused with great humility so great an honor, but the clergy entreated him so earnestly, that he felt obliged to consent, and carried the Blessed Sacrament through the town, assisted by the same priests as would have gone with the bishop, and with the same pomp as if he had led the procession. The meek and modest deportment of the servant of God, so mortified, even externally, caused great compunction in these people, and they held him in such high esteem, that many of high rank assumed the habit of pilgrims, and followed him on foot to different places where he gave missions, in the diocese of Camerino, S. Severino, Fermo, and Loreto. At San Severino the bishop, on presenting the crucifix to him at the beginning of the mission, took the occasion to play on his name, telling him that he was a lion, fighting against the powers of darkness, and desired him to roar loudly to save his people. And roar, in fact, he did, with so loud a voice that he banished sin, and effected a perfect reformation.

It happened during this mission, that a poor woman, desiring to hear the religious instructions, left her child, about two years old, sleeping in its cradle, and recommending it to the Holy Virgin, went to the church. When she returned the child was missing, and in great distress she set forth in search for him, and presently found that he had thrown himself from a window two stories high, but remained suspended in air by his swathing bands, without having sustained the least injury.

From Loreto he went to Rome, and having kissed the feet of the holy Pontiff Benedict XIV, who had been elected two months before, he humbly entreated him to say if he thought it was the will of God that he should be employed in giving missions, or if it was better for him to retire to his monastery, and think of his own soul, and prepare for death. The holy Pontiff replied that it was clearly the will of God that he should be employed in giving missions during the remainder of his life, and, like a brave soldier, die with his sword in his hand, fighting against the powers of darkness. This prediction was verified at the time of his death, as we shall see. His Holiness then intimated that he was going to proclaim the Jubilee, granted as usual in the first year of his pontificate, and that he should appoint him to give missions in five churches in Rome, viz., the SS. Apostoli, S Carlo al Corso, Santa Maria in Trastevere, S. Pietro in Vincoli, and S. Giovanni dei Fiorentini. Having received this order, he retired to his convent of S. Buonaventura, to gain renewed ardor and heavenly graces for the recommencement of his duties. On the 13th of November, 1740, he began the mission in the church of the Apostles, and having finished that, he gave in succession the appointed missions in all the other churches, which were attended by an immense concourse of people in every grade of life, and many were converted. In the church of S. Carlo alone he reformed ten women of bad character, whom he afterwards placed in the Conservatorio. In January, 1741, he went to Terracina, and the following letter, written on the 24th of January by Monsignor Oldi, bishop of that diocese, to the father-guardian of S. Buonaventura in Rome, will give some idea of the good he did there:

"The mission intended for the greater glory of God is ended in this town, and with extraordinary success; in the memory of man nothing like it has ever taken place, not only because it has been so well attended, but for the sincere compunction all have felt for their sins, and for the way in which they have applied all that was said, each individually to himself, with fear and remorse; they made general confessions, reconciliations, and restitutions. When he departed they fired the guns of the fortress as if for some illustrious person, and he had left behind him the fame of being a most devoted servant of God. He is universally reputed to be a saint, and such I hold him to be. Twice I have obliged him to bless me, in the presence of his companions. Would your reverence keep my letter, as we cannot tell what God may have destined in after times for one on whom He has bestowed so great gifts."

From Terracina he was sent by Benedict XIV to Gaeta, a place where he had for a long time been desired to visit; however, the people were much displeased that the time fixed for giving a mission should be when they were making preparations for the Carnival, as all would be thrown away, and a useless expenditure have been incurred. They were very much opposed to it, but the good missionary, unwilling that the devil should get possession of them entirely, told them he had not come to interfere with their amusements, but only to beg they would attend the sermons; with this assurance he quieted them, and began the mission. From the first day the attendance was most numerous, the crowd was so great that it became necessary to place a guard of soldiers in the church and around the confessionals, and also before the house where the missionaries lodged, to prevent any disorder which so great a concourse might cause. Three days after the missions commenced, the officers gave out a play, and sent invitations to all the gentry in the town. As, however, three only were accepted, they abandoned the theater and carnival, and gave themselves up to religious exercises and hearing sermons. One of the officers went in great humility to call on Blessed Leonard, to entreat his forgiveness on the part of the others for having opposed that which was manifestly the work of God; one, however, remained deaf to the Divine call, and determined to remain in sin, for which he was punished, and made an example to everyone in the town. When he was preaching on the miserable state of a hardened sinner. Blessed Leonard, inflamed with more than ordinary fervor, uttered these words: "My heart tells me that there is here one amongst us who is a hardened sinner, if he does not repent and reform, all is over with him. This very night the punishment will fall on him." The hardened sinner in fact was present, he was one who for some time had caused great scandal by his evil ways, from which not even the admonitions of the bishop had induced him to turn. Whilst he was at supper the same evening, he was suddenly seized with sickness, and died without the rites of the Church; his body instantly became so black and deformed, that it was fearful to behold. This event caused great consternation in the town, and the fame of the good missionary was higher than ever. In a sermon on the devotion to our Blessed Lady, he recommended everyone to forgive offences, and be reconciled to their neighbors. The mayor of the town, having for some time refused to salute with reverence his bishop, in consequence of the earnest exhortations of the servant of God, went in the presence of all, and kneeling, kissed the hand of the prelate when he was assisting at the mission. The bishop and all the officiating priests requested Blessed Leonard after he had ended the mission to remain there to give them some spiritual exercises, but as he could not comply with their request, they were obliged to content themselves with the benefit they had gained from his sermons. Archdeacon Conca, in a letter written on the 5th of March, 1744, thus described it to the bishop of Terracina: "You can form no idea of the abundant fruits gathered by means of the missions of the holy man, Father Leonard of Port Maurice, he has truly sanctified the town of Gaeta. Everyone felt during the mission an especial assistance of the Holy Spirit, and was moved by a zeal truly apostolic; so great was the esteem and veneration for the good missionary, that the crowd assembled to hear him was so great, that they were obliged to have a guard at the church door, many people were carried out fainting, and his leaving them was universally regretted. I shall not now enlarge on the subject, but reserve all further particulars till we meet."

Blessed Leonard left Gaeta for Rome on the 17th of February, where he remained during Lent and Holy Week, and gave the spiritual exercises as formerly, in the Rospigliosi palace, to the great edification of all who attended, especially the nobles. After Easter he went to teach in the diocese of Terracina for the second time, from whence he passed to Pontecorvo, and other places, and when he was giving a mission in Cavi, a town in the diocese of Palestrina, they gave him an image of the Madonna holding in her arms her divine Son. The pious missionary was much gratified with this gift, and admired it so much, that he gave it the name of the "Madonna del' bell' amore," and always carried it with him on his missions. So great was the fatigue endured by this indefatigable laborer, for the glory of God and the salvation of souls in the campagna of Rome, that whilst he was preaching his first sermon in Bocchignano, his strength was quite exhausted, and he fell fainting in the pulpit, from whence he was carried into the nearest house, and his life was despaired of, but on recovering from the fainting-fit, he intimated his intention of preaching the following day, which he did, and on ascending the pulpit he began with these words: "My flesh was weak yesterday, and I fell to the ground, therefore, I must chastise it, in order that I may not fail again." That he made light of these fainting fits, frequently occasioned by the great fatigue, will be seen on several occasions, and especially in Civita ducale, where he opened the mission the same evening on which he arrived, wearied and exhausted with a long journey made, as usual, barefoot, but before he had half finished his sermon, his voice failed, and he was obliged to sit down half dead. Everyone present thought that the function would end thus; however, he recovered a little, and resumed his discourse with so much energy, that he astonished everyone, and placing a crown of thorns on his head, and a chain round his neck, took a discipline into his hand, and would have scourged himself if the vicar-general had not, ascending the platform, compelled him to lay it aside. These are the kind of restoratives which he used for his body, which, like S. Francis, he used to call his beast of burden, and he treated it as such in his journeys and labors.

After this he went to give a mission in the town of Rieti, and on the same day, the 8th of June, 1742, they brought to him a woman possessed, and the evil spirit, speaking in her, declared that he had used every effort to destroy the effects of his ministry. In fact, some extraordinary accident had happened every day, contrived by the common enemy to prevent many attending the mission. When he was preaching the first sermon, a cat, which was believed to be the devil under that form, leaped from a high window on the head of a nun, who, belonging to an uncloistered order, was out of her convent, and pulled off her veil, which caused much talking and confusion amongst the people. One day some bricks fell from the church, on another an iron bar, but all escaped unhurt, though they were so crowded together; and on another occasion, when he was giving instructions in the Piazza, two bullocks, drawing a cart, ran away into the midst of the crowd, causing great alarm and confusion; however, no one sustained the least injury, but during all this the poor woman possessed laughed, and the devil within her boasted of having caused all this confusion, and declared his intention of causing still more. Blessed Leonard was desired to command her to cease from doing any more mischief, and having done so, he was allowed to finish the mission in peace. Amongst many other good works which he performed in Rieti for the glory of God, was that of undertaking the defense of some priests who had suffered persecution for the sole cause of having formed a society composed of priests and clerics, each of whom was to be employed, according to his capacity, in promoting the glory of God and the salvation of souls, they were to catechize the children, instruct prisoners, visit the sick, and labor to reform those who had gone astray. At an hour appointed they were to meet in each other's house by turns, and after reading a chapter from some pious book, and holding a conference, they were to finish with holy meditation. This society was formed of sixty persons, who besides the great gain to their own souls, were the means of leading others in the way of holiness, which excited the envy of the devil, who raised a storm of discord amongst the clergy. Suspicions arose against them; public censure and discontent prevailed in the town. They were accused of ignorance, rashness, and presumption, and there were even some who treated them as sectarians and lovers of novelty. Monsignor Camarda, then bishop of Rieti, being informed of all this, was determined to silence the slanderers, and make secure the peace and honor of these holy men, and gave orders that the conference and every other function should be held no longer in private houses, but in the church. But although the learned prelate attended these public meetings several times, as did also many well known ecclesiastics, the discontent and whispering did not cease, but increased every day, so that the members, fearing violence and danger to themselves; thought of giving up the association. About this time Blessed Leonard was giving a mission in Civita ducale, four miles distant from Rieti, and being informed of what was going on there, he sent a messenger to the clergy to entreat them not to abandon their pious association and the good they had begun. A few days afterwards he went to preach in the neighborhood of Rieti, when he took the opportunity of praising, both in public and privately, the above-mentioned priests, declared that he intended to employ them in the mission, and exhorted all present to attend their holy exercises, and bestowed on them the title of the congregation of the "Amanti di Dio." In concluding the mission he suggested the attendance at the exercises of the confraternity as one of the means of deriving advantage from it, and persevering towards perfection. This was quite sufficient to quiet the tumult and silence the detractors, and they very soon saw those whom they had slandered and condemned recommence their labors with so much profit that they became constant in their attendance at all their pious exercises. The confraternity was so firmly established, that the bishop, feeling confident of the great advantage resulting from it, obtained the pope's brief for them, erecting them into a congregation of secular priests, under the title of the "Amanti di Dio," and gave them a church in the town, where, by their daily ministrations in the confessional, continued preaching of the Divine word, and other pious practices, they opened to the people of Rieti and other places in the neighborhood a school in which to learn the way of salvation and the holy fear of God. The

Bishop, to make known the obligation he felt for the support he had given them by his zeal, spoke of Blessed Leonard in the following words: "All who have enjoyed these means of salvation ought, after God, to acknowledge that they owe very much to Blessed Leonard, for having supported this good work when it was in danger of being destroyed." He afterwards gave missions in several places in the diocese of Rieti and the abbacy of S. Salvatore Maggiore. When he was preaching in Belmonte, the Blessed Virgin testified in a singular and sensible manner how pleased she was with this faithful servant, for honoring, and leading others to venerate her by solemnly exposing her image to the people. During the last sermon, when the image was carried in procession, a star was seen shining over the stand on which the sacred image was, to the great wonder and admiration of all who beheld it. From Belmonte he went to Riofreddo, a place in the diocese of Tivoli, and whilst he was laboring there for the greater glory of God and the salvation of souls, he received an order to go to Rome, where the Pope wished him to renew the missions. Therefore in November, 1743, he repaired to that capital, and began his labors with admirable zeal and energy, first in the Church of the Holy Apostles, which mission was attended by many of the cardinals, and even the Pope himself, and afterwards in the church of S. Lorenzo. At this time he attended the deathbed of the Marchese Vincenzo Nunez, who having made to him his general confession, entreated him to remain and assist him in his last fearful struggle. The servant of God willingly complied with this request, and when the dying man faintly said, "Father Leonard, I consign my soul into thy hands," "and I," said he, "consign it into the hands of God," he rendered his soul to his Creator with meekness and resignation.

CHAPTER XIV

*Blessed Leonard Is Sent to Give a Mission in Genoa,
and from Thence to Lucca and Pistoia, and
Afterwards to the Island of Corsica.*

HE inhabitants of Genoa had for some time wished that Blessed Leonard would give a mission there, and having received orders he went from Rome to Florence, and from thence to Leghorn, where he embarked for Genoa. Great was the joy of these citizens on seeing him, for they had impatiently expected his arrival. The day following, which was Sunday, he was requested by the father superior of the convent of the Riformati to preach in their church, and the obedient and humble servant of God, although he would willingly have remained in private for some days, consented to give them a sermon. Scarcely was it known in the town that Blessed Leonard was to preach, when such a multitude assembled, that even the church, spacious as it is, was filled to excess, the convent and the Quadrangle were also crowded with people to hear, as they said, an apostle preach. He ascended the pulpit, and spoke of mortal sin in a tone of voice and fervor of spirit, that even at the beginning of his sermon lamentations and weeping were heard, and great signs of compunction were seen; towards the conclusion one might have imagined the awful day of judgment had come. To prove how abundant the fruits of this sermon were, the day following the penitents at the confessional were so numerous, that the priests were obliged to remain there all day hearing confessions. The bishop hearing of his fame and extraordinary zeal, gave him full power to exercise his apostolical ministry in all the towns on the banks of the Ponente. In one of these places some persons were found who opposed the mission, and others who refused to attend it, but they were punished by Almighty God. A person of some consequence in the place being decidedly opposed to the coming of the missionary, determined to leave the town as soon as he should appear, but before he had proceeded far on his journey he was overtaken by a violent storm, accompanied by thunder and lightning, which, however, did not arrest his progress; and as he was passing under a rock, a great portion of it became detached and fell to the ground, and he just escaped being buried beneath it. Everyone who heard of it declared it was a manifest warning from Almighty God.

A woman in the same place, instead of going to attend the mission, notwithstanding the remonstrances of her neighbors, went to work in the fields. When the storm came on she ran under the nearest tree, and climbed up one of the branches, but hardly had she done so, when she found herself suddenly thrown to the ground, and so severely hurt that she did not recover for some time. But if Blessed Leonard met with opposition in this place, it was very different in Port Maurice; the people rejoiced to see once more their fellow-citizen, from whom they had been separated for thirty-four years, and received him with extraordinary demonstrations of joy, and arranged everything with the greatest care, so that the mission should be properly conducted, and attended all the services with the most perfect devotion. When he was about to leave Port Maurice for Finale, four of his companions whom he had brought with him fell sick, and during their illness he was sent to give a mission in Genoa where he assembled such a multitude that they were obliged to raise a platform at the door of the church of the Riformati, so that he might be beard in the piazza as well as the church, both of which were crowded to excess. After this he went to preach in Bisagno, where it was computed that more than a hundred thousand were assembled to hear him. It was wonderful to behold that crowd.

No sooner had the missionary ascended the platform than

every voice was silenced, and all stood listening with the greatest attention. For a public and lasting memorial of the mission given by Blessed Leonard in Bisagno, the superior of the college gave orders that in the last place in which he preached three crosses should be raised, and a Calvary with an inscription, made of small black and white stones, of the words so often used by the servant of God, "Jesus, my mercy!" And as the zealous missionary, in preaching on the holy Name of Jesus, had recommended everyone to place the sacred monogram of the Most High over their doors, they had a very large one made of marble, beautifully carved, and in letters of bronze gilded the holy Name of Jesus, and that of Mary His Mother, and on the feast of John the Baptist it was placed over the door of the Monte Reale, and whilst they were carrying it in procession, the guns were fired, and the bells of all the churches were rung. The heads of the college assisted at high mass in the Metropolitan church, and the collect for the feast of the holy Name of Jesus was introduced in the mass, as also in all the churches in Genoa, by order of the archbishop. An order was also sent to all cities and fortified places of the Republic, to raise the monogram of Jesus and Mary over their gates.

In the meantime an order came from the pope for him to go to the island of Corsica, to which place he proceeded after having given missions in Lucca and Pistoia. Whilst he was giving the missions in Vioreggio, in the diocese of Lucca, the vessel which was to take him to Corsica was sent from Genoa, and cast anchor in the gulf of Spezia; the captain sent a felucca to Vioreggio, in which he embarked, to the great regret of the inhabitants, because he was obliged to leave the mission half finished; and from Portovenere in May, 1744, he passed to the island of Corsica. This island was at that time rent with revolutions, discord, rivalry, and factions, which were the cause of frequent murders, and rendered it a scene of desolation; and all this arose because the greater part of the inhabitants refused to be governed by the republic of Genoa. At so difficult and important a crisis, Blessed Leonard, fearless of danger, and ready to give his life for the salvation of souls, persuaded that he was doing the will of God, declared that he came authorized by the Holy Father, and only desired the peace and well-being and the sanctification of the islanders, telling them that he had come to give a mission, and would very soon land for that purpose. He was at sea two days and three nights, during which time he preached to the sailors and soldiers on board the vessel, of whom there were more than a hundred, and caused them to feel such great contrition, that on landing all made a general confession. They arrived at Bastia, the capital of the island, in the middle of the night, and were obliged to wait until morning to land, and the first thing after he had set his foot on shore, Blessed Leonard went to the convent of the Riformati, and celebrated mass, after which he called on the governor, with whom he held a long conference concerning the mission he intended to give.

The inhabitants of Bastia, who held him already in high esteem, the fame of his zeal and extraordinary holiness having reached them, made a request through the provincial and superior of the convent, that he would preach to them, which he easily granted. On the Feast of S. Pasquale after vespers, the governor having assembled the members of the senate, and most of the nobility in the church, the holy father ascended the pulpit after vespers, and preached to a numerous congregation, who listened with breathless attention, and many faces were seen bathed in tears. They wished him to give the mission in Bastia; but considering all the circumstances, the governor decided that it was better he should go first into the remote parts of the island, and afterwards give it With great solemnity in the capital. Therefore having received the necessary instructions, in order to regulate his ministrations prudently, he set off for the diocese of Mariana. As a presage of what he was to suffer afterwards, in this first journey he became so weak in consequence of fatigue caused by the rough roads, which had been torn up by a flood, and the finding no place of rest by the way, that he arrived at the convent in such a state of exhaustion that he could scarcely support himself. When they heard of the arrival of the missionary, a great number of people assembled to see him, but all armed with muskets, swords, and pistols. On beholding the people thus armed, and the ruin and desolation of the convent, which a few years before had been burned to the ground in a war with the French, he felt how true the report was of the ruin and severe loss to the island caused by disunion and discord, and without loss of time gave notice that he intended to give the first mission in this place; and being convinced that the prevailing sins were hatred and revenge, he began his sermon by inveighing against them. In order to induce these poor souls to lay aside all hatred and malice, he proposed to them two most efficacious means; one was to have the monogram of the most holy Name of Jesus printed in large letters on a board, which every day at the end of each sermon he should hold up to them, imploring at the same time the Divine Savior to restore peace to the island, he also recommended them to place the holy monogram over the door of their houses, and adore it every time they came in and went out, saying, "Jesus my mercy," with the intention of renouncing the sin of revenge. The other means he adopted was to place the stations of the cross in every church, and propose to everyone who attended this pious exercise to forgive all who had injured them, in imitation of our Blessed Lord, and to bear all injuries for the love of Him. So effectual were these and other efforts made by the zealous missionary to obtain what he so ardently desired, that he adopted them in the town of Mariana, where there were many living in open warfare; and his sermons made so deep an impression, that soon there was an end to all hostilities; and laying aside their arms, they embraced each other, and mutually entreated forgiveness. All this was effected so quickly, that those who had been mortal enemies for many years, at the voice of Blessed Leonard became not only reconciled in public, but ratified the peace by signing a public document.

On the day fixed for preaching the sermon on the devotion to our Blessed Lady, it happened that some men from the mountains passed through Mariana, all armed according to the custom, and seeing a great concourse of people, they inquired why they were assembled. They were informed that a mission was being given, when they became enraged, and raised their voices, saying: "Ah, this is the way we are treated by Genoese, sending their missionary to make us obey them, but we will have no Genoese here." Having uttered these words, they paused, desiring out of curiosity to hear the missionary, who by this time had nearly finished his sermon, and was in the act of putting the chain round his neck, asking pardon of the people, and kissing the feet of the priests. When they beheld this they began to feel compunction, their rage was changed into admiration, they declared peace, laid aside their arms, and throwing themselves at the feet of Blessed Leonard, gave public demonstration of their compunction and desire of amendment. Having heard of the wonderful success of the mission in Mariana, where peace had been so happily restored, the priests of Casacconi, which was in revolt and in arms, desired to have Blessed Leonard there; however he was not able to comply with their wish, because he was ordered to Casinga, but he sent them some persons called there "Parolanti," to treat with the offending party there, and assure them that if they would cease their warfare and hostility he would come in due time and give them a mission. They promised all that Blessed Leonard required of them, and faithfully kept this promise, as the Corsicans are wont to do. He then began the mission in the parish of Casinga, which was attended by the inhabitants of seven other neighboring parishes; the concourse as usual was so great that he was obliged to preach in the Piazza, when all were so touched with compunction that they waited from morning till night in the churches to go to confession; and those who, in consequence of the crowd, could not approach the confessionals, were much disappointed, and returned many times, until they succeeded in unburdening their consciences.

The rivalry and enmity which had prevailed in this parish was of a more serious nature, and of more frequent occurrence than our missionary had found in Mariana; but full of zeal, with the crucifix in his hand, he addressed them in so earnest and forcible a manner, that the hardest hearts were softened, and bursting into tears, they drew near, first to kiss the image of their crucified Redeemer, and then embracing each other, they were reconciled, and forgave all past injuries. It happened in this place that when the man of God, in one of his sermons, was loudly condemning those who made use of coarse and indecent language, and sang immoral songs, a countryman present began uttering the same in defiance, and in the hearing of his wife and some other women, who reproved him, but he still continued, and jested at the threatening of the missionary, and said it was only the way of the world. He had scarcely uttered the words, when he was seized with sudden illness, was carried home, and died very soon after, without the sacraments. The people were filled with horror, and the esteem and veneration for Blessed Leonard increased so much, that all desired to obey and fulfill his utmost wishes, fearing the wrath and chastisement of God. Immediately after the mission in this parish, according to his promise, he went to give one at Casacconi, where he found that discord and enmity had reached such a height, that it seemed almost impossible to restore peace. The sermons, however, were very well attended, and so many desired to go to confession, that the churches could not contain the crowd, and they were obliged to build confessionals outside, and for three days and three nights an immense crowd surrounded the house of Blessed Leonard, preferring to sleep in the open air, rather than not confess to him. But for all this he failed in restoring peace in some families, and much did it grieve the man of God to see so many souls in danger of being lost eternally; for it is frequently the case in Corsica, that hatred and enmity becomes a party thing, spreading through a whole class, as was the case in Casacconi, where seven hundred persons were divided into two contending parties. The last day of the mission came, and no signs of reconciliation, when the good missionary ascended the platform, and after having inveighed in the strongest terms against this revengeful, vindictive spirit, he turned towards them once more, and declared with Apostolic freedom, that not only he did not intend to give them his blessing, but even threatened them with the severe chastisement of God if they refused to be reconciled. He remained silent for some time, holding the crucifix in his hand, intending to conclude the mission, when there was a sudden movement in the crowd, and the belligerents presented themselves before the platform, weeping with much contrition, and laying aside their arms, called on each other to be reconciled, and in order to preserve peace for the future, they drew up and signed a solemn treaty.

A young man who lived in the neighborhood, having heard that a great number of people had assembled in Casacconi, went there with the intention of finding his enemy, and murdering him, as he afterwards confessed, and for the end came armed into the midst of the crowd, to give the fatal blow in the presence of all. When he heard the missionary preaching against the sin of hatred and enmity, he became impatient, and cried out with a loud voice: "When will that monk have done preaching peace?" He had scarcely uttered the words, when he turned quite black, fell down, and his limbs became so stiffened that he could not move, he was taken up and carried into a room in the convent, near where the mission was held. They laid him on a bed, and Blessed Leonard went to his assistance, and so skillfully did he minister to the miserable man, that he was soon restored to health, laid aside all enmity, made a good confession, and returned home contented and full of joy. The success of this mission was proved on another occasion. A man being obliged to go on business into the town where it was given, avoided attending it, or even going within sound of the preacher's voice, fearing that he might be persuaded to forgive his enemies. One of his sons entreated him to go and hear the missionary, if only once; but obstinate in his determination he mounted his horse and set off. He had not proceeded far when he was seized with violent pain and vomiting, and was carried to the convent, where those around him used every argument to persuade him to attend the mission if he hoped to be saved. An hour passed, and he remained in his obstinate determination, but feeling his pains increase, and becoming weaker every moment, he was at last reduced to promise them that he would, when immediately he was restored to health, fulfilled the promise, and publicly attested the fact. However, notwithstanding these striking circumstances, and the zeal of Blessed Leonard, who never spared himself in endeavoring to banish malice and hatred from the hearts of these people, many of them remained unconverted, and cherished vindictive feelings.

CHAPTER XV

The Mission Is Given in Many Other Places in Corsica.
The Various Occurrences During this Time

ROM Casacconi Blessed Leonard proceeded to Castel d'acqua, in which were four parishes, divided into two factions, which he was called upon to reconcile; there were more than two hundred people in arms, and a massacre was expected. When he beheld these people in the high roads and on the hill side all armed, and ready to fight, the man of God could not refrain from tears, but he lost no time in working a reformation; he began by entreating them to lay down their arms during the mission, and then by preaching and by private exhortations he labored hard to restore peace amongst them. They all attended the mission, but the church appeared more like a battlefield than the house of God, for on one side appeared one faction with its head, and a hundred men armed with swords and muskets, and on the opposite side, the other equally numerous, also armed, and in the midst, the missionary on the platform. What caution did he require to address these fierce contending parties, without irritating them; and how much did he fear that these bitter enemies, when they found themselves face to face, would take to arms, and slay each other in his very sight. This was the scene every day in the church, and seeing that he had no power over these misguided people, to promote the peace he so much desired he determined to leave them. The day for preaching the last sermon having arrived, he ascended the platform with the intention of taking leave of them, much afflicted to see them in such disorder, when suddenly he perceived them all advancing towards each other, extending their hands as a token of peace. The joy of Blessed Leonard was indescribable; he desired that the

St. Leonard of Port Maurice

Te Deum should be chanted, in thanksgiving to Almighty God for having in His mercy softened the hearts of these people; and they laid aside their arms, which they now felt to be a burden to them; all were reconciled, and peace restored. Revenge is the predominant passion of the Corsicans, and the cause of many other evils and disorders, as Blessed Leonard discovered in passing through the country, for on every side were seen farms and cottages in ruins, families dispersed, and troops of armed men going in search of their enemies, as if they were hunting wild beasts: he endeavored by every means in his power to root out of their hearts a vice so brutal. In every sermon he inveighed most strongly against it, and in the end succeeded. In Orezza, in the diocese of Aleria, when he was preaching against the same vice, some persons present, on the impulse of the moment jumped on the platform, and told him that they were ready to forgive their enemies, two of them even gave in writing a promise of forgiveness to those from whom they had received the greatest injuries. One woman, whose child had been murdered the day before, and another, whose husband had been murdered in revenge, came, full of contrition, moved by the eloquent preaching of Blessed Leonard, and publicly made peace together, even before the dead bodies of their murdered relatives had been buried.

In the same town of Orezza, a person, who, from his station in life, ought to have promoted the mission, opposed it with all his might, detracting from the merit of the holy father, saying that he was an impostor, working for his own ends, and not for the glory of God and the salvation of souls. This slander and detraction was most offensive to Almighty God, and was soon manifested by the strange and sudden illness of the wretched man; he was attended by Blessed Leonard, who desired his relations to prepare him for receiving the sacraments, for death was near, and, in fact, two days afterwards he died in great agony. This event was believed by all to be a just chastisement from God. Another man, on hearing of these occurrences, ridiculed them, declaring that it was not the hand of God, but chance, and that they happened according to the order of nature. Scarcely had he uttered these words, than he fell from a precipice, at the edge of which he was standing; his fall was broken by the trunk of a tree, which stretched over an abyss, and the unfortunate man remained suspended in this way, on the brink of eternity, without the possibility of helping himself, every moment expecting to be precipitated into the whirlpool below, as the weight of his body was tearing away his clothes. He cried aloud for help; the bystanders, however, who had heard what he had just been saying, did not care to go to his assistance, but said one to another: "This man would not believe in the mission, and declared that everything happened from natural causes, therefore, let us leave him where he has fallen." The unfortunate man, meanwhile, thus suspended in air, began to recommend himself to the mercy of God, at the same time declaring his belief that his misfortune was a just punishment sent by Almighty God, for having spoken against the mission. Then the spectators were moved with compassion, and bringing ropes, descended the precipice, and drew him up more dead than alive with fear. The great good derived from the missions of Blessed Leonard was spoken of through the island, and many who lived beyond the mountains wished to hear him, and requested him to go and give them a mission, but he was not able to grant their request, because he was sent to the dioceses of Mariana and Aleria, in which were many parishes. To these places many came from a distance of three days journey over the mountains to hear the sermons, and as the churches were not sufficiently spacious to contain the assemblage, they raised platforms in the chestnut woods, wherever a space was cleared. These poor people were so desirous to hear the divine word, and confess their sins to the missionary or some of his companions, that they came with only a little bread in their bags, which, with water, sufficed during all the days the mission lasted. The servant of God, seeing this, was encouraged more than ever, and, burning with zeal, hastened to these wild inaccessible places, and began preaching, giving instructions, hearing confessions, and reconciling enemies.

Frequently in going from one place to another he was obliged to travel by night, using a piece of lighted pine. On one occasion, going from Onesssa to Niolo, a place situated on the highest land in Corsica, he set off at six o'clock in the evening, in the month of August, carrying in his hand a pine torch, to enable him to see his way and prevent him falling down the precipices. After having walked ten hours through this rocky defile without resting, he found that he had still another ascent to make, of the distance of two miles. Faint, weary, and overcome by the excessive heat, he found it impossible to go on, and he was carried in the arms of two men who had come to meet him into a cottage. Exhausted as he was, and scarcely able to stand, he celebrated mass, which he always made a point of doing, even after a fatiguing and dangerous journey. Then, taking for his only refreshment a piece of bread, he pursued his journey, but his feet were still bleeding in consequence of walking barefoot over rugged rocks, and he was obliged to consent to be carried on a litter, made of the boughs of trees, to Niolo. The inhabitants of this place were accustomed to live the greater part of the year in the woods, or on the seashore; there remained in the villages the priests, who were ignorant and uncultivated, and some old women, part savages. Blessed Leonard set to work first in endeavoring to make the priests lead a holy life and perform their duties, and afterwards used every effort to prevent usury, robbery, concubinage, and homicide, which, with the Divine aid, he succeeded in doing. These poor people listened to his sermons with so much attention, that they were soon converted and reconciled to God. One young man only was obstinate in remaining in his sin. He desired to revenge himself on two brothers, who a week before had murdered his sister, and he declared he would not pardon or leave the murderers in peace, and so determined was he on this, that he refused to attend the mission, although his parents entreated him to do so, fearing that it might be the means of turning him from his purpose. Whilst he was thus protesting and giving his reasons, the cottage in which he lived took fire— no one knew how—and was reduced to ashes before they had time to save anything. Terrified and humbled, he went the following morning to confession and the sermon, and was reconciled in public to his enemies. Many were the instances, similar to this, by means of which Almighty God was pleased to confirm the words and actions of His minister; and the devotion of the people for him increased so much, that it sometimes exceeded the bounds of discretion. During the time he was giving a mission in Niolo, one day when he was in the act of ascending the pulpit a man rushed towards him to cut a piece off his habit, and accidentally wounded him in the hand; and another, when the servant of God was going from the altar to the sacristy after having said mass, rushed towards him in the same manner, and wounded him severely in one of his legs. In fact, they were obliged to watch the people for fear their indiscreet devotion should endanger his life.

From Niolo he proceeded to the parish of Corti, which formerly was a considerable town, but he found it ruined with internal feuds, hostility, and enmity. The fort was occupied by a large military force, amongst whom were many heretics, so that he found sufficient scope for his zeal. Amongst many conversions he made there, were two calvinists, who after attending the mission regularly, determined to make their abjuration of heresy to the missionary himself, in presence of the vicar-general of Aleria.

A shepherd being exhorted to attend the mission, refused, saying that if he left his sheep, the missionary would not take care of them. The same night two of his sheep died, and the following night three more; then the shepherd began to fear that he was chastised by Almighty God, and determined to go and hear the sermons, but only for one day, for as his faith was weak he thought his flock would be scattered and devoured by the wolves. That night five more of his sheep died, and he began to think seriously, and made a resolution to attend the mission, and recommended his flock to Divine Providence. On the last evening of the mission he returned to the country, and found them all in the same pasture where he had left them, not one having died or strayed away. It would take a volume to describe all that Blessed Leonard did for Corsica, what he suffered and endured.

The next mission he gave was in Isolaccia, in the parish of Prunelli, in the diocese of Aleria, where he found the people more barbarous and savage than any in the island, for it was the wildest and most remote part of the country. They subsisted by theft, never frequented the sacraments, and were entirely ignorant of their religion. For twenty years they had been divided into two factions, and the most horrible and cruel murders were frequently committed.

Blessed Leonard exerted all his powers to soften and subdue the nature of these savages, and one of them at last surrendering, began to attend the mission, and showed a desire to be in peace, but having for his chief a certain person named Lupo, who was more savage and fierce than any of them, he was prevented by him from following the dictates of conscience, and forbidden to go any longer to bear Blessed Leonard. All these unhappy people were thus under the influence of their chief, who forbade them to listen to any treaty of peace; so after laboring in vain amongst them for some time, the servant of God, deeply afflicted, determined to leave them and go elsewhere.

The night before his departure the house in which he was lodged took fire, and was very soon enveloped in flames. He was with his companions in a room into which the flames were bursting, and not being able to escape, he called out from the window, when some people came to their assistance, and with great difficulty they were saved. The following day he celebrated mass in the church, and preached a sermon on the occasion. The day after this, in passing from one room to another, a heavy beam became detached from the ceiling and fell upon him; some people who were waiting for confession, came to see what had happened, and found him breathless and half dead; they raised him, and gave him all the assistance they could, and in a little time he recovered. However, his companions finding that he was seriously injured, and that no medical aid was to be had there, resolved to take him to Bastia, which was some days' journey over high and rugged mountains, and not being able to convey him in any other way, they placed him in a chair supported by two poles, which was borne by two of the inhabitants of Isolaccia. Lupo hearing of the accident, and the way in which he was being conveyed to Bastia, offered the services of his men to assist, and even insisted on carrying him part of the way on his own shoulders. When Blessed Leonard was informed that one of those who assisted in carrying him was that same ferocious Lupo the chief, he who not only had refused to attend the mission himself, but forbad his faction to do so, he rejoiced exceedingly, and gave thanks to God. When they reached the place where the men were to relieve each other, notwithstanding his extreme suffering, he rose up, and burning with zeal, turned to Lupo, and said: "Come to me, Lupo, and kneel down." That fierce and cruel man became all at once meek and humble; the wolf was transformed into a lamb, and he fell on his knees. Blessed Leonard went on: "It is the will of God, and I desire that you should live in peace with your neighbors." Lupo, without making any resistance, replied: "Holy father, I consent;" and taking his gun, which he had placed on the ground, he fired it off in token of joy, exclaiming at the same time, "Peace, peace." At the example given by their captain, all the band fired their guns and returned home, crying out joyfully: "Let us give pardon and peace to our enemies." Those who have any feeling of religion and piety may imagine how the heart of the holy father rejoiced in this signal mark of divine grace. After this occurrence, he pursued his way in the manner already described, and reached Bastia, where every remedy was applied by the doctors to restore him; but Corsica being considered too cold, it was necessary to remove him to a more genial climate, and very soon he was sufficiently recovered to resume his missions.

CHAPTER XVI

After Traveling Through Several Provinces in Italy,
He Is Sent to Rome, To Prepare the People for the Jubilee

N November, 1744, Blessed Leonard left Corsica in a Genoese vessel, and after a voyage of some days landed at Porto Venere, where, in consequence of stormy weather, they remained five days, and having recovered from his illness, he embarked for Genoa, when he resumed his apostolic ministry. Although it was not the custom in that town to preach from a platform, the clergy erected a magnificent one, richly adorned for him. He began his mission with the approval and sanction of the archbishop and all the nobility. Scarcely had he begun his sermon when there was a universal exclamation, calling on God for mercy, with such expressions of compunction, that throughout the church nothing was heard but sighs and groans. A lady of some consequence in the town sent as an offering a gold heart, to be attached to the image of the Madonna, which was carried in procession during the mission; however, this true son of S. Francis returned it to the lady, saying that he thanked her for the generous offering, but it being inconsistent with the poverty he professed, he could not accept it, and recommended her to send it as a votive offering to the Madonna del Monte, assuring her that the holy virgin would graciously accept it. The lady took his advice, and was much edified by his entire detachment from earthly things and his love of poverty.

From Genoa he passed to different places in the surrounding country, preaching with his usual zeal and fervor, and bringing many to penance. Whilst he was giving a mission in Chiavari, he received a letter from the father-general and the secretary of state, ordering him to return to Corsica to finish the work of saving souls he had begun there. When he read the letter he kissed it, and said with reverence: "The will of God be done," and was ready to return to all the troubles and fatigue he had endured there, with the certainty of suffering again from the effects of the climate. He would have set off immediately, but the following day he received another letter, desiring him to wait for further commands, and he followed his intention of going to preach in the country. It was the time the Spanish and German troops were marching, and he wished to comfort the souls of the poor people, and exhort them to recommend themselves to God, that they might be free from those dangers which in such circumstances they might expect. Notwithstanding the state of the country, his mission was attended by an immense concourse of people, and great was the spiritual benefit derived from it. In Sestri especially, where the people were so terrified, it was considered a duty to attend all the sacred offices without missing one, so that during the mission the shops were shut, and they gave up every occupation to go and hear the servant of God. Blessed Leonard, however, seeing that in consequence of the war between the Savoyards and Genoese he could not proceed with his mission, took leave by letter of the archbishop, and, with the promise of returning, left Sestri for Lucca. He gave several missions in this diocese with much credit to himself, and abundant fruits were gathered in the compunction of the people, who frequently interrupted the sermon by their sighs and groans, and expressions of deep sorrow. From Lucca he went to Ferrara, and from thence to Bologna; during this journey he suffered much from wounds in his feet, which opened at every step, so that he arrived at Ferrara so weak and exhausted, that he could not stand without support. Notwithstanding this, he was anxious to begin his mission, which was so numerously attended that the church was not large enough to hold them; and during the last days be was obliged to preach in the piazza in front of the cathedral, which was so crowded that it was necessary to have a guard of soldiers to prevent the confusion which so great a multitude might occasion.

So great was the esteem in which he was held in Ferrara for having brought about so great a reformation, that to satisfy the devotion of the people he was obliged to have his portrait taken, which was afterwards engraved, to the great delight of everyone, who eagerly possessed themselves of it. He established the perpetual adoration of the Blessed Sacrament in this town, as well as other devotions for the glory of God and the good of souls, and left it for the diocese of Bologna. In this diocese he gave many missions, at Minerbio two cardinals assisted at it. Cardinal Doria, Legate of Bologna, and Cardinal Crescenzi, Legate and Archbishop of Ferrara, who, by being present at the procession of penitents, gave great edification to all assembled. Having recommended in a sermon on one of these days that the procession of the Blessed Sacrament should be conducted with the greatest honor when carried to the sick, it happened that same day that a very poor person, who lived half a mile from the church, was to receive the Holy Communion. As soon as the bell was heard, an immense number of people holding lighted candles assembled to accompany the Blessed Sacrament. The two cardinals before mentioned walked in the procession through the streets to the house of the sick person, with whom they remained sometime after he had received the Holy Communion, giving consolation to him and his relatives. The inhabitants of Ferrara were most desirous that Blessed Leonard should give them another mission soon; but being destined for the mountains of Bologna, he could not comply with their request, and set off at once for Treppio. He suffered much during this journey, which he made on foot; and before he reached Bargi he felt so weak, and his sight so failed, that he was unable to proceed farther without assistance, and night coming on, it became necessary for one of his companions to carry a lantern and show them the road, and the other to raise him on his shoulders, to carry him the rest of the way; and it was two o'clock in the morning before they reached their destination. The following day he became much worse, and was obliged to remain at Bargi, but the day after he made an effort to go on to Treppio, although still suffering from pain and weakness. So great was the anxiety of the inhabitants of Treppio to see and hear this new apostle, whose fame had already reached them, that an immense concourse of people assembled to attend his mission. Blessed Leonard was one of those who to the power of language united the force of example; by his virtuous actions inveighing against all vice, and animating everyone to virtue, he succeeded in subduing the hearts of his hearers. At the Baths of Porretta, scarcely had he arrived, and even before it was known that he was to give a mission, the people were so touched with compunction that all the confessionals were crowded with penitents. Many people came twenty miles to hear him, and the church could not contain half of them, so that he was obliged to preach in the open air. From this place he went to preach in Ravenna, where he did so much for the good of souls that it was publicly attested by the Archbishop Monsignor Guiccioli, who sent for him to give the missions in Ravenna, and in different parts of his diocese. In Argenta, although it was January, and the season very cold and rainy, many hundreds came more than thirty miles, walking in procession to see the servant of God, and hear his sermons. But Lent was approaching, and being unwilling to interfere with the usual preachers, he passed from Ravenna to Ferrara, being called there by Cardinal Crescenzi, who was then Archbishop. He here employed himself in hearing the confessions of several convents of nuns, and in preaching to them with such great profit to their souls, that all were anxious to confess to him. In Passion week he wished to perform his accustomed devotions and spiritual exercises and having none of his own order with him, he resolved to retire to the Certosa, where he remained till Holy Saturday, separated entirely from creatures, conversing alone with God. He came out of his retreat more fervent and zealous than ever, and recommenced his apostolical labors in that diocese. In Occhiobello and in Copparo the Cardinal-Archbishop assisted at all the sacred functions, and every morning after mass administered the Holy Communion with his own hands; he also walked in procession with the Holy Viaticum to the sick, and gave abundant alms to the poor. On returning to Bologna he gave a mission in the church of S. Giuseppe, belonging to the Servites, and amongst many conversions on this occasion there was one which for the greater glory of God deserves to be mentioned. There was living in Bologna a young woman about twenty years of age, married to a bailiff, and leading a most scandalous life. She was induced one day to attend the mission, and on hearing the voice of Blessed Leonard felt so moved by Divine grace that she was changed in a moment, and from a cause of scandal became an example of purity and modesty to all Bologna. A priest in the same town afterwards attested that she was most earnest in persevering in her new life, not only attending to her own sanctification by means of prayer, frequenting the sacraments, and the practice of good works, but becoming also deeply concerned in the salvation of others, going about the streets of Bologna, bringing the fallen ones to penance, and keeping the innocent from danger; she received fourteen of the latter into her own house, giving them employment, and instructing them in their religious duties. In this mission Blessed Leonard so earnestly recommended almsgiving, that five hundred crowns were collected, which were employed in contributing to the building of the church of S. Luke.

After the missions given in Bologna and other places in this diocese, he went for the same object to Ancona, where he received orders to proceed to Rome, and on his way there he stopped to preach at Spoleti, which he did with so much zeal and energy, though he had suffered much, traveling in the cold and rainy month of December, that even after his departure the people gave evident signs of compunction and piety. This was especially the case in Terni, where he had preached in the beginning of January, and recommended them to absent themselves from the carnival amusements, masquerades, and plays. Although the missionary was not there to remind them, they not only abstained from those pleasures, but from the 4th of February to the 27th of the same month, they attended to nothing but religious duties and works of mercy. Daring these days they had the exposition of the Blessed Sacrament by turns in every church, and besides the multitude of townspeople, the members of various confraternities went barefoot to adore their God with crowns of thorns on their heads and heavy crosses on their shoulders, some scourging themselves until the blood flowed, to the great edification of the beholders. On the last day of the carnival a solemn procession was conducted from the town to the convent of the Minori Osservanti, about a mile distant, to visit the stations of the "Way of the Cross" erected there. On this occasion many of the people walked barefooted, and all conducted themselves in a manner quite edifying. These were the blessed fruits gathered by this holy Father by his labors in Terni; although he was absent from them, his words and example were so deeply impressed on the minds of these devout people, that they willingly turned from the dangerous pleasures of the carnival, to occupy themselves with devotions so greatly to their spiritual advantage.

In the meantime Blessed Leonard arrived in Rome, and was sent to give a mission in the abbacy of Subiaco, from thence to Arpino and Aquila, all of which he performed with his accustomed zeal for the glory of God and the salvation of souls; the good he did was incalculable, removing abuses, converting sinners, and reforming morals. However, in consequence of his long and disastrous journey, the austerity of his life, his uninterrupted labors, and weak constitution, he often felt obliged to seek a little repose.

On one occasion when he was going, in the month of November, 1748, from Monterotondo to Magliano in Sabina, he was accompanied by two people, who, in order to shorten the way, took him through some ploughed fields, which at that season were filled with pools of frozen water. They were seven hours making this painful journey, and the servant of God found his strength fail, and was unable to proceed another step. In this difficulty they were obliged to send to Morlupo, a place not far distant, for a horse to carry him there, but when it was brought, they had great difficulty in persuading him to mount it, for he was most strict in the observance of his rule, which he feared by so doing to transgress; however, he was forced to consent, and in this way was conducted to the convent of the Riformati in Morlupo. Having ended the missions in Sabina, he received a summons to Rome from the pope, Benedict XIV, in order that he might prepare the people for the jubilee which was to be celebrated the following year. He was appointed to preach successively in the provinces and the city, which he did with so much zeal and fervor, to an immense assemblage of people of all ranks, and succeeded in making so deep an impression on the minds of all who heard him, that Rome became quite a different place in consequence of the reformation of morals. It would fill many volumes to give an account of all he did for the salvation of souls. The first crusade against vice was begun in the Piazza Navona, where the concourse was so numerous that everyone was astonished, especially at the last sermon, which was attended by all the nobles of Rome, and not only was that spacious square filled, but also all the streets which led to it. This mission lasted a fortnight, and the holy pontiff himself came four times to hear him; and as it was his custom before beginning his sermon to expose the Blessed Sacrament, and give benediction at the end, one evening the pope officiated in person at this sacred function, and every evening one of the cardinals officiated, twenty of whom always attended the mission. Blessed Leonard always gave first a meditation on the Blessed Sacrament, and after the sermon on the last day, the holy pontiff, who had remained to hear it, accompanied by the cardinals, ascended an open gallery, and gave the papal benediction to the countless multitude assembled below, and so ended the first of these most salutary devotions and exercises. But that which caused the greatest astonishment in this mission was the fact, that those who could not approach near enough to hear the voice and distinguish the words of the holy missionary, no sooner perceived him on the platform than they began to weep and express their compunction, and very soon throughout the crowd nothing was heard but weeping and wailing. Although it was in August, the hottest season, gentlemen and ladies of the highest distinction took their station in the piazza, and remained there exposed to the burning heat of the sun from the beginning to the end of the sermon, thinking nothing of what they endured from the time the man of God appeared; a sign from him was sufficient to cause the most perfect silence, so that you would hardly suppose there was a living person in that immense crowd. The other missions were given in the square of S. Maria, in Trastevere, and S. Maria sopra Minerva, and were honored by the presence of the holy pontiff. To conceive the fruits that resulted from these missions, it is sufficient to say, that although Rome was full of churches and confessors, they had to remain from morning to night hearing the confessions of the people, who crowded round the church doors before daybreak.

A few days after the missions were ended, and Blessed Leonard had gone to his retreat at S. Buonaventura, he was summoned by the confraternity of S. Giovanni Decollate, to go and convert a Sicilian, who a week before had murdered a priest; he was tried and condemned to execution, and the unfortunate man not only refused to do penance, but in answer to all entreaties, he only replied, "revenge," and obstinately persisted in his impenitence. Before they left the convent, the holy man said plainly to the Marchese Ximenes, who accompanied him, that he had no hope of the man's conversion, for in the inscrutable designs of Providence he had been abandoned; however, he used every means in his power to soften his heart, but in vain. As a favor granted to Blessed Leonard, the execution was deferred until late in the evening, but he remained in the same state, uttering the same cry, "revenge," in a loud voice, and was executed.

The holy missionary addressed the people assembled to witness this sad spectacle, from the scaffold from which the criminal was still hanging, with so much feeling and unction that he drew tears from the eyes of all, and among those who came and cast themselves at his feet to make their confession with great contrition, was a sinner who had not frequented the sacraments for more than twenty years. He came, declaring that he deserved death more than the man who had just been executed, and made a full confession of the sins of his past life. From this fact he took occasion to say, that preachers should never feel confident that they have done good to souls by their words, for that Almighty God had clearly manifested in the present instance, that it is His voice, and not that of man, which moves and softens the hearts of sinners, for His mercy is over all, as this man dying in impenitence had been the means of converting many.

Meanwhile, as the year of the Jubilee was drawing near, his holiness ordered him to give spiritual exercises during the month of November, in the churches of the Trinita dei Monti, S. Giovanni dei Fiorentini, and S. Cecilia, and in the following month, after having given missions in S. Andrea della Valle, he retired to the convent of Polveriera, for he said he had done nothing for his own soul whilst he was laboring for others; therefore he desired himself to go through some spiritual exercises. Accordingly he in the evening fell on his knees, and in the presence of all assembled in the refectory begged the blessing of the superior, and leave to perform the exercises, declaring at the same time that there was nothing of the religious about him but the habit; he then asked for the prayers of the community, and bursting into tears, was unable to utter another word. It may easily be imagined with what recollection and profit to his soul he performed these exercises: when he had finished, he presented himself at the feet of the pope, who having questioned him as to what he had gained, he replied: "An ardent desire to die, and enjoy eternal happiness." Some days after this, in going to confess and console a sick person, he hurt his foot, and, as was his wont, said nothing about it; the wound inflamed so that he could not stand, and he was obliged to keep his bed for a week.

As soon as the pope was informed of this, he came to visit him in person, and knowing how much he had suffered at different times from walking barefoot, ordered him to wear sandals, and on no account to leave Rome before he saw him again, and after having held a secret conference with him, which lasted half an hour, he departed, giving him his Apostolic benediction. When he was restored to health, his zeal and charity not allowing him to remain idle, he employed himself in hearing confessions in several convents, and giving spiritual exercises to some confraternities, amongst others that of the SS. Trinita dei Pellegrini, of which he was a member.

The Romans gave such evident signs of the good they had gained from the missions, by their devotion in visiting the churches, and all the services of the Church, that strangers were astonished, and the oldest inhabitants of Rome declared that they never remembered seeing them so devout and recollected as in this time of Jubilee, which might truly be called the "holy year."

With the same charity and zeal which employed him in various confraternities, he heard confessions in his own convent of S. Buonaventura, many of his penitents came from a distance, so that it might be said that during this year he saved as many souls in the tribunal of penance, as on the platform in giving missions. I shall only cite two facts amongst many I might bring forward, as a proof of what he gained by the missions given by him the year before the Jubilee. Whilst he was thus occupied, his fame reached distant parts, and a man who lived five hundred miles from Rome, whose conscience was laden by many sins, conceived the desire of going to Blessed Leonard, and for this end he set off to walk all the way to Rome. He arrived there in the course of time, but some days elapsed without his being able, for the crowd, to approach the servant of God, and he went to another confessor, and made his confession, but from a feeling of shame he concealed some of his sins, and received absolution, and thus adding sacrilege to his other sins, he returned home. Divine mercy, however, not willing to abandon him, caused him to feel in his heart such remorse, that he could neither find repose nor peace, and he seemed always to hear a voice urging him to return to Rome, and make his confession to Father Leonard. For the second time he set off on the same long journey, and arrived in Rome in August, went direct to the convent of S. Buonaventura, and having asked to see the holy servant of God, threw himself at his feet, and said: "Father, you behold in me the greatest sinner in the world." He then made a general confession, with many tears and signs of contrition, of all the grievous sins of his past life. Blessed Leonard raised him up, and embraced him tenderly, and with his usual charity encouraged him to trust in the mercy of God, and told him that he was much edified by the dispositions which induced him to undertake a journey on foot of two thousand miles to make his confession, and lost in wonder and admiration at the greatness and goodness of Almighty God, he loosed him from his bonds, and sent him away so contented, that he could not conceal the joy he felt in relating the especial grace he had received.

The other instance was that of a Prussian heretic, who having heard in his own country the fame of Blessed Leonard, went to Rome to see and hear him. He attended his sermons, and then seeking an interview, he expressed a desire to embrace the Catholic religion, but said that he had doubts respecting the papal supremacy and the invocation of saints, which made him hesitate. Blessed Leonard with so much clearness explained away his doubts that he was very soon convinced, detested his heresy, and abjured it, and made his profession of faith to the cardinal-vicar, and Blessed Leonard led him to the feet of the Pope, who gave him a plenary indulgence for every month, on condition that he went to confession and communion, and for his maintenance two giulios' a day. As they were near the close of the holy year, the Pope gave an order for a triduo to be given in the church of S. Andrea della Valle, to confirm the people in their devotion. It was commenced by his Holiness, who was present, and gave the benediction, and many of the cardinals assisted at it. The concourse of people was so immense, that even that spacious church could not contain them all, many were obliged to remain in the piazza. In this manner did the devoted servant of God finish his work during the holy year, with so much satisfaction to the supreme pontiff, who held him in the highest esteem, that he refused him permission to go elsewhere, and ordered him to stay in Rome, and to come to him every Sunday evening that they might converse on things relating to the salvation of souls, and the general good of his flock. However, sometime after this he gave him permission to give missions in Lucca and other places, as we will now relate.

CHAPTER XVII

Blessed Leonard Returns to Lucca to Give Missions, as Well as in the Archbishopric of Bologna, from Whence He Is Sent for to Rome, Where He Departs this Life in His Retreat of S. Buonaventura.

HE authorities of Lucca having petitioned the Pope to send Blessed Leonard to give them a mission during the year of the Jubilee at a time when he could not be spared from Rome, he was now ordered to go there. He began accordingly to prepare for the journey, and before his departure he was anxious to complete the work he had begun, the establishment of the Via Crucis in the Colosseum, a place sanctified by the blood of many martyrs. This was undertaken with the approval of Pope Benedict XIV, with whose permission he had instituted a confraternity of pious persons, giving them the title of "Lovers of Jesus and of Mary," who undertook to visit in procession the Stations of the Cross raised within the Colosseum, and also induce others to join in a devotion so holy and so acceptable to the Lord. He had already published a book, which he dedicated to the Pope, containing the rules for the confraternity, and the prayers to be said. For the completion of the work, nothing remained to be done but the blessing of the crosses, and he obtained leave for this on the 27th of December, the feast of S. John the Evangelist. The ceremony was performed by Monsignor the Vice-gerent of Rome, Patriarch of Constantinople; on this occasion he preached in the amphitheater, within which were assembled an immense multitude, and exhorted all to attend frequently the pious exercises of the Via Crucis, reminding them that besides gaining many indulgences, meditating on the Passion of our Lord at the fourteen Stations must necessarily cause a reformation in manners and morals. It might appear to some that such a devotion as this could not last, for several reasons, but it has boon proved to the contrary, for the "Lovers of Jesus and Mary" are still to be found in the Colosseum on the appointed days, together with many persons of distinction, who are living in the fear of God. Blessed Leonard intended to build an oratory for the confraternity, but death prevented him fulfilling this intention; however, the Pope at his own expense caused one to be erected near the church of SS. Cosma and Damian, in Campo Vaccino; and also, in order to provide for the good regulation of the confraternity, he appointed that the women should assemble in the church of the martyrs, and the men in the oratory, and gave them for their spiritual director the father-guardian of the time being of the convent of S. Buonaventura.

Having thus established the devotion of the Via Crucis, Blessed Leonard yielded to the entreaties of the authorities of Lucca to give a mission in that place, and began to prepare for his departure. On the 14th of April he presented himself at the feet of the Pope to receive his benediction, and when he heard his Holiness give an order for him to travel in a carriage, he stood in silent astonishment. The holy Pontiff repeated the same order, "I desire that you go to Lucca in a carriage, and in November I shall expect you again in Rome." The following day he set off on his journey, and in a few days reached Florence, where he found many people assembled to welcome him, amongst whom were many priests, regulars, and seculars, with nobles and persons of distinction; they all crowded around him as he passed to kiss his hand or habit, and it was not without great difficulty they could be prevented cutting pieces off his cloak. The archbishop of Florence and the bishop of Fiesole begged him to visit several convents of nuns, which he did with great satisfaction to the occupants. He found the convent of S. Francesco al Monte, where he was received, very distracting, in consequence of visits from seculars, therefore he removed to the Solitude dell' Incontro, which he had founded thirty-five years before in a secluded place, in the mountains of Tuscany, and here he stayed some days in the enjoyment of perfect peace and tranquility of spirit. On the 5th of May he went to Lucca, where he was held in great esteem for the holy life he had led there, and the good he had done to souls, he was received with the greatest demonstrations of veneration and affection. The missions were even more numerously attended than they had been the year before; the concourse was so great that the spacious cathedral of S. Martino could not contain half, and he was obliged to preach in the Piazza of San Michele in Foro. Although it happened at the beginning of the mission that the holy father, worn with age and very weak from unceasing fatigue, fell sick, and his mind gave way so that he was unable to preach for some days, he made an effort with his usual energy, and went on with his apostolical ministrations, and ended the mission; the tone of his voice was so touching, and his manner so impressive, that no one could refrain from tears. From Lucca he went to Camajore, and as he passed through Via Reggio, he was requested to preach a sermon, which proved the means of putting an end to a public scandal. A man in that place was living in the sin of adultery with a servant whom he kept in his house, and in consequence of whom he conceived a mortal hatred to his wife, so that she was obliged to leave the house, taking her son with her. Divine Providence led the servant to hear Blessed Leonard preach, his words entered her heart, she instantly felt compunction, and corresponding with the grace given wept bitterly, she detested her sin, and resolved to change her way of living. She returned home and spoke to her master with so much zeal and fervor, that he was alarmed, sent her away, and entreated his wife and son to return to him and be reconciled, asking their forgiveness, to the great joy of all in the place, who returned thanks to Almighty God, for having, by means of His servant, removed so great a scandal. Three days after, this man, who had so long been living in sin, was summoned before the tribunal of God. In Camajore there was also another most striking instance of the grace of God working in the heart by means of his powerful preaching. A woman whose son nine years before had been murdered, determined never to leave the murderer in peace, and her only surviving son had also made the same determination, and in reply to everyone who endeavored to reconcile them, they declared that no priest or missionary should ever induce them to forgive him. In these dispositions the mother and son went to hear the sermon on the devotion to the Blessed Virgin, which the pious missionary was accustomed to preach in his missions, they were both so softened and felt so much compunction, that they ceased to feel any animosity, and publicly declared peace with their enemy, to the great joy and edification of all in the place.

The Pope having ordered Blessed Leonard to begin his apostolic labors in the mountains of Bologna on the feast of S. Bartholomew, he gave missions on his way to that place in Brancoli and Gallicano, to which place many came from Lucca, Florence, and Modena, so that the influx was so great, that it became necessary to build two bridges over the Serchio, and at the last sermon thirty thousand people were assembled. He gave three missions in the country, and during the whole time he suffered so much, that he frequently fainted on the platform, and was unable to finish his sermon; he said frequently to his companions that these would be his last missions. To Father Diego, of Florence, who, for twenty-six years had accompanied him in his missions, he sometimes said that he only wished to preach him one more sermon. It was also observed, that instead of preparing his sermon as usual, he only held in his hand the maxims which he had drawn up in 1717, and which are to be found published in many forms. When he was seen giving his attention to these maxims, reading them over, and examining them with great attention, his companions used to ask him to lay them aside for the present, and to prepare for his sermon. "No," he replied, "these maxims are now all that are necessary for me."

These, and other similar things made them fear that his end was near, and that he was already warned of it. On the 29th of October, in reply to a letter he had received from Signor Belmonte, he wrote these words: "If it pleases the most High to permit me to arrive in Rome, I believe that I shall have accomplished His last will regarding me, for the vessel is frail, and no longer seaworthy. The month of November came, the time appointed by the Pope, who had lately written him a most affectionate letter, for his return to Rome, and he determined to set out on his journey. He went first to Ferrara, where he had been summoned by the archbishop, who desired to hold a conference with him.

From Ferrara he returned to Bologna, and set off on his way to Rome by the Loreto road on the 15th of November, he reached Loreto on the 20th, and Monsignor Stella the governor received him with the greatest demonstrations of esteem, and begged he would take up his abode in the palace; but this most humble servant of God, who in all his journeys had never deviated from his rule of lodging in monasteries, in order to be under obedience to the respective superiors, declined the invitation of the prelate, and went to the hospice of the Minori Osservanti, where he passed the night. In the morning he offered the Holy Sacrifice for the supreme pontiff, according to the request made by the archbishop the evening before; and after having heard another mass in the same chapel he departed for Tolentino, and arrived there the same evening. He lodged here in the convent of the Minori Osservanti, and it was remarked that he had never appeared so cheerful, and even joyous; his companions, not suspecting the cause, were astonished. When he left Tolentino in the morning the hills were covered with snow, and he suffered so much from the intense cold that he became as pale as a corpse. Notwithstanding this, however, on arriving at Ponte della Trave, he celebrated mass, took nothing more than a small piece of bread for his sustenance, and pursued his journey to Case Nuove, at which place he arrived late in the evening. As he stood before the fire, he was suddenly seized with a shivering fit; his companions went to his assistance, and inquired if he had a fever; he replied with great composure: "I do not know," and began saying the Divine Office. When he had finished this, he took some slight refreshment, and went to bed, but very soon he was seized with a fit of coughing, which convulsed him so much, that at the eighth hour of the night he called to one of his companions to light the fire, for he could not lie in bed any longer. When they inquired how he felt, he replied: "I am ill," which alarmed them, for during all the sufferings and fatigue he had endured for twenty-six years, they had never heard him say that he was ill, or even utter a word of complaint, for he bore all his pains with calm cheerfulness.

On the morning of the following day, he declared he was well enough to proceed on his journey to Foligno, where he wished to celebrate mass; his companions endeavored to keep him quiet for that day, for he was so weak that he could hardly stand; he replied with much feeling: "Brother, one mass is worth more than all the treasures of the world and then went to the altar, but he with difficulty finished, he trembled in every limb, and his voice was almost inaudible. On going the following day from Foligno to Spoleto, the driver mistook the road, and they found themselves in a narrow lane, through which the carriage could not pass; they were obliged to get out, and cross on foot a deep ditch. However he arrived at the convent of Spoleto, but quite exhausted, and in such a state that they feared he was dying; for all this he said the Divine Office, assisted by his companions. They entreated him to rest here, but he refused, saying that his holiness had ordered him to be in Rome in November, and pursued his journey to Civita Castellana, from whence, on the morning of the 27th, he proceeded to Rome. In this last day of his weary and painful journey he manifested more than ever his ardent desire of again finding rest in his beloved convent of S.

120

St. Leonard of Port Maurice

Buenaventura, and often enquired how far they were from Rignano, then how far from Castel Nuovo, where, as they halted three hours, he determined, though with great difficulty, to finish the office of that day; he then asked Father Diego when they would arrive at Pontemollo, and went on to say: "Brother, during these last missions in Bologna, I have often said I wished to speak to you, and preach you a sermon, now what I wished to say, is this. As soon as we shall have arrived at our convent of S. Buonaventura, I desire you will give the box containing my sermons to the father guardian, and tell him that I willingly give them up, for in my writing I have done nothing; tell him also to give those sermons to our community, for they will urge them to be active and zealous in the sacred ministry for the salvation of souls, and that if he does not do this he will have to render an account to God. Give also to the father guardian the key of the box which contains the image of the Madonna, the crucifix, and the other things we have used in the missions." He continued, "My brother, despoil yourself willingly of these things." To this Father Diego replied, that he willingly despoiled himself of everything. "I rejoice," continued Blessed Leonard, "that you are entirely detached from everything earthly, and I wish that your sole desire may be to do the will of God." He then went on to exhort him to keep strictly his sacred vows, to strive to lead a holy life, and be in peace, for then God would love him, and he would persevere to the end in the Retreat Soon after this he said: "I feel that death is near." Father Diego, to encourage him, said: "There is no sign of death;" he replied, "I feel that I am dying, but doubt not, my brother, that I shall always pray to God for you, having always loved you, and desired your well-being." He remained quiet for a little while, then sighing deeply, he raised himself up in the carriage, and said, "Brother, return thanks to God for me, for He has mercifully granted that which I have desired, to die in my dear convent." As soon as they had passed through the gates of Rome, he said to Father Diego: "Intone the

Te' Deum, and I will make the responses." And thus chanting the praises of God, he arrived at his convent of S. Buonaventura, on the evening of the 26th of November.

He descended from the carriage with much difficulty, and was so weak that they could hardly feel his pulse beating. He was carried to the infirmary, where, after having made his confession, he desired to receive the holy Viaticum, and an hour after his arrival it was administered to him, all the community being present. When the Blessed Sacrament approached, he fell on his knees in an ecstasy, making acts of faith, hope, and charity, with so much devotion and fervor, that all around him were moved to tears. After remaining for some time in prayer, he was told the doctor had come, and he begged that he would not order him to eat meat, anxious even to his last breath to observe the rule of abstinence, which he had done for so many years. He took, however, a cordial from the hands of the infirmarian, thanked him, and said, "Ah, well would it be if as much care was taken of the soul as the body." Having taken the draught, he added: "Brother, I cannot find words to thank God for the favor He has granted me, in permitting me to die amongst my religious in the Retreat. Soon after this he expressed a wish to write to his holiness, to testify his obedience, and asked for writing materials, but his confessor thought it better not to allow him to write, and said they would send a message to Monsignor Belmonte, who would apprize the pope of his arrival. That prelate came to him in the evening, and was much grieved to see him so near death; the servant of God on seeing him rejoiced, and with a smiling countenance, said: "May the will of God be done, and that which tends to His glory. Will you oblige me by making known to his holiness my sentiments of filial obedience." The bishop said: "Father Leonard, you are in the hands of God, and He will, I hope, give you possession of eternal glory, and I trust you will not fail to pray for his holiness, and for me." To which he replied: "I shall do so willingly." Monsignor Belmonte then went away, and the dying man, wishing to be more recollected, desired to be left alone, telling those who were standing round his bed to go and take some repose. The infirmarian alone remained, standing outside the door, where he heard him making the most fervent acts of the love of God, and invoking the Blessed Virgin, speaking to her as if she were present. In a little while the infirmarian approached the bed, and perceiving a bright hectic spot on his cheeks, touched him, and found he was in a burning fever. They administered the Sacrament of Extreme Unction, which he received with great devotion, and soon after, without a struggle, he slept in the Lord.

He departed to receive the reward of all his labors for the glory of God, and the salvation of souls, at the seventh hour of the night on Friday, the 26th of November, 1751, aged seventy-four years, eleven months, and six days, fifty-three years of which had been employed in the religious life, and forty in giving missions. Early in the morning a messenger was sent to convey the intelligence to the pope, who, when he heard it, said with much feeling: "Our loss on earth is very great, but we have gained an advocate in heaven," tears dropped from his eyes while he spoke. Scarcely had the news of his death spread through the city, than the church and convent of S. Buenaventura were crowded with people. To prevent disorders they deemed it wise not to expose the body every day, but only during the mass, and at the funeral, when it was placed before the High Altar. Monsignors Reali, Belmonte, and Giovardi, after the solemn ceremony was ended, carried the bier to the infirmary, where it remained the whole day. In the meantime, the crowd had increased so much, that the lane which leads to the convent was full, and they were obliged to place a guard of twelve soldiers at the gate. Towards evening, three cardinals, Guadagni, the pope's vicar, Bardi, and Monti, with Monsignor de Rossi, and other distinguished people, seculars, priests, and the religious of various orders, and everyone, on beholding that sacred body, said that a most faithful servant of God was dead, one of those men of whom the Blessed Savior said in the Gospel: "Come unto me, all ye who labor and are heavy laden, and I will give you rest." Some ladies of high rank, desiring, in their devotion, to see him before he was buried, came the same evening to the church, amongst them were the Duchesses Strozzi, Cesarini, and Carpineto, accompanied by many persons of distinction, who all came to pray for some grace which they desired. At one hour of the night the church was closed, for even then the multitude endeavored to press into it, notwithstanding the guard. They carried the corpse into the infirmary, where, after having gazed upon it for some time, they went away, and at daybreak the interment took place in the following manner. Monsignor Giovardi slept that night in the convent, in order to be present, as did also the notary, who drew up the deed in the presence of all the community, and the Father Provincial. The body of Blessed Leonard was then examined juridically, and found to be as soft and flexible as if he were living; it was then placed in a coffin, which was sealed, and by order of the pope, placed in a separate grave, in front of the chapel of S. Francis; a stone was placed over it with the following inscription:

D. O. M.

Hic Jacet
F. Leonardus a Portu Mauritio.
Mission. Apost. Ordin. Min. Reform.
Sacri Recessus S. Bonav. de Urbe.
Vixit Ann. LXXV. Obiit XXVI. Novemb.
MDCCLI.

We have now concluded our sketch of the Life of Blessed Leonard, a truly apostolic man, even the apostle of our times, the glory of the republic of Genoa, and of his native town, Port

St. Leonard of Port Maurice

Maurice, a light of the church, and an ornament of the order of S. Francis. It would fill many volumes to give an account of all he did by his teaching, and the force of his holy example, reproving vice, and causing virtue to flourish, converting the most hardened sinners, journeying through the country in all seasons, and exposing himself to the greatest hardships and fatigues in giving missions. His memory is still, and will be for ages to come, held in benediction with the people, his praise is in every mouth, and they never weary of speaking of the wonders done by him, all of which shall be described in the second part of this history. However, before we come to that, we shall refer to the rule of life established and exactly observed by him in the course of his missions.

CHAPTER XVIII

Rules Established by Blessed Leonard for the Conducting of the Missions, Which He Himself Faithfully Observed.

LESSED LEONARD knew well, that in giving missions, above all things order is requisite, and that good example is the soul of the apostolical ministry, without this all labor is vain, for, as says S. Bernard, "Example is better than precept, and makes a deeper impression on the mind than the most eloquent preaching." Before he began his first mission in Tuscany in 1712, he established rules, which were strictly observed by himself and his companions during the whole course of their ministry. They are as follows:

1. Before leaving the convent he requested the superior to appoint one who should be the president and director of the mission, and although he would not have the same authority as the guardian of a convent, it should devolve on him to see that everything was done in order and with regularity; he desired that the others should submit themselves to him, never undertaking anything of consequence, or going to distant places without consulting him; and the president was to give advice to the brothers, to enjoin them to live in peace, and, above all things, to observe the rules, which were to be read, at least once, at the commencement of every mission.

2. When they approach the place where the mission is to be given, they shall intone the Litanies, the Veni Creator, and other prayers to invoke the aid of the Holy Spirit, and recite the antiphons of the feast of S. Francis and of S. Vincent Ferrer, and the responsory for the Feast of S. Antony, so that these three saints, elected as patrons of our missions, may obtain by their intercession good success, and that all should redound to the

greater glory of God and the salvation of souls.

3. On arriving at the place they shall pay a visit to the Blessed Sacrament, and then go to the house of the parish priest to pay their respects, kiss his hand, and ask his blessing before beginning the mission.

4. The thing of most importance in the mission is to have the missionaries in union with God, that their words may have due efficacy, and that God may bless their labors. Every morning as soon as they awake, having given a little time to necessary things, they must all unite together and take the discipline, saying in a low voice the usual prayers, then they must read the points of meditation. After Prime and Tierce, they must employ an hour in meditation, and after this the president shall ring the bell, when they shall say the *De profundis*, and then go to confession every morning, that they may have a clear conscience, and be at peace with their God.

5. In the morning, the one having to give the instruction is not obliged to attend at meditation, but they must keep themselves recollected during the time, often raising their hearts to God in mental prayer; it is most important that they should be united to God in prayer, and use every effort to sanctify themselves.

6. After this they shall go to church, and pray before the Blessed Sacrament, that they may celebrate Mass with recollection. After Mass each shall go to the confessional appointed him by the president, and they are not to hear confessions in any other church without leave from the president.

7. The president shall fix the time, with the counsel of others, they shall employ in the confessionals, according to circumstances and the number of penitents. A quarter of an hour before the time appointed for the collation, which on feast days should never be before twelve, a lay brother shall warn the confessor to hasten the confession of the penitent; and if the

confession is so long that it cannot be ended in a quarter of an hour, he shall desire him to wait until after collation; and if he cannot wait, the confessor shall exhort him to come another day, giving him a written paper as a token, in order that he may be admitted the first to the confessional.

8. If the house in which they are lodged is far from the church, whoever is first in leaving the confessional shall wait for his companion, kneeling before the high altar, so that they may return home together. This rule, however, does not hold when the church is near, and is not to be observed when there is anything particular to be done; in that case, not finding any priest ready to accompany him, he may go alone, because necessity has no law. The president shall decide respecting the distance from the church.

9. The brother who is appointed to preach requiring more time to study, may be allowed to leave the church earlier, and take his collation alone, with permission from the president.

10. When they return home from the church they shall recite Sext and None, after which they shall make a short examination of conscience, and at a sign from the oldest among them, they shall gain the Indulgence by saying six Pater nosters and Aves, and end with the *De profundis.*

11. During collation no book is to be read, and they shall say one Ave Maria instead of the blessing, as is the custom in our convent, and also one in returning thanks.

12. After collation a sign shall be given by the oldest, and they shall retire to their rooms, in summer for an hour, and in winter for a quarter of an hour, to repose, if they need it, or to study, or read, as they please; a strict silence is to be observed during this time, and no confessions are to be heard at this hour; in this they must all be agreed, so that all things may be done well and in order. Let no one feel anxious on this point, for an act of obedience, ordered for the relief of an oppressed body, is more pleasing to God than attempts to convert the whole world. Only

on the day on which the papal benediction is given and the following days, are the priests of the mission allowed to hear confessions at this time.

13. After repose the president shall cause a bell to be rung, and they shall recite together Vespers and Compline, and those who do not require time to study may return to the confessionals, remaining there as long as their strength will permit, and those who remain to study, shall ask permission of the Father president to take the time necessary for preparation to discourse properly on the word of God.

14. During the sermons in the church they shall not hear the confessions of women, and if those of men are heard, they must be taken to some place where they are not seen by the congregation. If there are no confessions to hear each shall employ himself in some good work.

15. After the sermons they shall begin to hear confessions, if there be time, for then the penitents will be found in good dispositions; and a quarter of an hour before the time appointed by the president they shall be warned, so that they may act in the same way as in the morning.

16. As soon as they are all assembled they shall say Matins together, and afterwards make a short examination of conscience; and after having said the Litanies and other prayers, they shall say the prayers to gain the Indulgence, as in the convent. This manner of reciting the Divine Office together shall be observed as often as possible by all, excepting in cases of urgent necessity, such as having a penitent on their hands whose confession cannot be deferred, or to receive any person coming for advice. In order not to keep the others waiting, they shall make a sign to the Father president that this Father is engaged, otherwise they will disarrange the time for the common refection.

17. Before supper they shall give the blessing as in the refectory, and seat themselves in silence, and one shall read a

short chapter of some spiritual book, and one or two cases of conscience shall be read at a sign from the president. Then the reader shall close the book, and they shall begin to eat in silence; and when the first portion is finished the president shall say, "Tu autem Domine, etc.," and all shall respond, "Deo gratias." After this they shall be allowed to speak in a low voice, discoursing on matters relating to the mission, refraining from altercation or loud speaking, which might give scandal to the seculars, who mark every action of the missionaries, and everyone must be cautious not to say anything which might disgust or displease his companions; and although they may be allowed to indulge freely in conversation for relaxation of the mind, it must be with a holy freedom; they must be very careful not to indulge in anything approaching to licentious talking, or trifling jokes, which might dissipate the mind. It shall be the care of the president to reprove anyone who offends in this way.

18. After supper they shall return thanks as in the convent, and after sitting for a while to discuss things connected with the mission, the oldest shall say, "Tu autem Domine, etc." A strict silence must be kept, as in the convent, and all who retire to their rooms for repose must be very careful not to make a noise to disturb the others. The amount of time to be spent in sleep is to be settled by the president.

19. Two or three days after the mission is begun, they shall ring the bell at one hour of the night for hardened sinners, exhorting the people as usual; and the president, before the mission commences, shall write to the bishop of the diocese, not only for faculties to hear confessions, and give absolution where it has been deferred, but to apply the indulgence of forty days to all those functions which they shall judge convenient.

20. In our missions, which are given for the glory of God, the first object should be good example. For the holy father S. Francis attests, he expects from us that we should preach more by our example than by our words. We shall see how necessary it is to

131

practice retirement even more than in the convent; we must not let ourselves be seen except when we are preaching, saying mass, or confessing. No one is to go out without leave from the president, excepting the lay brothers, who are obliged to go for what is necessary, they must never go out alone.

21. During the mission no complimentary visits are to be paid, and not even the sick are to be visited, excepting when any dying person particularly solicits it: all the rest are to be left till the mission is ended.

22. No woman of any rank or station is allowed to enter the house on any pretext whatever; the rooms, however, are to be kept clean and in order. Anyone is allowed to sleep on the floor; and when they cannot bear this mortification, they must make up for it by their good example, so that our preaching may be efficacious in converting souls.

23. The missionaries must subsist by alms, using strict abstinence, and eating only the coarsest food. Neither the community, the parish, or the bishop, are on any account to bear the expense. In the first sermon he shall declare our poverty to the people, and that we desire to live by begging from door to door, according to the rule of S. Francis, and that we eat only Lenten food; and that if for the love of God they bring us what is necessary, we shall be spared the trouble of going to their houses, telling them that we require nothing more than bare necessaries, and that whatever remains is distributed amongst the poor. All this shall be declared to the people, but at the same time informing them, that though originally we eat only herbs, we are allowed one small portion of fish fresh or salted, and on the day of benediction something additional. It is most desirable that every ono should adopt this mode of living willingly, and live conformable to the good example given us by our seraphic Father S. Francis.

24. In order that good example may be accompanied by a proper sustenance for our religious, they shall inform the people

that though during the days they do penance and fast for them, yet they do not observe a rigid fast. That we take in the morning a pottage with various kinds of fruit, according to the season, and whatever is necessary is provided for those that are weak and indisposed, but that in community we only receive portions of fish on Sundays and feast days.

25. In the evening they shall give out the usual portions, viz., two of soup, and salad boiled or fresh, one portion of fish, fresh or salted. If anything remains it shall be given to the poor. If fishes should be sent in abundance, either they shall not be received or shall be sent to the neighboring convents, or given to the poor. Nothing must be done that could give scandal to the people, so that they may all know and feel that we desire nothing but the glory of God and their eternal salvation, and are willing to endure all things to gain that. Most assuredly the result of our labor, in a great measure, depends on this point; we may be certain that God grants an especial grace, and silences the adversaries of those who persevere in this mode of life. We read in the Life of S. Dominic, that being accused by some heretics of living well when he was giving his missions, he purposely went during Lent to lodge in the house of some protestants, and they observing that he ate nothing but bread and water the whole time, were so impressed by his self-denial, that they were converted to the true faith. The world thinks more of eating than anything else, thus they think that mode of life insupportable, which to us is so easy, and believe it supernatural; it is well that they so believe for the glory of God and salvation of souls. In the case of the sick, however, everything necessary is to be provided for them, whether eggs, meat, or whatever else, for no one should be scandalized to see charity used towards those who, from over fatigue or any other cause, are ill.

26. We exhort everyone to drink in moderation, for we declare that wine undiluted, besides being injurious to the health, has other very bad effects on those who have to be employed all

day in the confessional.

27. When the missionaries are obliged to travel by water a little more wine may be taken, but with care that they do not exceed the rule of holy poverty, and give scandal to the sailors. In conversation also during the voyage they must be careful not to give scandal, all must be admonished to conduct themselves prudently, and be always recollected.

28. When it happens in any place that they do not find things convenient, in consequence of the poverty of the inhabitants, or that they should not be well affected at the beginning of the mission, they must rejoice, and be willing to suffer all for the love of God, giving thanks for having an opportunity of experiencing the effects of holy poverty. By these means many souls may be gained.

29. In going to the place where the mission is to be given, no food of any kind is to be taken with them, unless they should have to travel by water. We must allow no one to eat with us and refuse to eat, in any house even that of a bishop, or some person of consequence who may press us to do so. Nothing is to be received but the bare necessaries of life, all besides this which they bring must be given to the poor. We do not beg during the time of missions, that all may know we seek nothing but the salvation of their souls.

30. In traveling from one place to another, that the thoughts may not be dissipated, after the usual morning prayers they shall each give an hour to meditation as they walk along, and then say the rosary of the Seven Joys; and when they approach the place where the mission is to be given, they shall keep silence for a quarter of an hour, making several inward acts, unless prevented by fatigue. In this way the soul will be united to God, and they will avoid many faults.

31. On every occasion they shall be exhorted to live in peace and charity, avoiding everything which may displease or give annoyance amongst them; and when the discussions lead to

altercations, the president shall put an end to them, whether the matter be trivial or for some good end.

32. The president on whom devolves the direction of the mission, shall take counsel in all things with his brethren, and when there arises a diversity of opinion, after having listened to all, he shall resolve what is best to be done, in accordance with the will of God, and all shall conform to his judgment.

33. Everyone shall feel indifferent where they hear confessions, for the place, church, and confessional shall be assigned by the president, and they must be ready and willing to confess either men or women, according as he shall judge proper.

34. In hearing confessions they must be very cautious, for one hasty or imprudent word is sufficient to destroy the effects of the mission. In giving the penance they must be moderate, and avoid private conferences, or interference in marriages, making promises, or adjusting differences, or any designs which might bring odium upon them, give an unfavorable impression, and destroy the fruits of the mission. They must not ask alms of their penitents, because that has been known to lead to great evils, even when it has been requested for the relief of the poor. In this everyone must be agreed, and on no account must they receive alms for masses, but all shall say mass, either for our own dead, or for the souls in Purgatory.

35. No one is to speak to women out of the confessional, excepting in cases of urgent necessity, and then always in the presence of a third person; they must not enter their houses excepting in cases of dangerous illness, when they must be accompanied by another priest, or some responsible person.

36. In the confessional they shall hear men on one side and women on the other, the young women, especially if they are spiritual, are not to be kept long in the confessional, for besides losing precious time, it might give occasion for comment to those who observed it. They must not call the women by name, or send for them, and studiously avoid everything which might cause

scandal.

37. It is forbidden to distribute rosaries and holy pictures in the confessionals, for various reasons; but they shall be given by one of the brothers at the end of the mission, that the penitents may come to confession for the love of God, and not to receive these things. A curtain shall be drawn before the confessional, so that no one shall see, or be seen.

38. The president shall see that the lay-brothers do not go out when there is no necessity, or enter houses unaccompanied by some responsible person.

39. They shall limit the number of candles required for the exposition of the Blessed Sacrament, they must not be less than twenty-four, or more than fifty, and they shall exhort the people to give alms for this end: any that is superfluous is to be used to provide torches to carry in procession when the Blessed Sacrament is taken to the sick, and for other things required in the church.

40. No small altars covered with superfluous ornaments shall be raised, for in so doing much time is spent which might be employed in doing things of more importance, and there is danger of the things lent being lost or spoilt. Permission is only to be given during the sermon on Mary to adorn the image of the Blessed Virgin in the usual manner.

41. They shall chant the usual hymns during the time the people are assembling, without any variation, viz., the "Salve Regina," "In Thee I believe, in Thee I hope," " Come all ye faithful," and the "Eviva Maria." They shall have no musicians without permission, excepting in singing the Miserere in the procession of penitents, when they must play for the love of God and charity.

42. In this procession the president shall take care that there is no disorder, and that the men and women walk separately, and the rule shall be observed without introducing novelties. They shall see that the penitents do not indulge in too severe

penances, because by so doing they will lose their health, and afterwards blame the missionaries. They must also be exhorted to dress themselves modestly, and in all things to give edification.

43. In these same processions they shall not force the priests to walk barefoot, and wear a crown of thorns on their heads and a rope round their necks, because violence might be injurious to them, but they shall modestly suggest what is done in other places, and leave them at liberty to adopt it. At the beginning of the mission they shall state what they wish to be done; it is most important that they should be on good terms with the parish priest, and the priests secular and regular, being armed with no weapons but those of humility and meekness.

44. The girls who attend the mission, and walk in the procession of penitents, must be exhorted to dress plainly and be modestly veiled, and without any display of vanity; against this sin they must inveigh strongly, so that they may bear it in mind after the mission.

45. One of the greatest benefits resulting from a mission, is to leave all the people in peace one with another; and the better to establish this, they shall elect some respected persons, either ecclesiastics or seculars, to whom they shall give the title of mediators; they shall take upon themselves the office of preventing any rudeness of behavior, and the smoothing over any apparent harshness in the missionaries, but they must not meddle too much in adjusting differences, but endeavor to promote peace between the contending parties; they must not bring them before the public, excepting in particular cases, and then they must consult the president beforehand to avoid disorder. When the parties are reconciled, they are not to go to confession in the morning, but after the sermon in the evening they shall induce them to go there, without using coercion, but with mildness and charity; if they have to deal with hardened sinners who make resistance, they must commend them to the

mercy of God, without troubling themselves further.

46. The missions are not to last less than a fortnight, or more than a month; some days must be employed after the papal benediction in hearing confessions, promoting peace, visiting the sick, and confirming the good done.

47. On the day the papal benediction is given there shall be a general communion, but as all cannot come in one morning, the people must be informed, that to gain the indulgence they may communicate the previous days, and they shall exhort them to divide their families, half coming one day, and the remainder the day following, that they may come more quietly and with devotion.

48. The principal functions of our missions shall consist as follows. In the morning, after having sung the "Salve Regina," an offering of the day's work shall be made to God, in which all the people shall join; then the instructions shall be given, and after this, the relics of the Blessed Virgin Mary shall be exposed, relating an example briefly: then follows benediction, so that this function shall only last an hour and a quarter, because the people must go to their daily labor; to keep them longer would do more harm than good.

49. When the bell has been rung for the sermon, the lay-brothers, clerics, and boys shall carry the cross, singing the Litany through the town to assemble the people. As soon as a sufficient number are in the church, they shall begin to sing some of the hymns before mentioned for a quarter of an hour. Whilst they are lighting the candles for the exposition of the Blessed Sacrament, one of the priests shall say the acts of Faith, Hope, and Charity. At the exposition there shall be sung "Vi adoro ogni momento," and the preacher shall say a few words upon adoration of the Most Holy Sacrament, and then a Pater and Ave shall be said for their benefactors. The almsgiving after the sermon shall be employed in the manner appointed; the length of the sermon shall be regulated, that this function last

only an hour and three quarters. After the "Laudate Dominum" nothing more shall be said.

50. There shall be a procession of penitents twice during the mission in the most populous parts of the town; they shall be conducted in the manner described above.

51. In cities and populous places, after a fortnight of fervent preaching, everyone shall go to confession, and they shall begin the public exercises. In the morning a brief "Riforma" shall be given, and after that the Holy Sacrifice celebrated, then an abridgment of the meditation; all this is to occupy an hour, the evening meditation is to last a quarter of an hour, when there shall be exposition of the Blessed Sacrament, benediction being given at the end.

52. On the first day, when the exercises are begun, a discourse shall be given, in which they shall be explained in order, that they may be better understood by the people, and they shall be instructed what spiritual reading and other devotions they are to perform in private.

53. The holy exercise of the Way of the Cross shall be introduced into every place where the missions are given, and an instructive discourse delivered at the same time, and making a procession accompanied by the people, the crosses shall be planted, not only in the churches but in the oratories, so that all may join in this pious devotion.

54. The day before the papal benediction a sermon shall be preached on Purgatory, to induce the people to give their prayers and alms to release the souls who are suffering there at this time of indulgence, when sinners are being loosed from their sins.

55. The great good which we hope may result from our missions, is to make the people feel contrition, and conceive a greater horror of sin, flying from every occasion of it, such as evil company, late hours, and idle conversations. The priests must be very particular in giving absolution only to the truly penitent; they shall endeavor to banish all hatred, promoting peace

everywhere, and inveigh loudly against immodesty in the women, persuading them to go to church closely veiled. All games at cards must be forbidden, at least in company, and for the sake of gambling; all who have cards in their possession shall burn them in public before the benediction is given. All books with an immoral tendency, all prohibited arms, such as Genoese knives, etc., shall be collected together and destroyed. They shall see that all learn by heart the acts of Faith, Hope, Charity, and Contrition, and often make use of the ejaculation "Mercy, O my Jesus!" wear a crucifix under the clothes next the heart, often attend the devotion of the Via Crucis, be very devout to holy Mary, especially to the sacred mystery of the Immaculate Conception, and inscribe the most holy name of our Lord Jesus Christ over the doors of their houses. In short, all our prayers, penances, and mortifications must be directed to one end, the reformation and sanctification of the people.

56. To obtain so great an end, those who are appointed to preach must prepare their sermons with the utmost care, weighing every word, and pondering over the subject; especially must they prepare for this by prayer, so that all who hear them may be moved and converted to God. Before ascending the pulpit they must prostrate themselves with their faces to the ground, declaring their insufficiency, and that the conversion of souls is the work of God; rising they shall say they have confidence in God, and desire to place their words in the sacred Heart of Jesus, that they may be dipped in His most precious Blood, and prove an instrument, by the grace of the Holy Spirit, to soften the hearts of the most hardened sinners.

57. The Fathers must be most cautious in the sacred tribunal of the confessional, and especially in asking questions of the women; and if there be any difficult case relating to the matter of justice, they shall not trust themselves to give an opinion, but consult some standard theological work, to be carried with them for this purpose.

58. Good example being the very soul of our missions, those who can and are willing to do so shall walk barefoot; those who are not able, from weakness, must be discreet and mortified, that their external deportment may be a living sermon, for they may be assured that every eye is upon them, observing their behavior. They must also be interiorly united with Almighty God during the whole time of the mission, with perfect purity of heart and with the sincere intention of seeking nothing but the greater glory of God; they ought to appear like so many images of holiness and meekness, being at that time truly a spectacle to the world, men, and angels. If any one of them shall hear the mission, or one of the missionaries, spoken against, they shall immediately inform the president, that he may prevent it, for hell trembles at being robbed of so many souls.

59. Every effort must be made to leave the people in peace one with another, and kindly affectioned; and before beginning the mission they must consult, not only the convenience of the chapter and parish priest, but the governor and authorities of the place. They should also treat with the regulars of the town for the well-being of the mission, going to visit them, and asking for their prayers, and treating them with due reverence.

60. The fundamental maxim in doing good, is that of being detached from the world and loving mortification. He who does not feel within himself a great love of purity, and a firm resolution rather to die than commit mortal sin, shall speak openly and sincerely to the superior; for it may be at the risk of losing his soul if he neglects to do so. It is most desirable that they should always be recollected, and engaged in all the prayers and exercises prescribed in these rules, they must be aware that all the admonitions here given, are founded on the experience of many years. If they act otherwise, they will find nothing but confusion and inquietude, and the missionary duties would be conducted without order, and cause scandal. Our fathers will be dissipated by them, and the people be disedified. Let superiors be

ever on the watch, as they will have to render an account to God.

61. Lastly, though at the beginning of the mission, the people shall walk in procession to present the cross from the parish priest to the missionaries, and after a short "fervorino" the Litanies shall be intoned, and they shall all proceed to the church, yet when the mission is ended, they must leave the place as quietly as possible, to avoid applause, not taking leave of anyone except the parish priest, kissing his hand, and asking his blessing, for they must seek nothing but the honor and glory of God. They must, during the mission, renew this pure intention if it be possible, at every breath, lest, "while preaching to others, they should become reprobate."

In the year 1704 Blessed Leonard was obliged, by order of the pope, Benedict XIV, to moderate and alter the rules for his missions, particularly in regard to diet, because his companions were often sick, and some even died, in consequence of the extreme rigor. Therefore, the rules drawn up in 1712 were remedied, and certain things left out, or added, according to the experience of past years. It is a certain fact that they were drawn up before he went to preach in Tuscany, and observed to the letter until his death, for we know, that the evening before his departure he knelt down in the middle of the refectory with a stone hung round his neck, confessing his fault in the presence of the father guardian, and recommended himself to the prayers of all the community. The day of his departure he asked the blessing of the superior and the companions to be given him, although he was allowed to select them for himself, according to the permission given by the holy pontiff Benedict XIV. He then went to the church, and having adored the Blessed Sacrament, left the convent reciting the Litany of the most holy Virgin, and other prayers ordered in the rules, without ceasing until they arrived at the place where the mission was to be given. During the time he remained there, he always rose an hour before his companions, keeping in his room an alarm to awaken him, and employed the time in prayer and preparation for celebrating the Holy Sacrifice, not allowing any one to enter his room, unless called there by himself.

THE LIFE OF

ST. LEONARD OF PORT MAURICE

PART II

CHAPTER I

Of the Faith of Blessed Leonard

T is by the grace of Almighty God that we become virtuous and holy, and by means of which men often become saints, and are raised by degrees to the highest perfection, and closer union with Him. Therefore, we must speak more at length of the wonderful degree of grace bestowed on Blessed Leonard, and his many heroic virtues, which caused his name to be held in benediction. Although we have often had occasion to mention them in writing his Life, for the greater glory of God and the edification of those who read it, we shall now enter more in detail on the principal and most noble of his virtues. But since many of these were hidden, and known only to God, we can only mention those which shone as bright lights in every action of his life. We shall begin with the first of the theological virtues, faith; the principle and foundation of our justification, the germ and soul of every virtue, and as S. Paul says, "without it we cannot please God." And as this is one of the interior virtues, we shall relate in what manner he manifested it, particularly in his devotion to the divine mysteries and the saints in heaven.

He proved his firm faith in every action from his earliest years, in giving instructions to his companions in the principal mysteries of religion, and preaching, in his childish way, as a prognostic of his apostolical ministry, in which for so many years he could not have persevered with so much zeal and fervor, oppressed with fatigue and suffering, without a firm and lively faith. He showed it in Rome, teaching the young men when he was only a secular, and drawing the people to catechism and sermons. After he entered the religious life, his faith was seen when in familiar discourse with his brethren; he expressed an

147

ardent desire of going to convert the heathens, and even to suffer
martyrdom for the Catholic Faith; he had this same desire during
his whole life, and he often lamented that he was not worthy to
give his life for Jesus Christ. He spoke with more feeling
whenever he heard that in China, where he desired to go in his
youth, missionaries had been tortured, and endured martyrdom.
So ardent was this desire, in consequence of his strong faith, that
I cannot forbear transcribing an extract from one of his sermons.
"If it be right," says he, "that a son should imitate his father, I
shall offer myself in the same way as our holy father S. Francis
offered himself when in presence of the Great Sultan." To prove
the truth of our holy religion he made this proposal, that if they
would light a great fire, he would throw himself into it provided
the barbarians would only listen to the word of God, and receive
baptism. "Yes, I would offer myself in the same way." He went on
to say: Light in that square a fire, and obtain for me leave from
the superior, rest assured if there be any one amongst us who is
wavering in his faith, in order to convince him, I would without
hesitation throw myself into the flames, to bear witness to the
faith which came down from heaven." Nay more than this, in the
eighth resolution drawn up by him in his retreat, it plainly
appears that he had taken faith for his guide in every action of
his life, doing all things by its light and guidance. In fact, the
light of faith accompanied him everywhere; by faith he believed
God to be always present, beholding Him in all things, and
seeking Him alone either in his interior or in external works. By
these acts of faith, with which he began all his works, he
acquired every day fresh fervor in laboring for the glory of that
God in whom he so firmly believed, and who was the sole object
of his desires, affections, and actions. To practice this virtue in an
especial manner, he made for himself a sort of mental solitude,
which he called the "land of faith," where, believing all
supernatural truth, and separated from things created, he aspired
to nothing, especially in prayer, but God and heavenly things. In

this "land of faith," he delighted to converse with God, and endeavor to transform himself to His likeness.

In this way, having God and His Divine attributes always in sight, contemplating them with the light of faith, he was often quite raised above the world, so that frequently when met by the religious and others, who saluted him, and asked him questions, without his even appearing to see them and without giving a reply, he would proceed on his way, quite absorbed and distracted in mind, lost in contemplation of that God, who by faith was ever present to him.

In faith he most firmly believed all the truths revealed by God, and proposed to be believed in His Church, all these mysteries he believed as if he had seen them with his own eyes, and even more surely than if he had seen them, because they were revealed by infallible truth. He endeavored to animate others to this faith in the Divine Presence, saying, as he did in the "Manual for Religious," written by him, that it was an easy matter, since it is sufficient that by faith we know that He is ever present, and that by the eye of faith we may behold Him even in this vale of darkness. He desired that all should possess this firm faith, and that they should never be exposed to the danger of wavering or losing it When he returned from Corsica to Genoa, and preached in that town, he recommended the people to enroll themselves in the confraternity of our "Lady of Succor," instituted for the support of the forces against the Corsairs, who often took as slaves those who were not well instructed, and who, therefore, ran great risk of losing their faith. To excite them to this devotion, he preached six sermons with so much zeal and fervor, that the report reached the Turks, who tried to capture him, as he mentions in one of his letters, in which he again expresses the ardent desire, cherished in his heart, of dying for the true faith. "In Tunis," he says, "the Turks have been informed that I have sought the protection of our Blessed Lady against them, and even say that Father Leonard has declared war against them, and that they are seeking after him, and if they succeed in finding him, he will soon be impaled, and thus made an example to the Christians, which I desire with all my heart." But if it pleased not God that His faithful servant should not go to heathen countries and give his life, as he desired, for the Catholic faith, he was permitted to exercise his zeal and charity in the conversion of many whom he found in a Christian country. Amongst many facts which might be adduced, I shall content myself with giving an account of one only. When he was giving a retreat in Leghorn, a young Turk, who, fortunately for himself, was in that port, went to hear Blessed Leonard preach, and although he understood very little of the Italian language, divine grace, working in his heart, led him to seek out the missionary, and make known to him the desire he had conceived of becoming a Christian. The man of God received him with joy, and encouraged him to carry into effect his holy resolution, and after having instructed him in the truths of the Catholic Faith, took him to Florence, where he was baptized. He had also the consolation of baptizing a young Jewess in Viterbo, who, being seriously impressed in hearing one of his sermons, resolved to embrace Christianity, sought an interview with him, and in a few days prepared herself to be received into the Church. Two young Hebrew women were converted about this time, but in a different manner. One of them was brought to the house of the catechumens in Rome, where several of her relations had become Christians; however, she was obstinately determined not to renounce Judaism until Blessed Leonard converted her by applying the image of the Mother of God, which he always carried with him, to her forehead, when she felt a change in her heart, and an ardent desire to become a Christian, and she afterwards consecrated herself to God in the religious life, feeling that she never could be sufficiently grateful to Him for so great a blessing. The other woman having received baptism, in hypocrisy soon after entered a convent, assumed the habit, and made her profession, and thus was in appearance a Christian, but in reality a Jewess. The convent was visited by Blessed Leonard, and when she came in her turn to confession he exhorted her with his accustomed gentleness and charity to open her conscience to him entirely. Then the unhappy girl, touched by the grace of God, made known to him her miserable state, and with great compunction entreated him to apply a remedy. Moved with zeal to bring this poor soul into the Catholic Church, he cleared away the mists of darkness, and illumined her mind with the light of faith, instructed her in the mysteries of religion, and so removed so great a disorder.

He manifested the same zeal for the true faith in the following occurrence. A sailor, a native of the place where a few years before Blessed Leonard had given a mission, having given way to the desires of his corrupt passions, in order to gratify them more easily determined to go to Geneva, where he very soon renounced his religion, and denied his God, but the Almighty in His mercy did not forsake him, but pierced his heart with true remorse, and made him feel an inward voice, which told him to return and confess to Blessed Leonard, who, when he found him truly penitent, would give him absolution and consolation. But very soon he full back, his heart again became corrupt, and darkened his intellect, and, insensible to the stings of remorse, he left his country and went to live amongst the Turks, and entirely renounced his faith. But although plunged in every sort of vice, his merciful God again made him feel remorse of conscience, which at last induced him to go to Rome, and make a general confession to Blessed Leonard. The wretched man, obedient to the dictates of conscience, set off on his journey, and as soon as he reached Rome, went to the convent of S. Buonaventura, and prostrated himself at the feet of the servant of God, related the wicked course of his life, and at the same time all the sins he had committed against the Catholic faith, first, amongst the protestants, and afterwards amongst the

St. Leonard of Port Maurice

Muhammadans. The good Father embraced with charity this prodigal son, and having instructed him to purge away the heresy into which he had fallen, reconciled him to his God and the church, and, finding that he was destitute, gave him the means of subsistence, and sent him to his own country much consoled. These are some out of the many instances of the strong faith of Blessed Leonard which animated his zeal for the conversion of sinners, and which encouraged him to persevere to the end of his days, oppressed as he was with constant suffering and fatigue.

CHAPTER II

On the Devotion of Blessed Leonard to the Most Holy Sacrament

T is by faith ever increasing that we are incited to adore the Eternal Truth, and as our holy Father practiced this virtue in an extraordinary manner, we shall see the blessed effects in every action of his life. As the Sacrament of the Eucharist is called, above all others, "Mysterium fidei," and the faith they have in it distinguishes Catholics more than anything else from modern sectarians, we shall say a few words on the great devotion of Blessed Leonard to this ineffable mystery. Without going back to the first years of his life, when we know with what wonderful reverence he assisted at mass, made visits to the Blessed Sacrament, and received the holy Communion frequently, it is sufficient to say that one of his resolutions was to constitute this divine Sacrament the end, aim, and center of all his affections, always reverencing by outward and inward actions Jesus there present, and inducing his young companions to do the same. When he was traveling, the first thing he did on arriving at any place was to visit the church, and prostrate himself before the altar of the Blessed Sacrament. He said mass every day with so much devotion, that all present were greatly edified; he prepared himself for the tremendous sacrifice by confessing twice in the day, and passed the time from compline till mass the following morning in preparation. He was most exact in performing all the ceremonies prescribed by the church, and communicated each morning as if for the last time, according to a resolve he had made some time before, and during the communion he made internally the acts of Faith, Hope, Charity, and Contrition, and an ardent desire to be transformed into Jesus. Before celebrating mass he always made these acts, and renewed them at the end, for he said, the greatest point for preparation and returning thanks was to have a pure and humble heart, which, enlightened by a lively faith, excited acts of interior humility, praise, love, and contrition. He assisted every morning at as many masses as his occupations permitted, and in the act of offering which he made, he formed the intention of hearing and offering to the Lord Almighty all the masses celebrated that day all over the world. He used to call the mass the Sun of Christianity, the soul of faith, and the center of the Christian religion, and the epitome of all that is good and all that is beautiful in the Church of God.

This was the faith he had in this great Sacrament, and hence his wonderful devotion to it, which was seen in his manner of celebrating; he never approached the altar without being girt with haircloth, and without having first offered thirty-three times to the Eternal Father the most sacred blood of Jesus Christ, praying to Him to grant, by virtue of this sacrifice, that his heart might be always pure and clean, free from every stain of sin. In vesting himself for the Holy Sacrifice he accompanied every action with such sentiments of lively faith and piety, that one could not fail to see outwardly the interior fervor which was glowing in his heart. In going to the altar he pictured to his mind the awful scene on Calvary, and saw with the eye of faith the Holy Trinity, surrounded by angels and saints, ready to receive the sacrifice he was about to offer. His deportment was that of a man raised above the world, recollected and absorbed in contemplating his God. He divided the Mass into five parts, to prevent distractions, and to keep the mind entirely fixed on God, viz., Preparation, Instruction, Oblation, Communion, and Thanksgiving. In the first, which lasted from the beginning of Mass to the Introit, he made an interior act of contrition and humility, confessing himself unworthy to offer so great a sacrifice. In the second, which extended from the Introit to the Credo, he paid great attention to the meaning of the words, in order, as he said, to gather those lights and graces which God might grant him. In the third, from the offertory to the communion, he endeavored to keep in mind these four ends, which everyone ought to have in offering the Holy Sacrifice, viz.: the giving of praise and glory to God; the satisfying His justice for sin committed; the returning thanks to Him for so many benefits received; and the supplicating Him to bestow others upon us. In the last part, from the communion to the end of mass, he accompanied all the prayers with a lively thanksgiving to Jesus, who dwelt within him, adoring Him with reverence, and making acts of love. If sometimes he was told that he was a long time in celebrating mass, he would reply, "Do you not know that my greatest consolation is celebrating the Holy Sacrifice, and my great sorrow is to see some priests celebrate it with so much haste; if all had a lively faith they would be unwilling to leave the altar. In fact, so strong was his faith, that he found his greatest delight in offering the Divine Son to the Eternal Father, especially in the consecration, when he appeared quite inflamed with love, and in the communion he was full of joy, as if he had been conversing with his dearest and most confidential friend, and during the whole time he was celebrating he seemed in an ecstasy. He was not satisfied with adoring the Blessed Sacrament himself with all these acts of devotion, but be induced others to do the same.

In all his missions he inculcated that in carrying the Blessed Sacrament to the sick they should do it with the greatest decorum and devotion, with a great many lights; and the effect of this exhortation was seen in many places, where, before he came among them, they had been very negligent in regard to this, but where they now accompanied the Viaticum in procession with due reverence and abundance of lights. This happened particularly in Ancona, where, in one of his sermons he had reminded them, that being a seaport, many strangers were there from almost every nation under the sun, who would be edified in seeing the Catholics carrying their God present in the Blessed Sacrament, with due reverence and devotion. This exhortation so impressed the people that they assembled in great numbers to walk in procession, with so many torches that sometimes as many as five hundred might be counted; this, united to the devotion of the people, edified and touched all who witnessed it. In one place in Sabina there was so much negligence in carrying the holy Viaticum to the sick, that the people were even ashamed to bear the canopy, and the priests were often obliged to wait a long time until some poor country men even could be found to carry it. The good missionary said much in condemnation of this, and after much labor he succeeded in persuading the people to employ themselves in so holy an office, so that all the country hastened, whenever they had an opportunity, to walk in procession with the Blessed Sacrament, persons of the highest rank bearing the canopy, and this they continued to do for the future. It happened at Minerbio, in the diocese of Bologna, that the Viaticum was to be taken to a poor dying man, whose habitation was a miserable cabin, half a mile distant from the church, and almost all the inhabitants assembled to walk in procession, amongst the number were two cardinals who were there at the time. The same thing happened in Occhiobello, in the diocese of Ferrara, and elsewhere, when he induced the bishops and other dignitaries to reverence in this manner the Blessed Sacrament, and for the same intention he exhorted the people to attend many masses with the greatest possible reverence. The devotion of Blessed Leonard even extended to asking alms to be employed in providing sacred vessels for the altar. Having at Ascolta collected two hundred crowns, he took from this a small sum to pay for the wax tapers consumed in the various offices, and with the remainder purchased five pyxes for churches in which they were wanted. In Castel San Pietro, in the diocese of Bologna, having found in the church only a very poor small remonstrance, unfit for so sacred a purpose, he was so diligent that before the mission was ended, he collected a sum sufficient to purchase a very costly and beautiful one. Having always expressed an ardent desire to establish the perpetual adoration of the Blessed Sacrament, he formed a confraternity for this devotion, attached to the church of the Rotunda in Rome. He published the indulgences granted to the pious members by the holy pontiff Benedict XIV, was enrolled himself as a member, and propagated it with so much zeal, that before his death he had the consolation of having established it in a hundred and thirty places where he had given missions, and of knowing that it was practiced even by the Catholics of Mexico. In short, from his childhood until his death nothing could exceed the devotion of Blessed Leonard to this great mystery, adoring it in every place and persuading others to the same. He gave a certain proof of his faith in the Blessed Sacrament in his last illness, when having arrived in Rome half dead, and having been carried to his bed in a state of complete exhaustion, at the sight of the Viaticum he raised himself up, and burst forth into acts of faith, hope, and love, with so much fervor that all present were moved to tears.

CHAPTER III

On the Devotion of Blessed Leonard to the Passion of Our Lord, and to the Holy Name of Jesus.

OST wonderful was the devotion of our holy Father to the Passion of our Lord, for besides meditating continually on it and having it imprinted on his heart, he spared no pains in exciting others to the same. "This is the way," said he, "to sanctify the catholic world, and free it from the power of Satan, to make all the faithful think often in their hearts of the Passion of our Divine Redeemer; to obtain this I would willingly give the blood from my veins, my breath, and my life." And well did he prove in his familiar discourses, and in his sermons, that he bore in his heart the cross of Christ, recommending all to meditate frequently on the death and Passion of their Lord, and he expressed, by his countenance as well as his words, how deeply he felt it. He usually began his prayer by meditating on some stage of the Passion, fixing in his mind the sufferings of the Redeemer, and particularly that of the crucifixion. Having arranged in order the points of the Passion on which he wished to meditate, he continued in prayer during every hour of the day, and sometimes during the night. Besides this he visited every day the Stations of the Cross, with so much devotion and tenderness, that he always shed tears of compassion in meditating on the sufferings of Jesus there described. He always carried on his heart a cross with five iron points, which were to remind him continually of the suffering of his Blessed Lord, and these words were found in his own handwriting: "I will bear Jesus Christ crucified impressed in my thoughts, and on my heart, and I will often fall at His feet to weep for my sins." Every

Friday in the year he ate wormwood and other bitter herbs, in memory of the gall which they gave the Redeemer to drink on the cross, and he fasted on bread and water. He frequently ejaculated these words: "May the Passion of our Lord Jesus Christ be always in my heart," and he pressed his lips with reverence to every cross he saw. His greatest care was to establish in every place where he preached, the pious exercise of the Via Crucis, and he caused the fourteen Stations to be erected, in which were represented the sorrowful way of Jesus from the Praetorium to Calvary, and which are so well calculated to induce the faithful to meditate on the Passion of the Redeemer. Having obtained permission from the pope to extend this holy and beneficial devotion, he very soon succeeded in introducing it into convents and churches were it had been until then unknown.

With the approbation of his Holiness he raised the fourteen little chapels in the Colosseum in Rome, which remain to this day, and where this pious exercise may be seen practiced by the confraternity of the "Lovers of Jesus and Mary."

Wherever he gave a mission he inculcated the practice of this holy exercise, representing to the people the great spiritual advantage to be derived from it. He wrote a little book containing meditations and devotions for the Via Crucis, so excellent, that many on reading it were induced to join the confraternity. At the end of the missions he always recommended the people to frequent it, and the chief advice he gave to confessors was, to enjoin their penitents to visit the Via Crucis, assuring them that nothing tended more to amendment of life, and perseverance in attaining perfection, than meditation on the passion of our Lord. He advised everyone to wear on his heart a small crucifix, to make them always bear in mind what He had suffered for them, and to serve as a sort of check against temptations, and the assaults of the devil. He also introduced the custom of tolling the bell every Friday at three o'clock, so that all who hear it may kneel down and say three Pater nosters and three Aves, in remembrance of the Passion of Jesus, Who for three hours hung in agony on the cross, and at the end of the third hour expired. This pious custom, introduced by him, is still kept up in many places, particularly in Rome, where at the same time they pray for impenitent and hardened sinners.

Since the name of Jesus signifies Savior, and as the Son of God was pleased to become man for our salvation, Blessed Leonard, full of devotion to Jesus crucified, reverenced with great piety His holy name, and promoted as much as possible its being reverenced by the people. He had it painted on a banner which be called his standard, under which were assembled the soldiers of Christ crucified, who were to make war against the powers of hell, imitating in this the two great saints of his order, S. Bernadine of Sienna, and S. John Capistrano, the former being the one who established the devotion, and the latter, who defended it. He converted many sinners and worked great wonders by virtue of this holy name, and preached a sermon expressly on this devotion, which he recommended with so much fervor and charity that he drew tears from the eyes of all who heard him. In every place where he gave a mission, he introduced the custom amongst the faithful, of saluting each other with these words: "Blessed be Jesus Christ," which is still in use in many places. From the great desire he had that this holy name should be reverenced, and the importance he attached to it, he was much grieved when he heard those bearing the name of Christian profane and blaspheme it. He inveighed in the most zealous manner against such persons, and desired that his words might be as so many darts to pierce their hearts, and incite them to love and reverence a name so sweet, so august, and so holy. To attain this end he used every effort, and succeeded to his heart's content. When he was giving a mission in Arpino, he found blasphemy more prevalent than any other vice, and consequently labored by preaching and every other means to extirpate so detestable a sin. He spoke one day from the pulpit to the children, and earnestly entreated them if ever they heard any one profane the holy name, to say in a loud voice: "Blessed be Jesus Christ." And the Lord blessed the labors of His servant, for it happened after the mission, that a man addicted to this vice was heard to blaspheme; he was immediately surrounded by a crowd of young men and boys, who reproached him so severely, uttering at the same time the well-known words "Blessed be Jesus Christ," that he was covered with confusion, and never heard to repeat his blasphemies. He also was most earnest in persuading them to have the holy name inscribed over the doors of their houses, feeling sure that if the faithful always had it before their eyes, they would be reminded to honor it. Almighty God vouchsafed to manifest clearly by signs how pleasing all this was to Him. It happened in Porto Ferrajo in Tuscany, that a Christian was prevented having the holy name inscribed over the door of his house, in consequence of a Jew living in part of it below, where he kept a shop, and not knowing what to do, consulted the good missionary, who advised him to place it over two windows of the same house. Soon after this, a fire broke out in the Jew's shop, and although that part of the house and all it contained was reduced to ashes, the flames did not reach where the holy name was inscribed, and left untouched the part of the house occupied by the Christian, to the great wonder of all, who acknowledged the miracle, and the power of the holy name.

Thus did Blessed Leonard honor the holy name of the Redeemer, because, with the light of faith, he knew the power, the merit, and the excellence of it. By the same light he knew the dignity and price of the Redeemer Himself, and professed the most tender devotion to Him; it seemed to him impossible that anyone should know and believe in Him, and yet not come to Him, and he held it for certain, that a serious reflection on what the Son of God has done for us, and the immense benefits we have derived from Him, is sufficient to excite the greatest love and gratitude. He used to say sometimes, that all the most noble thoughts united could not comprehend fully the dignity and greatness of Jesus Christ, and that it was impossible for man to conceive it. He was ever learning in the "land of faith," to which he often retired, and described it in his familiar discourses as a beauty so exceeding, that even in paradise one could not have a much higher enjoyment. To some he described it with a heart so full of love and tenderness, that he brought even the most hardened sinners to his feet, full of contrition, repenting of their sins. To others he described all the graces and benefits granted to those who love Jesus, exclaiming, "By our Blessed Lord, we are provided with so many adorable mysteries, so many holy sacraments, the Holy Scriptures, sermons, graces, the gifts of the Holy Spirit, good thoughts, holy affections, inspirations, and a thousand more treasures; in short, everything that tends to our sanctification comes from Jesus Christ." He then went on with increased fervor, exclaiming, " Ah, my beloved Jesus, take away my life, but give me only love for Thee, since on earth I possess nothing worth having but the power of speech to sound Thy praise; this, 0 my God, I desire to use, and will use to my last breath in praising and blessing Thee!" Sometimes he was unable to restrain the ardor with which his heart was inflamed in expressing the tender devotion he felt, and his firm faith in his Divine Redeemer. "Ah! my Jesus," he would say, "my only good, what would I not give that all my members might become so many tongues to make Thee known and beloved by all the world!"

CHAPTER IV

On the Devotion of Blessed Leonard to Most Holy Mary and to the Saints.

E may say that the devotion of Blessed Leonard to Holy Mary was born with him, and went on increasing with years, ever becoming more wonderful and affectionate. We described in the first part of this history his raising little altars when yet a child in honor of her, often asking her intercession, and inviting his companions to do the same, and with them going frequently barefoot to visit her image in a church two miles distant from Port Maurice. To understand how he advanced in this devotion, it is sufficient to read the sixteenth and three following of his resolutions, in the last of which he says, "I desire to have a tender devotion to the Holy Virgin, and declare, that in her hands I have placed the great concern of my eternal salvation, loving her with the most tender affection, the affection of a son towards his beloved mother, and desire that all may love and honor her in the same manner." He always spoke of her as his "dear mother," was exceedingly devout to her, and desired, as we find recorded in his own handwriting, to belong entirely to her both in time and in eternity. "I intend," said he, "not only to give her my whole heart, but also to strive to enkindle this flame of devotion in every soul, by proclaiming her glories, speaking and thinking often of her, and assisting in all the devotions that have been instituted in her honor." He recited every day the rosary of the Seven Joys, which originated, and is said in the Franciscan order; and when his various occupations prevented his doing so, he would make seven acts of love, in memory of the seven joys of the Blessed Virgin Mary.

He made every day twelve acts of humility in memory of the twelve prerogatives given her by the Holy conversion of sinners, declaring at the same time that he loved her with all his heart, and would continue to love her till his death as his Mother and Lady. Every time the clock struck he said a Hail Mary, and renewed his congratulations to Mary on her privilege of being immaculate, and the Elected Mother of God, and his thanksgiving to the most Holy Trinity for bestowing these graces upon her. At the accustomed sound of the angelus, he always fell on his knees and said the prayers appointed; at the first toll of the bell he renewed his vow of poverty in the hands of Jesus the Holy Child; at the second toll, his vow of obedience in the hands of Mary, and at the third, his vow of chastity in the hands of Joseph. He fasted every Saturday in the year in honor of the Blessed Virgin, and on the vigils of her feast he ate nothing but bread and water, preparing for the celebration of them with great devotion. Before the feasts of the Immaculate Conception, the Nativity, and the Assumption, he said a Novena and a Triduo before her other feasts, and employed the time in being more fervent in prayer, and using greater austerities to dispose his soul to receive from Mary on her feasts new graces and favors.

He always carried about with him a little wooden box, in which, in one division, was a picture of Mary, and the other, one of S. Vincent Ferrer, and often pressing to his heart this sacred image, he consecrated to his Holy Mother all his affections. When he was writing or studying, or whatever he was doing, he placed this image before him, often kissing its feet and entreating Mary's aid, and declaring himself her servant Since Mary was his most compassionate benefactress, he declared that all praise and honor was due to her, as he said in writing on this devotion: "As for me, when I consider the many graces I have received from Holy Mary, what do you think I seem to be? Listen to me while I publicly proclaim it to the glory of our Blessed Lady; I seem to be one of those churches in which are miraculous images of the Madonna, and where all the walls are covered with votive offerings and inscriptions, (Per grazia ricevuta da Maria). By a

grace received from Mary. The health of mind and body which
I enjoy, the sacred office in which I am employed, the holy habit
I wear, are favors received from Mary; every good thought, every
good desire, every good feeling of my heart, I owe to the
intercession of Mary. Read, read, for on my heart and all my
members the name of Mary is written. On my soul, Oh would
that you could see it, is written 'Per grazia di Maria.' On my
heart is written "'Per grazia di Maria,' on my tongue is written
'Per grazia Maria.' Blessed forever be my compassionate
protectress. I shall sing in eternity the praises of Mary, for if I am
saved, it will be through the intercession of my great protectress
Mary." In declaring his obligations to the Blessed Virgin, he was
most desirous to be made worthy of her protection. In giving
missions, and in his private discourses, he was inflamed with
holy zeal in exhorting all to be devout to holy Mary, and offer
her their hearts. Besides recommending this from the platform
with wonderful energy, entreating all to have recourse to her in
their wants, and exhorting the rich to give alms to the poor, on
condition that they should say the rosary every evening; in every
mission he preached a sermon on the devotion to the Madonna,
with so much zeal and fervor, that the most hardened were
touched. Innumerable were the conversions after this sermon;
and in speaking of them Blessed Leonard used to say, "In
preaching on the devotion to my dear Mother, I have
accomplished that which the fear of eternal torments and the last
judgment have failed to do."

So great and extraordinary was the fervor with which he
preached this sermon, that all who heard him might see how his
heart was inflamed with love and devotion to the Queen of
Heaven. To understand it in some measure, I shall give an
instance of the language he used. "I desire to die," he was wont
to say, "and to live with Mary. Ah, my beloved brethren, I do not
say this as a mere matter of form, I say it in truth, with my heart,
with my whole heart; ah! dearest Mother, receive me in your

arms, behold a poor sinner, who desires to come to you, beloved Queen of heaven. Do you, my brethren, say a Hail Mary for me, to obtain for me the grace to fall down dead, even here on this platform, that so I may go and live with Mary. By the grace of God, my conscience does not accuse me of sin, and I hope to go to Paradise, and be admitted to see our Blessed Lady and true Mother; if I am not worthy of this, at least, let me expire breathing the words, 'I wish to die, yes, I wish to die, to live forever with most holy Mary.'" He spoke these words with so much affection, feeling, force, and fervor, that everyone felt convinced they came from his heart. In continuing to animate the people to a tender devotion to the Mother of God, he taught them that to be truly devout, they must honor her every year, every month, every week, every day, every hour, and at all times; and after having instructed them in the various ways of paying the tribute of reverence and devotion to her, he concluded by saying, that the most acceptable devotion, and without which all their doings are nothing worth, was to fly from sin and the occasion of it. Anyone truly devout to Mary, finding himself in danger of falling into sin, ought to say. "This will displease my Holy Mother, I must not grieve her by doing it." Sometimes he would say in preaching, "Give yourselves with fervor to the devotion to the Blessed Virgin, and you will be saved. But who is truly devout to her? He who is truly the enemy of mortal sin." To undeceive many false devotees, of whom there are many in the world, even the Catholic world of our times, who, plunged into sin of every sort, believe they will be accepted by the Blessed Virgin for saying the rosary, or visiting one of her images, he said in one of his sermons, "This is to pretend that the Mother of God is the patroness, not of sinners, but of sin! To be numbered amongst the truly devout children of Mary, we must be truly converted to God."

I should never end were I to relate all that he said and did to promote and establish amongst the people the devotion to the

St. Leonard of Port Maurice

Blessed Virgin, and how he honored her himself by every act of veneration and love, and the pleasure it gave him to see her image, which he carried about with him in his missions, honored by the people, and carried in procession with a great many lights, with all the reverence and honor which the means of the place admitted.

As Blessed Leonard adored and loved God, and reverenced with great devotion His blessed Mother, so he reverenced and invoked the saints in heaven, the faithful servants of Jesus Christ. He was most devout to his guardian angel, and as he recommended in his eighteenth resolution, whenever the clock struck after having said a "Hail Mary," he saluted him with great devotion, thanking him for the assistance given during the past hour, and begging him to be with him during the coming hour. These acts were also made by him during the night, if he happened to be awake.

Having chosen for the patrons of his missions the seraphic Father S. Francis, S. Vincent Ferrer, and S. Antony of Padua, besides invoking them and saying the antiphons of their feasts before he began to preach, he reverenced them every day with particular devotion. "I propose," said he at the introduction of his resolutions, "to imitate, as closely as possible, the great virtues of my seraphic Father S. Francis, asking his paternal blessing on all my undertakings." He had also a singular devotion to all the other saints, honoring them, and having recourse in all his wants to their aid and intercession. At night before he slept he recommended himself to all of them, invoking them in the Litany he had composed. In order to die, as he said, fortified with the sacraments, he said a Pater and Ave to S. Barbara, virgin and martyr, asking her to obtain for him this grace. He constantly invoked the aid of his angel-guardian, speaking to him and asking his counsel in doubts, and assistance before he began to preach or pray, or any spiritual exercise.

St. Leonard of Port Maurice

This was the devotion of Blessed Leonard, originated and produced by that faith which made him believe in all the mysteries of religion as if he had seen them with his own eyes, and even more surely, because they had been revealed by Almighty God to His Church.

CHAPTER V

On the Firm Hope of Blessed Leonard

LESSED LEONARD had a firm hope that he should be able to obtain all that God has promised in His infallible Word, and the only desire of his life was to gain the blessing of heaven, and to be provided with only just what was necessary for the support of the body. Very strong indeed was his hope of eternal bliss, for the attainment of which he labored unweariedly as long as he lived. "I propose," he says in one of his resolutions, "to practice the virtue of hope with as much confidence as if I were secure of my salvation, and was already in Paradise. I will found my hope, and will look for grace, glory, and all things that are not opposed to the glory of God, upon these four foundations, the justice, the faithfulness, the mercy, and the omnipotence of God, for He is able, is willing, and has promised to save us, giving us as our ransom His Son Jesus Christ, by whose grace I hope to live holily, and be saved. I hope that having assisted the souls of others, God will save my soul, for I am resolved never to lose an opportunity of giving spiritual aid."

This did he, hastening wherever he was sent to give missions, converting sinners without heeding the length of the journey, rain, snow, heat, or cold, bad roads, or any dangers and impediments. To make his hope more firm and steadfast he endeavored to conceive so great an idea of the mercy of God, so that relying on the infinite merits of Jesus Christ, he hoped that he might be saved without going to Purgatory, although he was disposed to accept the pains and sufferings of that place willingly and thankfully, if such was the will of God. "And this hope," he added, "cannot be injurious or presumptuous, but may be profitable, because it does not exclude a holy filial fear resulting in the honor of God, and will make me more diligent, since for this end I propose to avoid not only mortal sin, but venial sin, and the least imperfection." He frequently used the ejaculation, "Jesus, my mercy," to obtain all graces, and particularly that of persevering to the end in the love of God. The hope he had of being saved never left him, and he not only consoled himself with full confidence in the Divine mercy, but encouraged others never to despair, but to believe, that notwithstanding our imperfections, and the venial sins we often commit, Almighty God remembers our weakness, and is merciful. He exhorted them to bear in mind the merits of Jesus Christ, and the sacrifice He made for our sins, the intercession of the saints, who pray for us, the indulgences to be gained, and other similar things, which may lead us to the hope of gaining Paradise.

Such was the courage with which he inspired one of his brothers in religion, by whom he was asked if he hoped to go to heaven without passing through purgatory: "Yes," he replied, "for I hope to be made worthy to do so, if I try not to fall into mortal nor even venial sins deliberately, and God will mercifully accept the works and hardships which for His glory I shall perform, to merit in some measure His Divine mercy." Frequently when he was speaking with his brothers in religion, he would fix his gaze on heaven, full of trust and confidence in God, and exclaim: "Ah! when shall I see death, when shall these bonds which bind me to earth be broken? When will that happy day come when I shall behold my God?" He took a very high view of the virtue of hope, and would not endure the idea of its being restricted to the limitations of human prudence. On one occasion when he was called upon to give his advice in strengthening the faith and trust in God of a poor soul, he thus wrote: "Desire the poor girl to place herself before the tribunal of God, as one who depends on him for every want, offering Him the sacred Blood of Jesus, and reminding Him of His promises." We may see from this how well-founded was his hope. In hearing confessions, in preaching, and on all occasions, he encouraged everyone not to lose hope, but however grievous their sins might be, to hope in God, and feel secure that with His gracious mercy and assistance they would attain eternal salvation. He not only hoped for eternal blessings from God, but even the necessaries of this present life. With a firm trust he looked to Heaven for support in the most difficult cases, without ever failing in courage. When he was sent to give missions in Corsica, a country rent with factions and disorders, which might well cause fear, he was most courageous, and when he was about to commence his mission he thus wrote to a priest: "I am going to Corsica, the dangers are great, however, I feel as if I had the heart of a lion." And bold as a lion he was in making war against vice amid so many perils, as we have seen.

When the monastery of S. Francesco was founded in Florence, to which the Grand Duke contributed with great liberality for whatever was required for the support of the community, without their being obliged to beg, Blessed Leonard, at that time superior, returned his thanks to the prince for his generosity, but entreated him to allow them to live by asking alms, since if they acted otherwise, it would seem like a want of trust in Divine Providence. To live in hope and trust in God was all he desired, and amongst the regulations observed in his missions, one was this: In going to any place, no food of any kind is to be carried, excepting when making a sea voyage. No one is to be allowed to eat with us, nor must we eat in the houses of others, even that of a bishop or person of consequence, who may invite us. Nothing is to be received but the mere necessities of life, and all beyond this which is brought is to be given to the poor. He observed this rule with so much exactness, that during the many years he was giving missions, and the many journeys he was obliged to make, he never departed from it in the least degree, even though he exercised his Apostolic ministry for forty-four years, in various provinces and places; he never accepted food or anything that was offered to him, although he was often obliged to walk from morning till night in desert places, and roads almost impassable; he never carried any provisions, not even a piece of bread, to restore his wasted energies. He always said to the people who offered him food to refresh him by the way, that he had a good God, who had graciously promised to provide for his wants, and whose word had never failed during many years, and never would fail, for He was his Father, in whom he trusted, feeling secure that He would provide for every necessity. When he reached the place where the mission was to be given, he always refused to be maintained by any one particular person, except in the last which he gave in Rome, when he was obliged to obey. He ever wished that the support of himself and his companions should be bestowed by God's daily Providence, sure and certain that if they labored for the glory of God and the salvation of souls, they would not be left unprovided with means of support. And the Lord Almighty failed not to encourage the hope of His servant, providing for him in most extraordinary and unexpected ways. In the year 1716, a short time after he had refused the generous offer of assistance from the Grand Duke, it happened there was a scarcity of oil in Tuscany, in consequence of the olives having been injured by the frost the year before. All that remained in the convent was a very small quantity in a jar, and the brother appointed to collect alms much concerned, not knowing how to provide for the want, applied to the superior, explained the case, and told him that in a few days they would be left without oil, for the small quantity they had would soon be consumed. Blessed Leonard, not in the least disturbed at this intelligence, said very quietly: "Trust in God, and doubt not that He will provide for us." Meanwhile, the oil diminished gradually, and was almost exhausted; the lay brother went again to the superior, to inform him of their want; Blessed Leonard turned to him as before with perfect calmness, and repeated the words: "Trust in God, and doubt not that He will provide for us," adding, however, to encourage him that he must hope in the mercy of God, "Do you think, brother, that having left all things for the love of God, and refused, trusting in Him alone, every offer of assistance from the Grand Duke, that His mercy will fail us now?" It was as he predicted, for just at that time God put it into the heart of some benefactor to send eight barrels of oil to the monastery. He experienced another similar instance of the care of Providence in the same place, when all the altar-linen was stolen from the sacristy, and they knew not how to replace it. The brother who had the care of these things expressed his difficulties to Blessed Leonard, who replied: "Brother, trust in God, He will provide for us in all our wants." And so it was, for the robbery reached the ears of the Marchese Ferroni, who not only replaced all the linen that was stolen, but also undertook to supply whatever was required for the altar as long as he lived. In many other circumstances Blessed Leonard experienced the beneficence of Divine Providence, receiving from the God in whom he trusted all that he required for the missions and his convent. He never failed him in the many journeys undertaken without provisions, and in all difficulties.

Once when they arrived at a strange place late in the evening, they could not at first find anybody to give them a night's lodging, but this was permitted by God to try His servant, as a person was afterwards found to receive them until morning, and minister to their wants. From these, and many other instances he was more than ever encouraged to trust in God, and fly to Him for succor in perfect peace; even in the most unlucky and distressing accidents he looked for and received seasonable aid, as in the following instance. In the year 1749, a fire broke out in the convent of S. Buonaventura in Rome, and the flames spread so rapidly as to threaten the total destruction of the building. The monks were all sleeping unconscious of the danger which threatened them, until the flames had reached the roof, and were bursting from the windows. Great was the confusion and terror of all, but Blessed Leonard, with his accustomed trust in God, went direct to the sacristy, put on a cotta and stole, then took the Blessed Sacrament from the tabernacle and gave benediction, having done this, whilst the monks, with other people who had come to their assistance, hastened to extinguish the flames, he went with calm devotion to visit the Via Crucis, and then returned to his cell, where he gave himself a long and severe discipline, and prayed without ceasing till the fire was out, and all danger was over. Such was the firm hope in the mercy of God which Blessed Leonard testified on every, occasion, because he believed. Him to be just, faithful, omnipotent, and merciful, feeling certain that if he labored for the glory of God, with the help of divine Providence, he would, through the merits of Jesus Christ, attain the eternal bliss of Paradise in the life to come, and in the present life all temporal aid required for that end. He endeavored by every effort to excite this hope in others, especially in sinners and those in tribulation, encouraging the former to ask for, and hope in God for the pardon of their sins, and the latter, to hope from the same merciful God for consolation and comfort in all their troubles and afflictions. From hope arose an entire detachment from all perishable and earthly things, so that he was willing to be poor, as we shall see in the following chapter.

CHAPTER VI

Of the Holy Poverty Practiced by Blessed Leonard

MONGST the many virtues practiced in so heroic a manner by Blessed Leonard, certainly poverty was one, which, having made a solemn vow to observe, he determined to practice in the same way as did his seraphic Father S. Francis, and his companions. He proposed to follow their maxims, and love the inconvenience and hardships attendant on poverty; and he encouraged himself in this resolution by the contemplation of the great reward, in imitation of S. Francis, who found all pain and privation delightful in expectation of the recompense to be received for it. One day he was speaking of the holy apostles SS. Peter and Paul, who had appeared to S. Francis, and said that to those who in the most perfect manner practiced the virtue of poverty until death, their salvation was sure, and they were numbered among the blessed. He went on to say: "I love this virtue with all my heart, not only for the reward promised, but for its being well pleasing to Jesus, who was willing to be born poor, to live in poverty, and to die poor and naked on the Cross. He always spoke of poverty as the distinguishing mark of his order, and used to say, if poverty was taken from a Franciscan monk, he would cease to belong to the order of S. Francis.

In one of the memoranda which he wrote and always carried about with him, the following words are found: "I desire to observe the rule of holy poverty with all the strictness and rigor with which S. Francis and his community observed it, and to use every means to introduce it in all its rigor into the convent. He divided poverty into three kinds, viz., poverty of body, which concerns temporal things, poverty of soul, which consists in keeping under restraint all the affections, and the being entirely detached from earthly things, and poverty of spirit, which consists in detachment from spiritual sweetness, and even the gifts of God. Regarding temporal things he observed the most strict poverty, so that he never asserted a right to anything, but was ready to leave it in the hands of the superior; he was never known to depart in the least degree from the professed rule of poverty. One who was his confessor for many years gave his testimony to the fact in the following words: "So great was Father Leonard's love of poverty, that if he had not been prevented he would have carried it to an extreme in his dress, eating, furniture, convent, and everything, and he endeavored to infuse this spirit into the minds of all the religious, and rejoiced whenever be saw this virtue shine pre-eminent. He never wore a new habit, but one which had been used by others, and was almost worn out, which he had patched, and rejoiced when it became torn and ragged. Once only he put on a new one, and that was in the year 1746, when he was sent to give missions in the dioceses of Bologna and Ravenna; the weather was very cold, and as he was advanced in years, the superior of the convent of S. Buenaventura in Rome having compassion on his infirmities, sent him a new one, with an order to wear it, which in obedience he was obliged to do, but in order to show his poverty he had it covered with old patches. During all seasons he never had more than one habit, even in winter, when he was sent amongst the mountains; his thoughts were occupied in saving souls, not in keeping himself from the cold; he was often seen trembling from head to foot. He never wore an under vest, though the rule of his order allowed it, excepting when giving missions, to prevent his losing his voice from the effects of cold, and in his journeys he sometimes, in obedience, wore a piece of woolen cloth. He exhorted his brothers in religion with great earnestness to observe holy poverty in their dress, telling them that it was most unbecoming to appear vain under a poor and humble habit; and as a rich and costly dress is the ornament of a nobleman in the world, so a worn and patched habit is becoming in a poor religious, the follower of Jesus Christ. When he was guardian of the convent in Florence, he introduced the custom of patching the new habits, so that they might appear old, and make holy poverty more apparent. He exhorted his fellow religious, not only by preaching, but by his own example, dressing himself as we have said, girded with a coarse rough rope, and barefoot, so that to all who beheld him he appeared like one who truly loved poverty, and despised the world, and its vanities.

Not less was his poverty in food, which he always took sparingly, and of which we shall speak when we come to the subject of his temperance, always taking care, that in this he was conformed to the strictest rules prescribed by his order. He ate only herbs, vegetables, and fruit, and of these most sparingly; and if sometimes he was desired to eat something more to strengthen him when he was undergoing so much fatigue, he replied: "He who makes a profession of poverty ought to feel the effects of it, and if he satisfies every want without enduring inconvenience, he is not conformed to this holy state." At other times he would say, "In consequence of the vow of poverty which we religious have made, our benefactors give us alms, of which we ought to render a strict account, since we take what belongs rightly to the poor, and great is the debt we owe to God." When he saw that his religious deprived themselves of things necessary, and missed some of the usual dishes in the refectory, he rejoiced, and said: "Today we are truly children of S. Francis." For the same love of holy poverty he refused, as we have seen in the preceding chapter, the support offered by the Grand Duke of Tuscany to his monastery, and in all his journeys he would never take any provisions, or even accept letters of introduction offered to him that he might be lodged in a comfortable house, saying that a true lover of poverty, which he professed to be, ought to go and beg for a lodging. If during the mission he perceived that the soup was better than usual, he would refuse to eat it, saying that he had no appetite. "My brothers," he would say, "straw is sufficient for the ass, there is no occasion to give it oats." If he was offered anything for his maintenance, his reply was always this: "I cannot think of such a thing; my only thought is to convert souls to God; temporal things I leave for my companions to arrange." He was in fact so detached from the things of this world, that he took no thought for anything, eating only what was barely sufficient for his support.

In his room there were only two boards, on which to sleep, a covering, one chair, and a small table for writing. During the nine years he was superior of the convent in Florence, the only table he had was a board nailed against the wall, and for a seat he had nothing but the end of the board on which he slept. Hung round the walls were two or three pictures without frames, and the crucifix which he wore when he gave missions; he would not have by him even those little devotional things which the superiors of convents are accustomed to have. He did not even possess necessary articles, such as scissors, penknife, and needles; if he wanted any of these things he borrowed them of others, and returned them as soon as he had made use of them. His room contained nothing besides the things mentioned excepting a little box, in which he kept his writings, his breviary, his rule, his spectacles, a hair shirt, two disciplines, and a wooden cross with spikes of iron, which he wore next his skin, his rosary, and a small case, which contained the images of the Immaculate Conception, and S. Vincent Ferrer, with which he used to bless the sick. These were all his riches, and the furniture of his cell, for the books and other things required during the missions were left to the care of his companions.

His love of poverty often induced him to retire to poorer convents, like S. Maria dell' Incontro and S. Angelo di Montorio, in these he delighted to dwell, spending his time in spiritual exercises. The same love of poverty incited him to be strictly frugal in the smallest thing, knowing well that this tends to perfection in virtue, and how greatly it is esteemed by the saints. Therefore in writing to persons of distinction he took just sufficient paper, which he covered all over with his writing, and if sometimes he was reminded of the rank of his correspondent, and asked to write on a sheet of paper in order to show his esteem, he would reply: "Not thus am I taught by holy poverty; he knows that Father Leonard is poor, and will commend him for writing as a poor man." For the same reason he never gave or received a gift, even of the most trifling value, nor had he ever given a rosary or image, and when anything of the kind was offered to him, he always replied: "Change the subject; do not talk to me of such things; I never accept anything, and desire to observe strictly my vow of poverty."

It frequently happened in places where he was preaching that offerings were made to him and his companions of food and other things, but he invariably returned them with thanks. After he had given the mission in Ferrara, the Archbishop Monsignor Crispi sent him a box full of beautiful pictures, images, and rosaries, in token of gratitude for the good he had done; but the servant of God, without even opening it to look at them, returned it by the messenger who brought it, thanking him for his good will, and saying that his labors were abundantly recompensed by the fruits seen in the people, who had given decided proofs of repentance and reconciliation with God. The vicar-general of Frascati, seeing the great fatigue he underwent, preaching morning and evening, sent him some preserves and sweetmeats to strengthen his stomach and voice, but scarcely did this lover of poverty and enemy of every delicacy see them, than he said: "Take them away to the vicar, and tell him that these things do not become the poverty I profess. I must think of nothing but converting souls to God, and He will preserve my health and make my voice strong for preaching, if it be His holy will, so that I need none of the delicacies so inconsistent with true poverty." Two days after he had begun the mission in Civita

St. Leonard of Port Maurice

Castellane in 1735, the holy Bishop Monsignor Tendirini was attacked by a severe illness, which reduced him to the last extremity; however Almighty God, for the well-being of His Church, restored him to health. Blessed Leonard attended him with the greatest care; celebrated Mass every morning in the palace chapel, and gave him communion with his own hands. The day on which he was accustomed to preach on the devotion to our Blessed Lady, the good bishop begged the missionary to bring her image into his room, in order that he might pay her that devotion and reverence in private which his illness prevented him doing publicly. Blessed Leonard complied with his request, and brought the image to his bedside, and after having kissed the feet with much devotion, he offered in token of his reverence and affection for the Mother of God, a gold cross and a chain, but Blessed Leonard would not on any account accept it, but as the bishop insisted, and would not be deprived of the merit of making an offering, he replied, "Monsignor, in the present case the Madonna will be satisfied with the good will you have shown, but such offerings I cannot receive, since I profess poverty according to the rule of S. Francis." The bishop could say no more.

There would be no end were I to mention every instance of his refusing similar offerings, it so frequently happened during his missions. He never appropriated even the smallest sum from the alms which were collected in such abundance after his sermons, but left all to be distributed in other ways, he did not even touch it, but recommended that some part should be given to the poor, and the remainder to provide tabernacles, canopies, and things required for the exposition of the Blessed Sacrament. In fact, his poverty was most rigid, as all can testify who knew him; he was not satisfied with the exact observance of it in his own person, but used every effort to infuse the same spirit into the minds of his brothers in religion. As superior, he exhorted all most fervently to be poor and detached from earthly things; and it often happened, that moved with the force of his words, they came and threw themselves at his feet, giving up all they possessed, which was contrary to the rule. He desired that poverty should be seen in the refectory, in the cells, and throughout the convent, and even in the church and sacristy, and in drawing up the rules and constitutions for the convent in Florence, he strictly prohibited the use of silk in making the vestments, and desired that the albs and cottas should be quite plain, without embroidery or valuable lace. From this poverty, which we may call external, may be seen how detached he was from all transitory and perishable things. He had placed all his hope in God, and aspired to nothing save the possession of heaven, taking no thought for the things of this life, believing, with S. Bernard, that nothing is more hurtful to the soul than self-gratification, and that it is a hindrance to the pure love of God, which it was the ardent desire of this true lover of holy poverty to attain to.

CHAPTER VII

Of Blessed Leonard's Love of God

Y faith our holy father believed God to be supremely good and infinite, that He contained in Himself every possible perfection, without end, and that he was worthy of all our love and affections, and declared that we should love Him with all our heart, soul, and strength, and that every thought, word, work, and action, should be directed to Him. He resolved to make interior acts of love very often, rejoicing in God's infinite perfections; of benevolence, desiring that every soul should serve and bless Him; of preference, that all should esteem Him above all created things, and consider as nothing all that is not God. He made besides, seven times a day, an interior conversion to God, as if he were only beginning his spiritual life, protesting that he would love Him forever, and most fervently, and have nothing else in view but His glory in all things. And as he kept in mind that sentence of our Blessed Lord, "If you love me keep my commandments," he resolved never voluntarily to commit a venial sin, and always to keep himself detached from earthly things, giving no place in his heart to anything but God. "And although," he added, "I may commit many faults, I shall feel that this is my desire, to love God with a perfect love, and always to be employed in doing His holy will." He often declared that the love of God was the end of all his works, and although he had a particular motive in exercising every virtue, he endeavored to exalt them by that of charity, directing everything to God.

Whatever his occupation might be, either in the convent or in giving missions, his own personal affairs, or those of his neighbor, all was done to please God, and promote His glory and honor; and as charity is the more perfect the more it is divested of human interests, he loved God in purity of heart, because He is worthy of being so loved, and attained so great a degree of perfection in charity, that he was often heard to say, although he knew for certain hell should be his destiny, still he would love God with all his heart. "I intend," he used to say, "to love God with the greatest and most perfect love, because He ought to be so loved, and in this I will not be excelled by anyone on earth, whoever he may be." When he was engaged in performing certain acts for the love of God, one might see by the expression of his countenance how his heart was inflamed with charity.

A person having written to ask him how to love God, he replied, "Love Him without bounds, without measure, and not with a weak affection, which consists in tears and tender sensibilities, but a strong interior love, which proceeds from the light of faith, which makes us know and feel the beauty, goodness, and greatness of God, who must be loved with the whole heart." Such was the divine love which inflamed the heart of Blessed Leonard; it never became tepid, for he determined never to do anything which might diminish this ardent love, but always to seek after that which he thought would be most pleasing to God. He often said that our hearts were made for God alone; they should not be divided, but solely employed in loving Him.

If anyone came to him for advice concerning spiritual things, he would say with great fervor, "My son, love God; bear this in mind; love God. Every morning make this covenant with Him, 'Oh, my God! every time that I shall repeat these words, Jesus, my mercy, it is with the intention of making a most fervent act of love towards Thee, and as often as I shall repeat the ejaculation during the day, I shall make so many acts of love of Thee.'" To a person of distinction whom he found in sorrow he said, "The maxim I give you, is to suffer, and love; that which you suffer in your body from desolation, consent to endure for the love of God; this is pleasing to Him, and will be profitable as a cross, if it be accompanied by love." In a letter to the same person, who bad confessed to him that he loved the son who had been taken from him with an excessive love, he replied in these words: "All the love we give to creatures belongs to God alone; love your children, but love them as the images of God, and with such a holy detachment, as not to engross the thoughts, still less the heart; our nearest relation is the great God, from whom we have everything. Love Him with the whole heart, and remember that the world does not contain anything so worthy of our love." He did not inculcate this maxim upon others, without being deeply impressed with it himself, for after having exhorted this person to suffer and love, he went on to say, "I exhort you to suffer whilst I am free from all pain, since for forty years I have never been ill enough to require a doctor. I desire, it is true, to suffer, but God knows it would not benefit me, and so He does not send it. Pray to Him to send me the most severe illness that ever mortal man suffered, but at the same time to give me fervent love, with which I shall desire to suffer even more, and long for the much desired moment when I shall see and enjoy eternal blessedness. I desire to die under the weight of the cross, and to be burnt to ashes in the fire of Divine love." And as he who truly loves desires to be near to and to converse with the object of his love, so Blessed Leonard desired nothing more than this union, and his every thought was employed in contemplating the Divine greatness, and in familiar communion with God in prayer. When he was in the convent, he never failed to make the three hours meditation by night and day, as prescribed in the rule of the retreat; and if sometimes be was obliged, by obedience, to leave the choir, he either made up the time he was absent from the common prayer, or he endeavored to keep himself recollected, whilst he was occupied with works of mercy, being thus at once in communion with his Creator, and ministering at the same time to the wants of His creatures. When in the choir, engaged in mental prayer with his brothers in religion, he appeared like a stone figure, kneeling quite motionless without support, which was his habit even during the last years of his life, when he had become feeble and worn out with incessant toil. If he was called to hear a confession, or any other exercise, they were often obliged to speak to him several times, and even shake him; so absorbed was he in the contemplation of God, that he seemed quite unconscious of anything passing around him. Although the greatest part of his life was employed in missions, he regulated his time so well, that he was never prevented from performing his devotions and prayers at the appointed hours.

During his frequent journeys after having said the usual prayers with his companions, he continued praying apart from them, so entirely raised above the world, that he walked like one out of his senses, not seeing the path, and frequently hurting his bare feet against the stones, and sometimes he was found up to his knees in the ditches and bogs. Even when he was reading over the sermon he was to preach, he was meditating on the maxims he desired to impress on the minds of his hearers, and used to say that it was of more importance to be united with God in prayer, than to trust to any other care in saving souls. When he was giving missions he always kept an alarm in his cell, to awaken him before the dawn of day, that he might make the meditation, which he never omitted, notwithstanding the very great fatigue he had endured the preceding day in the pulpit and confessional. He was not satisfied with his daily devotions, but twice in the year he went to make a retreat, in order that he might be quite alone and in undisturbed communion with God. He came out of his solitude with renewed zeal, and more than ever inflamed with the love of God, with more courage to instruct the people and convert souls, never sparing himself, and making it evident that the love of God will overcome every difficulty, and give support in the greatest toil and fatigue; and indeed what else was it but Divine love, and the desire he had to please God, that gave him strength and enabled him to endure a long life of incessant toil, penance, and bodily suffering. He was often heard to say: "To give glory to God, and be well pleasing to Him, I am ready to endure any fatigue and suffering, even to die a thousand deaths, and be doomed to the torments of hell." It is not then a matter of surprise that with this ardent love of God, and earnest desire to please Him, he should hate sin, for he well knew how hateful it is in the sight of God, and his great desire was that it should be rooted entirely out of the world; and he often said with extraordinary fervor, "I declare that in this world I have only one enemy, and that is mortal sin, and I have sworn to make war against it as long as I live." It is related of him that from his earliest childhood he triumphed gloriously over it in himself, and always held it in abhorrence, so that according to the testimony of those who heard his general confessions, he never in his life committed mortal sin. To prevent it in others and free them from it, he often exclaimed with a sigh, "Ah, if God would give me grace to save one soul, or at least to prevent one mortal sin. Willingly would I give my life if I could prevent even one mortal sin, which is so displeasing and so odious in the sight of God." To this end all his energies were directed in the pulpit and the confessional; to rid the world of sin he undertook long and painful journeys in the most severe weather, and even desired to go to heathen countries to give his life to prevent sin against God, and to proclaim his love for Him. In fact, Blessed Leonard lived in holy indifference to everything earthly, and with a fixed determination to do only the will of God, and he thus wrote on the subject: "The only thing to which we ought to give our thoughts is to follow in all things the holy will of God, made known by our superiors and spiritual fathers." Whatever he was desired to do, however difficult, such as to interrupt the missions when he was reaping great fruits from them, or to take a long journey by sea or land, or to leave the solitude to which he had retired to give, as he said, a mission to himself; immediately, without saying a word, he left all, and went about the work he was ordered, thus to perform the will of God, which he acknowledged and adored in these commands. So heartily did he desire to do the will of God, that whenever he was about to undertake any work, he tried to assure himself of the will of his superior, feeling certain that that would be the will of God, and well pleasing to Him.

And as conformity to the Divine will is more meritorious when accompanied by holy dispositions, Blessed Leonard made it his study not only to surrender his will to that of God, but to believe that whatever God appointed for him was for the best, conduced to His greater glory, and was profitable for his own salvation. For this reason he was constantly repeating this ejaculation, "May Thy most perfect and holy will be done, in me and for me, now, henceforth, and forever. Amen."

If by chance he found that any one in adversity and affliction was giving way to impatience and lamentations, he would say in the most affectionate and earnest manner: "My brother, we have a good and loving Father in heaven who loves us, can you think that a God so beneficent will decree anything that is not good for His children, for whom He has done so much, and for whom, if they will only be obedient, he has prepared a paradise?" To others, in order to make them think always of God, and be conformed and united to Him, he would say: "The more you think of God, the more you will be inflamed with love for Him." These words clearly indicated that he was always thinking of God, and loved none but Him, and sought only to be conformed to His divine will. Such was the charity of Blessed Leonard, as it appeared in the whole course of his life, as well as in his "Resolutions" which have been published, and to which we have often referred, a love at once most pure and ardent. He thus wrote to one of his penitents the year before his death: "I wish to die, and go to enjoy eternal happiness in that blessed land where God is perfectly loved. I am old, and now I know by experience that in this world we never arrive at the perfection we desire, and instead of increasing in love, we halt by the way. But for all that, I desire nothing but what God wills for me, having no other end or aim but the perfect accomplishment of His most Holy Will."

CHAPTER VIII

The Charity of Blessed Leonard Towards His Neighbor

HE command given by our Blessed Lord to love our neighbor, is in some measure similar to that of the love of God, because it arises from the same motive; therefore, as our good Father advanced in the love of the Creator, so did he in charity to the creature, made in His image and likeness; beholding them as such, he loved them with the greatest tenderness, procuring them every possible advantage, keeping them from evil, and always being ready to do them good. He was never heard to say a word that could offend anyone, but found something to praise in all; even with those who had given cause for blame and reprehension, he with charity tried to extenuate and excuse their defects and failings, and began to speak of their good qualities. He was ever moved with compassion on seeing the poor and destitute, and relieved them whenever he had the means.

The Florentines knowing the high esteem in which he was held by the Grand Duke Cosmo III, came daily to him in great numbers, to beg that he would make known their wants to the good prince, and Blessed Leonard, recognizing in these poor people the person of the Lord Jesus, without hesitation presented their petitions, and obtained for them all they required. But as these requests were continually being made, and the good father went with their petitions almost every day to the court, he began to fear the prince would be weary of him, and one day when he presented himself as usual, he began by saying that he feared to offend him by such frequent applications, but seeing so many destitute people, he felt his heart moved to pity, and his poverty not enabling him to relieve them, he could only endeavor to induce others to do so. "Bring me all the petitions that are given to you, without any such fear," replied the Grand Duke, "and I shall do what I can to relieve my poor people, and I assure you that to prevent them sinning against God, I would give half, my kingdom." After receiving this gracious reply, Blessed Leonard became the means, through his charitable mediation, of doing much for the people, obtaining employment for the men, marriage portions for the young women, and support for many destitute persons.

His love for his neighbor induced him to exhort the companion who went with him on his missions in places where there was much poverty, to cook something every day for the poor, and distribute some of the provisions which were sent for their use. If anyone came to him who was infirm as well as poor, he was so moved with compassion, that if he had nothing else to give, be stripped himself of some article of clothing. One morning he was called to confess a poor man, and seeing him half naked, trembling from head to foot with cold, in pity he took off a piece of woolen cloth he wore under his habit, and gave it to him; his companion seeing him so affected by the cold, suspected what he had done, and informed the superior, who quickly restored what he had given away.

When he was unable to relieve the wants of the poor himself, or by the means of others, he prayed to God to provide for them, or stirred up the people to give alms for the same intention, declaring that he would give them money if he had it. "I have the desire," he said, "of giving alms largely, but I cannot do it because I am poor, but I may, however, please God and help my neighbor, by offering to Him my intention, and praying to Him to provide for them."

His. Charity was not restricted to particular persons, but extended to promote the public good. At the time Florence was threatened with destruction by an earthquake, he being guardian of the convent dell' Monte, gave himself a long and severe discipline, together with his community, to appease the wrath of

God, and in the morning visited in procession all the churches in the city for the same end. Soon after this a pestilence broke out amongst the animals, the mortality was great, and it was feared the infection would extend to men, for a great many deaths had occurred. On seeing the gates of Florence closed, and all the people in great fear, he called together his community, and represented to them what a great act of charity it would be, to offer their lives to God in the service of the pestiferous. "I," added he, "am resolved to sacrifice myself, and shall consider it a happiness to die for love of my neighbor." He spoke with such fervor, that all present with one accord offered themselves to follow his example, and confirmed it with secret vows: the danger passed, but they had the merit of their good dispositions.

Not less was his charity for his brothers in religion, and although towards himself be was most rigid and austere, he was with them most indulgent, mild, and benignant, full of compassion for everyone, and rejoiced when all were provided for according to their state and profession. When he was guardian, he desired that all that was necessary in the way of food should be prepared for the community, but always refused to partake of it himself, saying that he was healthy and robust, and could abstain. The same charity induced him to moderate the rigor of the fasts which they kept during the missions, and because his companions were very often sick in consequence, he allowed all of them to eat as much as was necessary, whilst he took nothing more during the day than a cup of water mixed with barley and wormwood, although he had gone through the greatest fatigue. So also in his journeys he walked barefoot, but desired his companions to wear sandals; his feet were often bleeding from the rough roads and intense cold.

He was extremely charitable to the sick, not only in the places where he gave missions, where he visited and consoled them, exhorting them to make a good confession, but whenever he was called to assist them he went quickly, whether it was

195

night or day, without stopping to consider the rough roads or stormy weather. After having exhorted them to suffer willingly and with resignation the pain sent by God, and after giving them spiritual aid, he prayed that if it was the divine will he might take their sickness on himself, and that they should be restored to health. One of the monks in the convent of S. Buonaventura having lost his sight, went to Blessed Leonard for consolation, who said to him that blindness was a treasure, and he ought to rejoice in having one enemy less to contend with, for it was through the sense of sight that so many sins were committed, and so many souls lost. To this the brother replied, that the only thing which made him regret the loss of sight was the not being able to celebrate the holy sacrifice. Blessed Leonard then said, "Let us do this: you pray that the will of God may be fulfilled in you, and I will pray with all my heart that if it be His good pleasure, I may become blind, and you have your sight restored, and willingly shall I consent to lose my sight, since you will have the consolation of being able to satisfy your pious desire of saying mass."

He extended his charity in a wonderful manner to all the faithful departed, procuring for them all the prayers he could to release them from purgatory. He preached with so much fervor on this subject, and excited so much compassion for the suffering souls, that abundant alms were always collected, which he distributed for the purpose of saying many masses for their repose. Every morning he made an intention, to gain all the indulgences he could that day for the release of the souls in Purgatory; and every time he passed a church where many indulgences could be gained he entered it, saying to his companion, "Let us go and pray for the faithful departed." During the time he was giving missions and could not visit churches, he obtained from the holy pontiff Benedict XIV for himself and his companions the power of gaining three times in the day the indulgences of the Holy Land, made applicable to the souls in Purgatory. He exhorted all to pray for the dead, and so great was his charity towards them that he offered all the merits of his labors, prayers, and penances for their release.

In his charity towards the living, it is impossible to detail all he did to save their souls; his life was one continued exercise of charity and incessant toil in converting souls to God, and He alone knows the numbers, which, by means of preaching, admonishing, and confessing, he drew from the depths of sin and the road to hell, to paradise. In hearing confessions he held it as a maxim to treat his penitents precisely as he would desire in a similar state to be treated, and when sinners came to him laden with iniquities, who for many years had not frequented the sacraments, he said to himself: "Brother Leonard, if you were at the feet of this poor man would not you wish to be treated with indulgence? do then to others as you would have them do to you." With this thought he received them with extraordinary affection, encouraged them not to be overcome with shame, never interrupted or hurried them, or showed any weariness in listening to them, but assisted them in every possible way, speaking kindly to them, and making use of every means to gain them. He recommended them to the care of their angels' guardian to assist them in their confessions, and in giving them absolution he realized that he was pouring over their souls the precious Blood of Jesus Christ, which would cleanse them from sin; his manner was so fervent that his penitents were filled with compunction and comfort at the same time. His greatest consolation was that of seeing at his feet some great sinner, and rejoicing at seeing him brought to penance, he would so move him by means of his wonderful zeal, that he would burst into a flood of tears of contrition. Many of these he had the consolation of confessing, and having given them absolution and instructions, they amended and changed their lives.

During the many years he was employed in giving missions and preaching in different nations and places, he found sinners of every kind, and some of the most notorious, who came to make their confessions to him, and he invariably and with great satisfaction gave them absolution, and embraced them, returning thanks to God, that He had, through His blessing, cleansed them from their sins, and brought those poor wandering souls again into the fold. We read in the first part of this history how the devil, foreseeing the great loss he would sustain in the conversion of so many hardened sinners, tried by every means to prevent the good effects of the missions, and how Blessed Leonard, not being overcome by his assaults, desiring only to gain souls for heaven, courageously surmounted all opposition.

All the time the mission lasted he filled up the time in hearing confessions, and the penitents came in such numbers, that he was often employed the whole day, and even part of the night, so that he went without sleep or food. If it happened in some places that he had not time during the mission to confess all, he remained for some days in order to hear them and give instructions. Having done this in a place near Sienna, where he had no clock, many of the people came at three in the morning to call him, he went immediately to the church, and remained in the confessional till daybreak, when he said mass, and returned again to his confessional, persevering in his labors without food or sleep for thirty hours, until he had heard all with the greatest charity and patience. The electress Anna di Medici being informed of this, sent him an alarm, so that he might regulate his time, and not wear himself out in his apostolic ministrations.

The most certain proof of his charity toward his neighbor, are the many missions he gave in the course of forty-four years, journeying through many lands with admirable zeal for saving souls, for which he cared not how he toiled, or what he suffered from fatigue, and even risked his life by long voyages by sea. In adversity and misfortunes, instead of his courage failing, it became greater, and if he met with opposition, or extraordinary inconvenience in his missions, he hailed it as a good sign, and rejoiced, saying: "You see the missions displease the devil, so we may hope for good success, and we must offer to God what we have to endure, He will give more grace to these people, that they may be converted." Having for four months suffered great pain in his foot, in consequence of walking barefoot, he was obliged to have it lanced, to extract a splinter of bone, and when he was reproved for having suffered the pain so long without sending for a surgeon to cure it, he replied: "Do you not know it is the glory of a soldier when he can shew the wounds he has received in fighting the battles of his sovereign." On another occasion when he was returning from Corneto to Rome, walking barefoot through the snow, his companion perceived that five of his toe-nails had dropped from his feet, which were bleeding; he felt much distressed at the pain the holy father was suffering, although he gave no sign of it, but walking on as if nothing had happened, said joyously; "Brother, you have no cause for distress, for I regard these wounds as treasures, five nails are lost for the love of God, but five crowns are gained for paradise." If on any occasion he heard them speaking of the sufferings and dangers to which he was exposed in giving missions, he used to say that they were nothing to what the saints had suffered, and that he should consider it a high destiny to die laboring for the glory of God and the salvation of souls.

When sometimes he was weak and exhausted, and they entreated him to put off preaching for some days, he replied with admirable zeal: "A soldier would feel ashamed when he has received a wound, to put down his sword, but would even fight with greater courage." In confirmation of this, a short time before his death, he thus wrote to a religious in Rome: "I am old, and my days on earth cannot be many more, but I desire to die with my sword in my hand, fighting against sin and hell, delivering souls out of the power of the devil, and restoring them to God." In short, it may be said of him and his zeal for saving souls: "Aquae multae non potuerunt extinguere charitatem."

And, in truth, during the forty-four years he was employed in the holy office of missionary, he endured endless fatigues, observing the strict rules prescribed in his "Resolutions," which he drew up for his missions, charity towards his neighbor enabling him to overcome every obstacle, every toil and fatigue, scorn and reproach. During this time he gave missions in eighty-eight dioceses, preached in two hundred and sixteen different places, and gave three hundred and sixteen missions, with what result we have already heard. Nor was he satisfied with doing so much for his neighbor himself, but he exhorted others to do the same, saying to them with great fervor: "Does it seem a small thing to you to gain one soul? a soul the price of which is the blood of Jesus Christ?" He was most desirous that the number of missionaries should be increased, and praised those priests, secular and regular, who were ready for this work, exhorting all to go and hear them preach, and he went himself whenever he was able. He used often to say that the name alone of a mission was sufficient to make the people feel compunction, and also added: "There are two things to which God in an especial manner gives his blessing, to spiritual exercises for devout persons, and to missions for all, especially the uninstructed." A wealthy citizen of Florence, who had founded some charitable institutions, was desirous to spend more money in the same way, and went to Blessed Leonard to ask his advice, who said to him; "Now listen, Jesus Christ gave Himself, and was willing to shed His precious Blood for the salvation of souls, for this reason I cannot give you better advice than to employ your riches in promoting the conversion of the same. Give your money to the missions, and you will share the merit of the conversion of many poor souls." This advice pleased the good citizen, and he bequeathed a large sum of money for this pious purpose. I should never end were I to relate all the deeds of Blessed Leonard to promote the well-being of his neighbor.

I shall only mention that he wrote many instructive books,

amongst others, the "Manual for virgins consecrated to God," "Instructions for hearing mass," "The method of meditating on the Passion of the Redeemer," the "Way of the Cross," the "Directions for making a general confession." The rules for the confraternity he founded of the "Lovers of Jesus and Mary," and several small tracts, which will remain an everlasting monument of his ardent charity in the salvation of souls. So great was his love for his neighbor, that his greatest consolation was that of hearing of the conversion of a great sinner. On this subject he once wrote in the following words to a priest: "In October, if God prospers my journey, I shall arrive in Rome, where I am obliged most unwillingly to stop, for being near the end of my days on earth, I wish to labor night and day to prevent sin, which prevails so much in the world." He was often heard to say in his discourses, public and private, that so great was his love for souls, that he not only desired that all should be saved, but that he would be contented to be placed at the entrance of hell to stop up the way, not caring how his senses would suffer, provided he could prevent anyone falling into the fearful abyss. In accordance with this expression of his desire, he would say when he was going to give a mission: "I go to make war against the powers of hell."

CHAPTER IX

On the Prudence of Blessed Leonard

ELIEVING, as we do, prudence to be a cardinal virtue, which suggests all the means requisite to enable us to attain Christian perfection in our work, we shall thus speak of it in this chapter. With this great virtue, which is the soul and rule of all the other virtues, Blessed Leonard was so enriched, that it ruled and regulated every action of his life, and enabled him to lead so many to the blessings of eternal happiness. In all that concerned himself, he acted with so much circumspection and prudence, that he never placed any impediment in the way of grace, and by means of prudence all his works were perfect, pleasing to God, and most profitable to the souls under his care. He was so afraid of doing things rashly, that he never undertook anything without advice, invoking the Holy Spirit, and depending in all things on his superior and spiritual father. We have seen when he was called by God to the religious life, what pains he took, and how anxious he was to be certain of his vocation; he was not satisfied with the decision of one confessor, but he would have four, knowing that in a "multitude of Counselors there is wisdom." Such a way of proceeding when he was in the world, joined to an exemplary and virtuous life, as if he had embraced one of the most rigid orders in the church, clearly proved, even when a secular, and young, how adorned he was with the Christian virtue, prudence. After he entered the religious life, he never allowed that light to be extinguished which God had granted him, but was ever occupied about the sanctification of his soul, and gaining heaven. Great prudence was that which induced him to appoint all that he was to do during each day, during each week, each month, each year, and at all times, and to make at the end of each day a strict examination, to correct every failing he discovered in the fulfilment of his duties. From all this we may believe that in his wisdom and prudence he fixed his gaze constantly on the end for which he was created, that of knowing, loving, and serving God in the present life, to pass to the enjoyment of a better, in which consists the true prudence of the saints. He measured all his steps, weighed each word, watched all his actions, and regulated them in such a manner, and with such prudence, as was pleasing to God and profitable to himself.

But if he was thus prudent in regulating his own conduct, he was no less so in directing that of others who had recourse to him. Valuable indeed were the instructions he gave to each of them to encourage them in virtue, and cause them day by day to advance in it, and it is impossible to relate the many instances of his leading the most hardened sinners to God. Many were the persons, even of the highest rank in various places, who, owing to his advice and prudence in directing them, walked generously in the way of virtue, and some of them died in the odor of sanctity. He used to say amongst other things for the instruction and regularity of those who desired to attain perfection, that it is absolutely necessary to raise a high standard, and that those who were content with mediocrity in virtue, without aspiring to great things, are not guided by the Spirit, and are liable to be easily led away by their passions, and to fall miserably. In the direction of virtuous persons, he instructed them in the way of attaining perfection by the same means as he adopted himself, pointing out to them with great prudence the most certain way of gaining eternal happiness.

On one occasion, when he was conversing with a religious on the subject of internal peace, and how he was to attain it, he was requested to give in writing all the rules he had prescribed, with which he readily complied, and wrote in the following manner: "Four foundations are essentially necessary to attain peace of mind and heart, without which we cannot profit ourselves or assist others. The first is to be dead to the world, to creatures, and to oneself, and to all that is not God, keeping the heart free from earthly things, so that all that does not pertain to God shall be esteemed as loss than a grain of sand. The second is, so to live that all the occurrences of the day, important or trivial, propitious or adverse, may always be attributed to the disposal of Divine Providence, that whatever God permits must be considered the best, most just for His glory and for our eternal salvation. The third, to love suffering, whether of body or mind, rejoicing in the contradictions and contempt of men. The paradise of heaven is full of joy, the paradise of earth is full of suffering; let us look to Jesus, who had for His companions sorrow, contempt, suffering, and poverty. The fourth is, not to undertake many affairs upon us, even in doing good, and not to act rashly or inconsiderately, but with calmness and discretion, being modest in every action, word, and deportment. For myself I daily make an examination of conscience, and always find that I have failed in something; I trust that your reverence will profit more than I do by observing these rules."

By these extracts from letters, we may judge in some measure with what Christian prudence he led his penitents in the way of heaven and the practice of every virtue. It is not to be wondered at that so many persons, in every grade of society, rich and poor, men and women, nobles and peasants, seculars and ecclesiastics, religious of many orders, well qualified to teach and renowned for their theological learning, came to seek his counsel and direction in regulating their lives, for he gave them instructions according to the state and condition of each. Thus it was that all, acknowledging his wisdom and prudence, proclaimed him to be a man of God, gifted with extraordinary lights, to teach an easy, short, and sure way to paradise. During the short time he remained in Rome, when he was not giving missions, a great number of people went to the monastery of S. Buonaventura to confer with him on the most important of all affairs, the salvation of their souls.

It was astonishing to see sometimes twenty people assemble at the same time, consulting him on different matters, and he replying in a few words, as if he had studied the subject for some time. These brief instructions served afterwards for a rule of life to each to walk safely and surely in the way of heaven. He gave to each the most suitable advice, and sent them away contented and satisfied. Greater still were the number of those who wrote to him from a distance, when he was in his convent, and also when he was giving missions. By almost every post he received letters of this description, to all of whom he replied, clearing up their doubts and difficulties, and giving advice according to the wants of those who wrote, with so much wisdom and prudence, that all reverenced him as the servant of God sent for their instruction and profit.

Although the prudence of Blessed Leonard excelled in directing and instructing those who were walking in the paths of virtue and perfection, even more brightly did it shine when he was employed in restoring those who had been leading a sinful life. When he had succeeded in gaining these, which was frequently the case, he treated them with kindness and affection, as prudence suggested, and he knew exactly how to apply to each one either severe correction or affectionate exhortation, according as it was required; consequently the most hardened sinners rose from his feet humbled and filled with compunction. He was persuaded that with penitents it was better to use gentleness than severity, for the greater their sin the more they are to be pitied. Besides being governed himself by this maxim, he persuaded other confessors to act in the same way, adding even more, that when in their office they feel obliged to refuse or defer absolution to anyone, they must do it with so much prudence, and speak to them in such a manner, that the penitent shall feel assured that it is for his spiritual good alone. On this point he has left the following advice in writing: "Those confessors are greatly to blame, who with rough manners and harsh words exasperate poor penitents. They ought to receive them with affection, composure, and meekness, making them understand that they are desirous for nothing but their spiritual good, and enlightening their minds in such a manner, that they see the necessity of, and willingly consent to what is imposed upon them."

That he observed these rules himself is certain, since amongst the many sinners who came to make their confessions to him, not one was ever known to leave him dissatisfied or discontented. After having patiently listened to, and assisted them in making known to him all their sins, and encouraged them not to be overcome by shame, he spoke to them in a way so proper, so gentle and efficacious, that they instantly put in practice all that he suggested to them as necessary. Those who returned to receive absolution were seen to weep bitterly, and more than one, after having made his confession, was heard to thank God, and joyfully exclaim, "Father Leonard has saved me from hell!" If it were not too long, I might bare mention the numerous conversions he made in every place in which he lived or preached, since they were not less the effects of his prudence than his zeal.

One of the most arduous duties, and one which requires the greatest prudence, is that of giving missions. It is an office so difficult, that if it be not regulated by prudent conduct, it may become the means, not only of not gaining the souls of others, but also of losing our own. The going from one place to another to preach to people of different dispositions and manners, the duty of extirpating vice and effecting a perfect reformation, the open war against hell, is an undertaking so hard and laborious, that to succeed in it requires the greatest prudence. Now, since our holy father having been employed in it for the space of forty-four years in different countries, succeeded without there having occurred the least difficulty or disturbance, everyone must agree in saying that he regulated all with the greatest prudence, although, wherever he went, he found many thorns and many tares to uproot, and often the devil put forth every effort to prevent the mission, or when it was begun, never failed to disturb or interrupt it; he was never cast down, but used every effort to extirpate vice, and in the end gained the hearts of all; and when the mission was finished, those who had opposed him saw him depart with deep regret, weeping bitterly, and would gladly have kept him longer amongst them.

When the inhabitants of any place were found leading corrupt lives, immediately Blessed Leonard was sent to give a mission; and when it was thought almost impossible for him to succeed in reforming them, he soon made himself master of all who came, often even on his first appearance on the platform. His words came with such force, that he succeeded in penetrating the hearts of the most hardened. He was so prudent, that in holding up to odium any particular vice, he never offended those who were addicted to it, from whence it ensued, that amending their lives, and detesting sin, they conceived a great esteem and affection for the holy minister of God, who had in so excellent away opened their wounds, and extracted the poisonous matter without increasing the pain.

Perhaps his great prudence was more exercised in Corsica than in any other place; he was sent there, as we have related, to give missions. The island was rent with revolutions, tumults, envy, and hatred, and divided into two contending parties, the more powerful of which, treating with contempt the Genoese government, were continually committing murders. In fact, the island had become like a forest of wild beasts. Amongst these people was Blessed Leonard sent in 1744, to preach penance and induce them to lay aside their hatred, and be reconciled to their God. Whoever reflects on all he did there, may conceive what his prudence must have been. A Genoese himself, and sent by the Genoese government, he was obliged to act with great caution, to weigh every word, and regulate every movement and action, in order not to irritate these people, already so excited; yet with such earnestness and prudence did this holy man of God comport himself under circumstances so critical and dangerous, that although they heard him reprove their excesses, they soon learned to love and revere him, listened to him with attention, and dared not refuse the penances he thought proper to impose on them. In every place where he preached, he succeeded in reforming the customs and putting an end to the disorders, and would have restored peace to the island had he not been called away suddenly. As we have seen how Blessed Leonard ruled all his actions by prudence, so that it shone in all, even the most arduous and difficult, we may surely say that he possessed this so useful and necessary virtue in a high and heroic degree.

CHAPTER X

How Carefully Blessed Leonard Observed the Virtue of Justice

LTHOUGH under the name of justice is comprehended every virtue, and those who possess it are called just, as we find in the Scriptures this name given to Noe, Job, S. Joseph, spouse of the Blessed Virgin, and others, still we shall speak of it here as a single virtue, which teaches us to render to all their rights. As man is debtor to himself, to his God, and his neighbor, we shall see in this chapter how just Blessed Leonard was to himself, always endeavoring, when a secular as well as when a religious, to promote his own spiritual good, and the attainment of the end for which he was created, in the practice of every virtue, as we have seen. He most jealously kept his own soul free from all sin, as all who knew and conversed with him constantly affirmed that he had kept his baptismal robe spotless, for well he knew that the least sin would make him unhappy, both in this world and the next. He used to say that he valued purity of conscience more than all the treasures of the earth, and held in abhorrence even venial sin; for although it does not deprive the soul of the grace of God, it is the means of chilling the fervor of devotion and charity, and endangers the falling into mortal sin, than which there could not be a greater misfortune. He was persuaded that one deliberate venial sin does more evil, and carries with it more weight, than all the profit that was ever gained in missions; it was his maxim, and he endeavored to instill it into the minds of others, that no sin in the sight of God is trifling or small when we view it as an offence against our Creator.

In writing to a nun to induce her to guard against all sin, he thus expressed himself: "Is it not sufficient that venial sin is offensive to God to prevent you falling into it?" And to this reason he added another; "It prevents the advancing in Christian perfection; all who ardently desire this and to possess every virtue, must abhor and detest all sin."

Regulating his life on these principles, and continually thirsting after justice, he formed a perfect method of practicing every virtue proper to his state of life; and his ardent desire to be just, and in the possession of every virtue, may be clearly gathered from a memorandum written by him, and found after his death, which is as follows: "Having performed the spiritual exercises in this convent of S. Angelo di Montorio, in the year 1732, during the month of July, and until the tenth of August, and having reconsidered my 'Resolutions,' I have renewed them, determined to practice them to the letter; and since perfection consists in loving God and our neighbor, in the observance of these two precepts I am resolved, without however, making a vow, in consideration of my weakness, always to do that which is most perfect, in conformity with the advice of my confessor, and to live a life of angelic purity inwardly and outwardly, with the desire to exercise every virtue in the most heroic manner, as far as I am able, with the help of God; and I am determined not to let any occasion pass of mortifying myself, to be dead to myself and to the world, for I love God, and am willing to give my life for Him.

"In the observance of the second precept, although I do not make a vow, still I propose to spend night and day in the earnest desire of converting the whole world, of obtaining, as far as I am able, that all souls shall be brought into the right way, and I will never spare myself when the conversion of a soul is in question. I will employ myself in ministering to the temporal wants of my neighbors in the manner proposed in my 'Resolutions,' and according to my state and ability. In short, I propose never to rest from seeking God, loving Him, and trying to be in closer union with Him. For this purpose I will, during the day, often renew my resolution, turning sweetly to God, to ascertain His pleasure,

His desire, and the fulfilment of His most holy will in all things, whether small or great.

"When at my particular examination of conscience at noonday, and my general examination in the evening, I shall find that I have failed in any of the resolutions, I will give myself some penance, especially if I have been tardy in making the renewal of spirit, and communion with God, which can be done in the midst of distractions and noise; and still more if I have failed in charity, whether positively in speaking, or doing anything, however slight, to offend my neighbor, or negatively, by drawing back from assisting him, especially in his spiritual necessities. For any failing in these things I will inflict upon myself a penance, either a *Miserere*, an act of contrition, or prostration on the ground in the form of a cross."

From these sentiments, nourished in a heart desirous of reaching the highest degree of perfection, in the attainment of which he lost no time and spared himself no fatigue, one may see clearly how just he was to himself, procuring for his soul so much merit in the practice of virtue, and that glory which God has promised in heaven to those who do His will on earth. He knew that he had received a soul from God, and that He had appointed him to labor in His vineyard, and in the end to attain eternal salvation; therefore he justly esteemed it his duty to give all his thoughts to this end, doing that which ho believed to be for the best, to attain merit here on earth, and the greatest possible amount of glory for his soul in heaven. Having always in view this obligation, he hastened to save his soul, never losing sight of it, and using every effort to gain that great end. When he was ordered to preach, he never left off his accustomed austerities and penances, or any of his exercises of virtue and piety, but generally added to them, saying with the holy Apostle S. Paul; "Lest when I have preached to others, I myself should be a castaway."

Those who were the companions for many years of Blessed

Leonard, and eyewitnesses of all his actions, have since declared, that they always admired in him the possession of so many virtues, and one of them, in speaking of himself, said, that if he felt tepidity in devotion, he had only to consider the tenor of the life of our holy Father, to excite him to renewed fervor. A priest, who had for a long time lived in the same convent in Florence with Blessed Leonard, in his juridical attestation, after having spoken of his many virtues, thus concluded: "In fact, during the many years I conversed daily with that blessed Father, I never detected one fault in him, and in truth it may be said of him, *Videtur in homine isto Adam non peccasse,*[1] but he was full of zeal and charity, humility, obedience, and patience. All this I declare on oath, and I cannot in conscience say anything to the contrary, but I believe and assert, that if he be not a saint of our times, I know not who can be. I have since his death felt myself strongly animated to virtue, and I have so firm a faith in his holiness, that I feel sure that whatever I ask from God, through his intercession, will be granted me, and I never speak of him that I do not feel compunction and extraordinary fervor, and regarding him as a saint, exclaim, 'God is wonderful in His saints!'" In the same manner, others who had conversed familiarly with him, agreed in representing him as one who had hungered and thirsted after justice, unwearied in the practice of every virtue, and the fulfilment of that duty which tends to perfection and sanctity; and one who was his confessor, thus said of him: "From the reflections I have made in observing his interior, and every action of his life, having been his confessor for some years, and the director of his conscience, I never saw anything in him but the most perfect harmony in every virtue. In short, our holy father was just to himself, constantly intent on sanctifying his soul and adorning it with the virtue of justice, which comprises every other virtue." And here it must be considered, that living

---

[1] In this man, it is as if Adam never sinned.

as Blessed Leonard did in a religious community, in which nothing was thought of but the attainment of perfection, and where every action was observed, if he made himself worthy of so much love and admiration amongst his brethren, one may imagine how wonderfully perfect his life must have been, and the fervor with which he advanced in the way to heaven. He knew that the profession of a religious imposed on him the obligation of seeking after perfection, that such was essential to his state, to neglect it, or not to be diligent in the endeavor, was the same as if he ceased to be a monk, therefore, he daily increased in virtue, and in the end attained that for which he so ardently longed. He kept this obligation ever in view, and we may easily believe, that since he was just towards himself, he endeavored to fulfil it. The conviction also that a greater degree of perfection is required from religious than seculars, for they are commanded to be so in the gospel: "Be ye perfect as your Father in heaven is perfect," constantly stimulated him to perform great things, and always increase the store of merits for his soul, deeming this an act of justice owing to it. For the same motive he practiced every virtue, as we have already related, in so heroic a manner, that he never spared himself the greatest toil and fatigue in being just to himself, and in acquiring much merit in this life, and glory in the life to come.

CHAPTER XII

How Blessed Leonard Excelled in the Virtue of Religion

IN speaking of what is justly due to God, we allude to the adoration and honor paid to Him by external acts of veneration and reverence, in which religion consists, and we shall see with what fervor and exactness Blessed Leonard paid to Almighty God the first tribute of reverence and adoration in the most perfect manner possible, especially when he celebrated Mass, in the Divine Office, and in prayer. We have seen how great was his devotion to the Blessed Sacrament of the altar, and with what dispositions he every day celebrated mass, and with what devotion he heard it when he did not celebrate, and how he never lost an occasion of celebrating, or never allowed sickness, fatigue, or suffering, during his long journeys, or any of his multifarious and serious inconveniences, to prevent his offering the Holy Sacrifice.

On one occasion, in 1742, after having made a journey of twenty miles on foot, on arriving at the convent of S. Buonaventura in Rome, although he could scarcely stand from fatigue, without resting a moment he went to the sacristy, and celebrated mass with as much devotion as he could have done were he not suffering from weariness. Another time, he set off on a journey in August; after having given a mission in Chianciano, in the diocese of Chiusi, he and his companions lost their way, and made a long tour exposed to the burning rays of the sun, and he felt himself quite overcome and faint from the excessive heat. After wandering for some hours they found the road, but were so exhausted and tormented with thirst, that having found a ditch, in which was some water, his companions began to drink it eagerly, and pressed him to do the same, for in consequence of extreme exhaustion, he was scarcely able to speak, he, however, as if insensible to such suffering, replied: "No, my brothers, for a little water I will not be deprived of the consolation of saying mass."

In fact, on arriving at Monte Pulciano, he went directly to the altar, although his throat was so dry he could scarcely be heard, and it was with difficulty he swallowed the sacred Host, he said to his companions when they expressed their astonishment: "The pain has now passed, and I have celebrated the holy sacrifice thereby proving that nothing is impossible to those who really love God. And to others in a similar manner who were astonished in seeing him celebrate mass when he was half dead with suffering and weakness, he replied: "Do you not know what mass is, and how pleasing the offering is to God, and how acceptable is the worship with which we honor Him in celebrating one mass? In the other mysteries of our faith, we renew the memory of that which we represent. On the feast of the Nativity the Birth of our Lord is represented, but it is not true that our Lord is born again on that day. On the feast of the Ascension and Pentecost, we represent the ascending of our Lord into heaven, and the coming of the Holy Spirit on earth, but we do not believe that our Lord ascends again into heaven, or that the Holy Spirit visibly descends again on earth. We cannot, however, say the same of the Holy Sacrifice, since in this we do not make a simple representation, but we offer the same sacrifice, in an unbloody way, which was consummated on the cross in the shedding of blood. That same Body, that same Blood, that same Jesus who offered Himself on Calvary, we offer daily in the holy mass, and shall I allow a little fatigue to prevent me celebrating it? The sacrifice which we have in our holy religion, the mass, is a most holy, perfect, and complete sacrifice, with which all the faithful give honor to God, declaring at the same time their own unworthiness, and the supreme dominion which

He has over us, and it is called for that reason the sacrifice of justice; and shall I for any trivial motive abstain from offering to God such a sacrifice?" Thus we find it written in an exhortation made by him to certain persons, to excite in them a fervent devotion to the mass: "In the holy mass God is honored as He deserves with a fitting adoration, because our God and Lord Jesus Christ, coming down from heaven in reality on our altars, with inexplicable submission adores the Holy Trinity; therefore, let us, who are united together with Him in offering this great sacrifice, give to Him infinite adoration and reverence; the soul which assists with devotion at the Holy Sacrifice, gives more glory to God in this than the saints and angels in heaven, because as they are simple creatures, their devotion and reverence is bounded, whereas in the mass, Jesus Christ humbles Himself, and this humiliation is meritorious, and of great price, therefore the adoration which we through Him give to God in the holy mass is infinite." Being persuaded of this, Blessed Leonard, however tired or weak he might feel, offered every day the Holy Sacrifice of the mass with so much devotion and joyousness of heart, that after he had celebrated, he was frequently heard to exclaim: "Oh! my most loving God, why have I not an infinite number of tongues to render infinite thanks for the treasure so great which Thou hast given us in the holy mass."

Much as he loved to give to God the glory and honor due in the celebration of the Holy Sacrifice, he showed it no less in reciting day and night the Divine Office, in which he offered to God with his lips the sacrifice of prayer and praise. When he was in the convent, he was so ready to go at all hours into the choir, that at the first sound of the bell, he left whatever he was employed in, to go and praise God, and considering the choir a paradise on earth, he often declared that reciting the office was one of his greatest consolations. As soon as he entered the choir, he prostrated himself and made an act of adoration of the Blessed Sacrament, and with other acts of virtue, he prepared to offer to

God that devotion of prayer and praise with the greatest fervor. He declared himself unworthy to stand in the Divine presence to praise Him with the community, and therefore begged his Angel Guardian and Patron Saints to supply his unworthiness, by praising, adoring, and blessing the Lord for him. He then entreated the Blessed Virgin to vouchsafe to offer for him praise and thanksgiving to the most Holy Trinity, and with the deepest humility entreated the Redeemer to offer the same to the Eternal Father. He then raised himself up, and with an act of great confidence in God, protested that he wished to join his voice to those present, and his praises to those of the angels and saints in heaven.

He did not satisfy himself with vocal prayers, but raised his heart to God, and fixed his thoughts on heaven, so that he seemed in an ecstasy, or out of his senses, and the better to fix his attention, he took a point for meditation during each psalm. He was also most ingenious in moving his fingers, thus intending to make certain acts of virtue, according to a plan formed beforehand. Although in his order the office is said slowly and although they always recite the psalms standing, so that the Matins, with the meditation, often lasted hours, two and a half or three hours, he was never known to lean against anything, or show any signs of weariness; not even when he was advanced in years, and exhausted with toil and fatigue. If it happened that he was obliged to recite the office out of the choir, he knelt on the ground, and went through it with the same devotion, making the same acts and the same meditations as in the choir. During the time of missions, he said the office with his companions in a low voice, but with the same devotion as in the convent, and was so exact in paying to God this tribute of praise that even to the last day of his life, when he was traveling, or even seriously ill, he always managed to recite the whole of the Divine Office. When he had not time to say it with all the pauses and meditations which he prescribed in his fifth "Resolution," he made these acts implicitly, saying: "I believe, I hope, I love, I am sorry, I return thanks," intending in this way implicitly to make acts of faith, hope, charity, contrition and thanksgiving.

Having described the attention and reverence of Blessed Leonard in celebrating mass, and reciting the divine office, it now remains to see with what fervor and assiduity he gave himself to private prayer, to offer to God the glory and honor due to Him, and practice the most noble virtue of religion. He always spoke of prayer as the daily and continued food of his soul, for, in fact, in all his works his mind was ever fixed on God, and in the midst of the most distracting occupations, he remained in communion with Him. Sometimes he said in his heart, "Jesus, my mercy," intending by that ejaculation to ask of God the grace to live religiously, and to do in all things His most holy will. Sometimes he would raise one finger, indicating by that that he desired to make some particular act of virtue, and in many ingenious ways he thus excited his fervor, and in the desire of being united to God, he made use of every means to pay Him adoration, praise, and thanksgiving. When he retired for mental prayer, and to be alone with his God, which he did several times during the day and night, it is impossible to say with what sentiments of piety and devotion he performed it. He considered this manner of praying of such high importance, that he used to say that all the troubles and disturbances of our times arose from the neglect of mental prayer, and he has thus left it written for our instruction: If for only one quarter of an hour in the day we thought seriously of eternity, and the blessings of God, the obligations of our state of life, the dangers of the world, and still more of the bitter Passion of our Redeemer, we should not see so much scandal, so much vanity, so much luxury, so much evil feeling, and so much profligacy amongst men." For this reason he delighted to retire to his cell, if charity or obedience did not oblige him to go out; where he conversed with God, meditating on His greatness, and adoring and returning thanks to Him by various acts of virtue. He usually began his prayer by meditating on some point in the life of our Blessed Lord, especially the crucifixion, which he dwelt on inwardly, and breathed forth the tender affections of his heart Having formed within himself a mental solitude, in which all things of earth were forgotten, he sought nothing but God, holding communion in prayer with Him alone. He called this solitude his little earthly paradise, and all the time he had to spare from his many occupations, be employed in it, retiring to pray and commune with his heart. Indeed, meditation had become so familiar to him, that whether he was studying, or whatever his occupation might be externally, he never left this mental solitude; in this school he acquired more knowledge of himself, and felt an increased desire in his heart to please, honor, and praise God, and to cause Him to be adored and praised by all, as his whole life bears testimony. He learned in this school to understand, as far as it is possible in this mortal life, the Divine Mysteries, and to feel the deepest devotion and reverence for the Blessed Virgin, and the saints in heaven. In this manner he gave to God in prayer the adoration due to Him, and became ardently zealous in adoring Him still more, and using every effort to induce others to do the same, and he drew from this fresh vigor and light to venerate deeply everything that belonged to God, for in this consists the virtue of religion.

CHAPTER XIII

On the Perfect Obedience of Blessed Leonard, and His Justice Towards His Neighbor

THE virtue of justice requires that we should give our neighbor his due, and we shall see how Blessed Leonard satisfied his obligation in this respect: and since obedience obliges those in the religious life to fulfil the will and wishes of their superior, as the minister of God, in whose name he commands, we will see first how he fulfilled his duty in being obedient to his superior, and afterwards speak on the zeal for justice he showed towards all, desiring that each should have his due. Our holy father was so jealous of the virtue of obedience, and so loved it, that he never undertook anything without having first ascertained the pleasure of his superior and sought his advice believing, with S. Bernard, that "obedience makes the monk." On this he depended, and allowed himself to be guided in all things, performing with readiness all that was required of him, just as if he was a novice a few days old. In order that his superiors might feel more at liberty to impose on him whatever they pleased, he placed himself at their feet, and with humility and resignation, declared his resolution to obey them willingly in all things, and at their command he was seen to leave whatever he had in hand, obeying them as if the order came directly from God. It was astonishing to see with what solicitude he learned the inclination of his superiors to anticipate and obey their wishes. If it happened that he was sent to visit a sick person, the order was scarcely given, than he was seen at the gate of the convent, waiting for the companion appointed, and he went wherever he was conducted, sometimes without even inquiring the name of the place or the person, but allowed himself to be led there like a child. But that which caused the greatest edification was, that whenever he arrived at a strange convent, where he was only to stay a few hours, he placed himself under obedience to the superior. When it was known that he was expected at a place to give a mission, and was received in a monastery, many people came to consult him on things relating to their souls; however tired he might be, he was ready to comply at once, and be under obedience to the superior, ready to do all that was required of him. Not less anxious was he for obedience when he was out of the convent employed in missions; he never decided any point himself, but always referred it to his superiors, writing to them and doing nothing without their permission. When he received an answer, he performed with exactness whatever he was desired to do, making it clearly understood that he had no other will but that of his superiors.

Although he was aware of the good effect produced by his preaching, he declared that if he was ordered to give up the missions entirely, he would obey readily, even joyfully; and he used to say that obedience was a virtue most pleasing to God, and without it every good work lost its merit, and was defective. Frequently when he was employed in giving a mission he received an order not to proceed to the places adjoining, in the same diocese, but to turn back to begin one in a distant part of the country, and after that to return to the place from whence he came, and notwithstanding the unfavorable season and the pain and fatigue he endured from walking barefoot, he set off without delay, not considering for a moment the inconvenience. He thus wrote to a religious on the occasion of one of these sudden journeys: "I allow myself to be led here and there by Divine Providence, feeling certain that in obeying I cannot err." To another, who wrote compassionating him in being sent about so inconveniently, he wrote in the following terms: "I willingly perform the office of a driver, plying hither or thither, for by that means I gain my bread." And to one who exhorted him to explain to his superiors the difficulties he found at his advanced age in executing some of their orders, he wrote thus: "My father, we must obey, you touch the most delicate point in my conscience; I declare that for fifty years of my life in religion I have never had to confess having failed in holy obedience, and do you think that now I am old, I will fail on this score?"

The love he had for this virtue was the cause of the great personal esteem he had for his superiors, and the reverence with which he spoke of them in discoursing on obedience. "In it," he used to say, "we practice in an especial way the three theological virtues, for when we obey our superiors we obey the will of God, and it follows that in perfect obedience we make an act of faith, in a most perfect way, regarding in the person of the superior that same God from whom he has authority to command, or forbid, whatever he deems proper, for the good regulation of those under him. We practice hope, placing all things in the hands of those who rule over us, in confidence that we are directed with the especial aid of Providence, giving up our own will, and being ruled by that of others, secure in the hope of being guided in a way most suitable for our advantage. And finally, we practice the virtue of charity in loving the divine will, and refraining from disputing what God, by means of our superiors, disposes, and willingly doing their pleasure." He held obedience in such high esteem, that whatever was imposed upon him, however difficult and arduous it might be, he always said, "When we have made the vow of obedience let us give even live ours for it, I shall consider myself most fortunate if I die for obedience."

He was often called upon by persons of distinction, and even by cardinals, to do some important work, but he always pointed to his superior, if he was present, and replied with humility, "Please your Eminence, this person stands to me in the place of God on earth. I cannot say anything for myself: since I made my religious profession, I have had no will but that of my superior, who governs me in the place of God." His esteem for his superiors was such, that besides speaking to them with reverence, he always listened with attention, his eyes cast down, and to whatever was said to him he showed the sincerity of these sentiments by placing himself in their hands, ready to obey whatever they commanded. It was most edifying to see the old man, venerable on account of his age and great merits, kneeling at the feet of his superior, humbly asking leave to go out of the convent on some work of mercy, perfectly indifferent as to who might be his companion on the occasion. He asked leave every time he had to reply to a letter, change his habit, and other similar things, kissing the ground each time, as if he was a novice; every time he passed the cell of the superior he uncovered his head, and stopped, making a profound bow, and if he were asked why he did so, he replied: "This is a sacred place occupied by my superior, and for that reason worthy of all reverence, for he stands in the place of God to me." He never inquired into the reason or cause of any order, and reproved those who refused to obey until they had examined the motive of the superior, and used to say to them, "It ought to be sufficient that the order given is not offensive to God, in everything but that it becomes us to bow our head in obedience." And to a nun who mentioned to him some doubts she had about obedience, he replied: "Plant in your heart this truth. The superioress may err in giving orders, but those under her rule, who desires only to please God, can never err in obeying." Persuaded of this himself, he left or undertook all his works according to the pleasure of superiors; and although he had determined to observe strictly the "Resolutions" above mentioned with the approval of his superior and confessor, if either of them, to test him, or for any other reason, desired him to abandon or moderate them, without giving the least sign of reluctance or vexation, he quickly obeyed. In one of these "Resolutions" you thus read: "I beg my spiritual father after having read these 'Resolutions' if he approves of them, to give me his blessing, that I may do all with the merit of holy obedience."

He used often to say that he only desired to be carried about like a staff in the hands of those who stand in the place of God on earth, obeying them in all that is not sin, and in exhorting others to rule themselves in the same way, he thus wrote in a letter to a religious: "Whatever may be prescribed for you in holy obedience, throw yourself into the sea of Divine Providence, doing all your superior desires. This is the way to live in peace, and die in peace, and we may be certain that the more frequently we place ourselves to be turned and tried in obedience, the more perfect peace we shall have. Let us make this generous declaration to our superiors, 'Fathers, behold us at sea, guide us to shore, we are ready for any obedience without reservation, and when we have made this resolution we shall be at peace.'"

All the superiors to whom he had been subject, attest that they always had reason to admire his obedience in the most trivial, as well as the most difficult and important concerns. In the fear of losing the merit of obedience, he dreaded nothing so much as being appointed superior; he loved being subject to the rule of others, and for this reason he had great reverence for the bishop of the diocese in which he preached, depending in all things on his decision, and he treated the parish priests with great respect, kissing their hands and asking their advice in giving the mission. He even obeyed the lay brother who was appointed to accompany him in his missions, whatever he advised him to do, that he did without saying a word. As the perfection of obedience consists in doing whatever is ordered promptly and cheerfully, our holy father always expressed in his countenance the joy of his soul in obeying; he used to say, "In perfect obedience under all circumstances I am sure not to go wrong, for I rejoice more in an act of obedience than if I had converted the whole world." He often had on his lips "Our duty is to obey." Finally, having declared that he would be obedient to death, he fulfilled his vow in his last journey from Bologna to Rome, since the holy pontiff had given him an order to return there in the November following, and had written to him in these words: "I hope that you will soon be in Rome." He left Bologna, as we have seen, on the 15th of November, and was taken ill on the road, and although they entreated him to stop at several places, he insisted on proceeding on his journey to Rome, in obedience to the pontiff, as he explained to his companion, saying to him, "You know, brother, that his holiness desired, when I left Rome, that I should return in November; you know that he wrote to me in Barbarola: 'I hope that you will soon return to Rome, and when the pope says, 'I hope,' we must take it as if he said, 'I command.' My conscience will be very much troubled, if, in consequence of this illness, I fail in obedience. Let us then go on to Rome, and if I die on the road, it will be an especial favor granted by my Heavenly Father, which I have so long desired, to die in the exercise of obedience." In short, a few hours after he arrived in Rome, he departed this life, with the consolation of being obedient unto death.

Not only did Blessed Leonard practice justice towards his neighbor in obeying his superior, but he was zealous to promote this virtue in others, by reforming abuses, putting an end to usury, and preventing oppression. It often happened that he found the poor oppressed by avaricious tyrants, who, by means of unlawful contracts which had passed into a law, and pressed hard upon them; he was moved with compassion in such cases, and inveighed loudly against their persecutors, and in his zeal for justice he labored hard to put an end to oppression. He held up to odium the enormity of the imposition, and the injury done, taught them the way to bargain honestly without going beyond the bounds of justice by oppressing their neighbors, and at the same time spoke in the most impressive manner to those who for the sake of sordid gain and usury were in danger of losing their souls. He was most unflinching in defending the rights of the poor, and preaching against the extortions of the rich, and all that offended against justice, by usury, robbery, not paying what was strictly due, or fraud of any kind; he spoke so clearly and with such vehemence, that it was easy to believe how he loved justice and hated the contrary vice.

Sometimes he was charged with imprudence, although he only spoke in general terms in his sermons, and avoided personality; however, he was informed of this charge, and declared openly from the pulpit that he was engaged to combat against vice, and to exterminate it, and whether he found it in the cabin of a countryman, or the palace of a nobleman, covered with rags, or clad in purple, that he, as a minister of God, was debtor to all, and would render to all their due.

So far from relaxing in his love of justice, on being told that some persons disapproved of the strong language he used in speaking of those who had defrauded the poor of their rights, he became even more zealous on the subject, and frequently expressed himself thus: "They will say that Father Leonard is highly culpable for endeavoring to reform abuses now become so common; they will say that he is a fool, and does not know what is necessary to support their dignity, but let them say what they like, I should be unworthy of the apostolical ministry, and betray their souls, if seeing them sin against justice, I were silent, and failed to remind them of their duty. It matters not to me what they say, I would give my life for justice, a most necessary virtue, for the neglect of which so many souls are unhappily lost." In this way did Blessed Leonard preach against the transgressors of justice, and by rendering to all due honor and esteem, he strongly inculcated the principle and teaching of the holy apostle S. Paul, "in honor preventing one another."

CHAPTER XIII

On the Love of Blessed Leonard for the Virtue of Temperance

HE virtue of temperance is that which renders our appetites subject to the law of God and of reason. It is perfect when a person abstains not only from unlawful things, which every Christian is bound to do, but also consents to deprive himself of that which is permitted, this tends to perfection in the way of the Lord. As Blessed Leonard practiced every virtue in the most perfect way, so he did that of temperance, mortifying his senses, and denying himself the use of them, even in things lawful. He held it as a maxim, that gratifying the taste and refusing to suffer is sufficient to prevent a soul from being united to God, and declared it was the desire of his heart to endure every kind of mortification, great and small, and make a continual war against his senses, powers, and passions. He was always most severe with himself, and never indulged in any earthly gratification, and was never contented unless he was mortifying and afflicting himself, and depriving himself of pleasures, however lawful they might be.

He acquired, with the aid of divine grace, such a dominion over his passions, that he seemed to live in the body, as if out of the body, and so far was he from indulging his flesh, that he mortified it on all occasions. He was never seen in a passion, or with the least expression of displeasure or internal trouble on his countenance, whatever happened; master of himself, he wore the same serene and composed expression, because he received all things from the hands of God, and so, as beneficial to himself. For this reason he was never melancholy, and if any one of his companions appeared so from fatigue and toil, he used to say: "Let those who are in a state of sin look melancholy, we who are laboring for the glory of God ought to be joyful, knowing that we serve a God who keeps a reckoning of all our deeds to give us a great reward in paradise."

He attained this tranquility of mind by watching carefully over himself; so that he never allowed his memory to dwell on anything that was not for his soul's good, or for the glory and honor of God. He subjected his intellect to the judgment of others, and when occasion required him to speak his own sentiments, he proffered them most modestly, without forcing his own opinions, and frequently yielded to those of others. He was always the most implacable enemy of his own will, contradicting it in everything which was not conformable to the perfection he so ardently desired. Not less was his temperance in restraining his corporal senses. In the many journeys he made in different countries, he never looked at anything rare or curious, and in walking through the fields, he kept his eyes fixed on heaven, or bent down to the earth, never indulging in the sight of beautiful scenery.

When he passed through a village, he was observed to be so abstracted in mind, and so absorbed in God, that he never noticed anything in passing, or even knew the road he was going. He never distinguished the monks in the convent whom he met daily, for he passed them with his eyes cast down, so absorbed and recollected that they were quite edified, and touched with compunction.

To keep a guard over his sense of hearing, he avoided all useless discourses and idle talking. If it happened that such was ever introduced in his presence, he in the most gentle manner changed it for profitable conversation, or turned his back and walked away. Greater still was his care in the custody of his tongue, never uttering a word that did not tend to the glory of God, or promote the good of his neighbor. He used to say: "The tongue is the pulse of the heart, and that to know the mind of a religious it is sufficient to converse with him; if his conversation turns on holy things, it is a sign that his heart is with God; if otherwise, he is nothing more than a hollow reed, given to levity and foolish talking." He held this maxim, which he inviolably observed: "I will not lose time in idle talking, and never speak but from necessity or charity." He rarely spoke, and lived retired and solitary in his cell, which he never left but to do his duty to God and his neighbor. He gave the following advice to a nun: "I will tell you the great secret of pleasing Jesus in your conversation. Always be the first to introduce holy subjects; do it, however, with judgment; listen sometimes to the common discourse, but in order to raise the tone, begin by degrees to mingle something sacred, but in so gentle a way, that Jesus will be always with you." In speaking to those of his community he always weighed all his words, and during the time of missions, he left his companions after supper, that he might not be tempted to talk, and retired, keeping a perfect silence. In short, he was so careful in the custody of his tongue, that at noon and in the evening he made a strict examination of conscience regarding it, and if he found that he had failed in the least point, he gave himself a penance, constantly repeating that the tongue is a great enemy, and if we do not often punish and mortify it, in the end it will be found intractable, and do much harm.

Since the virtue of temperance principally consists in moderating the senses of taste and touch, let us now see how strict Blessed Leonard was on these points, reserving the subject of his chastity for the following chapter. In regard to taste, he was so rigid in not gratifying his palate that he astonished everyone, for they could not understand how, with such severe fasts and mortifications, he could support himself, and continue to exist under the weight of so much toil and fatigue, especially in old age. For the space of forty-four years he never ate either flesh-meat, eggs, or fish, his only food was pottage, herbs, and salad, and he never altered his diet; even on the principal feasts of the year he satisfied himself with soup and a little fruit. It might with truth be said that he kept one continued fast. Besides the fasts of six months during the year, observed in the Retreat, Blessed Leonard never took more than one plate at dinner or supper; at dinner he took soup, and at supper the first thing offered, when it was usually a salad with a little fruit, even of this he sometimes only ate salad, and offered the fruit to the Infant Jesus. He was often seen to pour cold water into his soup, concealing the mortification by some pretext, and he never took salt with his food, even though it consisted of raw herbs, preferring the insipidity rather than lose an opportunity of mortifying himself.

He always refused to eat anything sweet, saying that those things were too good for him, and that his body (which he called his beast of burden) deserved neither oats nor caresses, but only straw and blows, and for that reason he always abstained from lemons, oranges, sauces, and everything which might please his palate. He was most temperate in drinking, never satisfying his thirst, and his beverage always consisted of more water than wine, or rather was water just tinged with wine. He was never heard to find fault with his food, however it was seasoned; and he used to say that many persons impeded their progress in the way of perfection by not mortifying their taste: "They overcome in all other things, but are overcome in this, and that fervor which was gained in the choir is lost when they come into the refectory." In the fear of falling into any excess, he seemed to measure every mouthful, and often he was seen to weep whilst he ate. Everyone felt that though his body was there, his mind was with God; he used to say: "Now and forever let us renounce all pleasure in eating, seeking only to do the will of God." He was even more temperate when he was giving missions in the country, although he underwent continual fatigue; he began all his labors fasting, being contented to eat only in the evening, but with his usual charity and discretion he allowed his companions to take some food in the morning, taking nothing himself but a little sage water to strengthen his voice, and fearing that this was too good, he changed it into a mixture of wormwood and water. For a whole year he never tasted anything in the morning but this bitter draught, until his companions having informed the vicar-general, he was ordered by him to take some bread, and a cup of wine, when he obeyed, and continued to do so until the end of his life. In the evening, however tired and worn out he might be, he ate nothing but salad, or the pottage with oil, and if occasionally his companions, moved with compassion for him, seasoned it a little better than usual, as soon as he perceived it, he refused to eat any more, saying that it was too rich, and would disagree with him. All who were with him at these times agree in declaring the excessive rigor of his fasts, and although in 1742 he was ordered to moderate them by the holy pontiff Benedict XIV, and consequently was obliged to eat something more at his usual supper, such as a small portion of fasting food, he refused to touch anything made with milk, or meat. He was never induced, either in the convent or out of it, to eat the least morsel before or after the usual meals, and even in his long journeys in the greatest heat of summer, they never could persuade him to drink even a little water to refresh him; he always replied quickly, "Do not urge me for a little water to lose the great merit and reward of self-denial; shall not I consent to suffer a little thirst, since my Savior suffered it so much for me on Calvary?"

Finally, the temperance of our holy father was seen in the way in which he treated the sense of feeling, torturing his body with the discipline so severely. He wore every morning for many hours next his skin a hairshirt and iron belt, he put this on before he went to celebrate mass, and never left off this custom, whether he was in the convent, on a journey, or giving missions. He used to say, "Our bodies are like wild colts, which, if they are not continually curbed, will carry us over the precipice." Besides the frequent use of the discipline, he scourged himself in public with iron chains two or three times before he began to preach, as well as every night in secret. When he was living in a house with seculars, in order that he should not be discovered, he made use of a discipline of small chains armed with points, this he carried with him on his journeys to flagellate himself without being perceived. All, however, saw the manner he treated his body on the platform, the fierce blows he gave himself until the blood flowed, and after his death the scars and wounds were visible. After having with fasts, hair shirt, and discipline, mortified his members, he gave himself a brief repose, lying on a board, taking for his pillow a log of wood. Having occasion to pass the night in the house of one of his benefactors, he slept on a chest, or on the ground, but for three years before his death he was induced, through obedience, to lie on a sack of straw. In the most severe cold weather, although he never wore anything but an old thread-bare habit, and always walked barefoot, trembling with cold, still he rarely approached the fire, and if by chance he came near it he drew back directly, calling himself a coward; and if anyone asked him to warm himself, he replied with great humility; " The more we give to our body the more it will require, and to whatever we accustom it, that it will endure." In this heroic manner did Blessed Leonard practice the virtue of temperance, in which he persevered to the end.

CHAPTER XIV

On the Spotless Chastity of Blessed Leonard

OUR holy father having made a solemn vow in his profession to practice the virtue of chastity, he kept it most faithfully, avoiding during his whole life everything that could stain or tarnish it. Not only did he preserve it pure and spotless from the time he made a vow so to do before the altar, but even from his earliest youth when he lived in the world. From his childhood, as we have seen in the first chapter of this Life, he proved how much he loved chastity. He was even then so modest in his manner and appearance, that all who knew him declared he was an angel on earth. He added to modesty penance and prayer, and induced his companions to have a tender devotion to the Blessed Virgin, to obtain this virtue so pleasing to her. Having attained the age when young persons are exposed to the greatest danger and temptations, he redoubled his caution, and determined never to converse with any but those who were spiritual, and made choice of a good confessor, under whose direction he frequently received the sacraments of confession and communion, the surest means of preserving chastity. After he entered the religious life he often thanked God that he had taken this vow, regretting that he had not done so when he was younger.

He expressed this sentiment not only in private, but publicly in preaching, and we thus find it written by him: "To Thee do I turn, sweet Jesus, and with tears in my eyes thank Thee for having placed me in that state of life in which I have made a solemn vow of perpetual chastity. Ah! why, from the time my mother held me in her arms was not this light given me; Oh! that I had made this vow in infancy: Oh! what joy in heaven for a soul who lives chaste and pure." He never ceased praying to God for grace to keep this vow inviolably, and to grant him an angelic purity, so greatly did he fear to blemish this virtue in the least degree. To prayer and this ardent desire he joined the necessary means for preserving his chastity, and he used to say that it mattered little having the will, if we do not carry into practice all that is necessary to prevent us from contracting any stain. Therefore he constantly fled from every occasion, however remote, which might excite in his mind the least desire that was not perfectly pure. He avoided all needless conversation with women, and whenever they came to consult him, he stood before them with his eyes cast down, and dismissed them as soon as the business was ended, even if they happened to be ladies of the highest rank and distinction. Although his usual manner in conversation was easy and good humored, with women he was always grave, and almost severe, carefully avoiding every expression which might seem familiar or tender, and giving his advice with seriousness and earnestness, as he deemed best for the good of their souls. His companion used to say to him, that with some very devout ladies he might bestow a little more of his time, and not be so austere, but he always replied: "Brother, supposing they say I am uncivil, rough, and harsh, what does it matter? with regard to personal purity we cannot be too cautious and watchful over ourselves?"

On another occasion he said: "Know you not that the lily is more secure the more it is surrounded by thorns? If those ladies were somewhat annoyed by my harshness, it matters not, for they will eventually be edified, and purity will be well guarded." Whenever he was obliged to converse with women, he occupied his mind with some good thought, and he used to say for the instruction of others, that when a religious is obliged to speak to women, he ought to act as do those who come in contact with infection; although they cannot fly from the sick of infectious disorders, they may hold in their hand some perfume which will prevent their taking the infection; so the religious, when he has to converse with women, should make use of the perfume of holy thoughts to keep him from danger. In hearing the confessions of women, he was ever more grave and severe in manner, and on this point he often said: "The confessional is a sacred place, an earthly tribunal, where the priest stands in the place of God; it is a soul-cleansing fountain, in which all who come can cleanse their souls from every sin, and for this reason we ought on no account to allow any discourse but such as directly tends to an end so sacred as that of purifying a soul from sin. The minister ought then to make use of such language, and regulate his conduct in such a manner, that it may breathe of nothing but purity, so that in healing the wounds of others he may not receive hurt himself."

When he heard the confessions of women he never turned his face to them, but listened with gravity and seriousness to all that was necessary for the right administration of the sacrament, and gave the instruction they required without asking a question or hearing a word that had no reference to what was confessed. He had a curtain hung before his confessional, which he drew as soon as he had seated himself, without looking at the person who might be kneeling there waiting to make her confession; and before he entered this sacred tribunal, fearing that the devil might put some impure thoughts into his mind, he earnestly entreated his angel-guardian to be with him, and keep him from such danger. He took the greatest care during the missions that no woman entered the house he inhabited, and never spoke to them out of the confessional excepting on occasions of urgent necessity.

He always kept to the resolution he had formed of never going out alone, not even from his house to the church, and was most vigilant in seeing that his companions observed the same; and if it happened that he or one of them was sent for to confess a sick woman, he desired that they should be accompanied by a priest, or some responsible person, who during the confession

239

should remain where he could see the confessor and the penitent. To those who expressed their astonishment at such caution, he used to reply: "The virtue of chastity must be practiced by everyone, but especially by those who are employed in leading souls to God, for the shadow even of the contrary vice is sufficient, amongst other evils, to destroy all the good effects of our teaching; it is not sufficient for a missionary to be pure in the sight of God, but he must appear so in the eyes of the world, for it is good to give evidence always of his holy life."

For the same end, in traveling from one country to another to give missions, he never allowed a woman to accompany him, however devout and spiritual she might be, for he always held this maxim: "A religious should not only avoid evil, but even the appearance of it in the eyes of the world, which is always too ready to judge unmercifully." He never permitted anyone, especially women, to touch his hand, and when the people used to press round him in the towns through which he passed, to kiss his hand, he presented his habit or cloak, and without ever stopping he went on his way quite abstracted. For this reason he wore his cloak in the hottest weather, to his great personal inconvenience, and on being asked why he burdened himself with it, he replied with sincerity: "Those simple people wish to kiss my hand, and there are many women amongst them, and although I keep my hand in my sleeve they try to take hold of it, which displeases me much, because I do not think it according to holy purity that a religious should allow, even on the score of devotion, his hand to be touched, especially by a woman. I wear my cloak that they may kiss it, and I may be free from the danger of being touched by any one of them."

In a letter to a nun we find these words: "If you desire to be chaste and pure, this is the way; be retired, modest, and mortified." What he taught to others he practiced himself; he lived so retired when he was in the monastery that he scarcely ever went into the garden to breathe the air, and when he was on a mission, he never left his room except to go to the church, or on some work of mercy. He often had these words on his lips: "If anyone in religion does not love retirement, they will be sure one day to encounter something which, if it does not offend against purity, will at least put it in danger, and not guarding against such occurrences by being retired, is a sign that purity is already lost, or in danger of being so." His modesty was so perfect, that walking always with his eyes cast down and with singular composure, he breathed holiness in his deportment, so that many declared they felt touched with compunction on beholding him, and others who knew him well for many years affirmed, that in every word, action, and gesture, his modesty shone resplendent.

In admonishing young men he used to say to them: "If you are not modest and discreet, you cannot be chaste; those who sin against holy purity begin by being indiscreet." Regarding the mortifications of his body, and the other necessary means for the preservation of chastity, we have given sufficient instances in the preceding chapter; we shall only add, that the doctors who attended him declared, that considering his mortifications, his labors, and the way he used the discipline, his continuing to exist so long was quite miraculous.

To all the necessary means for preserving chastity, he added that which is of all the most important, prayer; feeling sure that man could not of himself keep this inestimable treasure, he often said: "Of ourselves we can do nothing, and we above all things in this particular require the help of God." To obtain this end he prayed without ceasing to God, asking for the grace to keep perfectly his vow of chastity, and foreseeing dangers, however remote, he frequently had recourse to this ejaculation: "Jesus, my mercy." Although he adopted these and many other means to preserve the lily of purity, he had no self-reliance; and in exhorting his companions and others to be vigilant in the custody of this precious virtue, he thus expressed himself: "My brothers, old as I am, I have so much fear on this point that I would not risk even raising my eyes from the ground, knowing that many men adorned with every virtue and holiness, by a sudden temptation have fallen miserably." At other times he would say: "Let us fly from danger, fear all things, and recommend ourselves to God, for there is nothing of which we ought to be so jealous as chastity. The devil never sleeps, and stands in wait for the old as well as the young; if a religious unfortunately falls, it is from a great height over a precipice."

To make himself more secure, he proposed to reveal to his spiritual father minutely all the dangers to which he was exposed against this virtue, and exhorted others to the same, saying, "Ah, if you knew how the devil is daunted when he sees himself discovered, and when we make known to our confessor his suggestions with sincerity, and allow ourselves to be ruled by his wise counsels, for thus beholding his designs discovered, he flies in confusion; but if he sees us deceiving ourselves, and we allow his temptations to lie concealed in our hearts, flattering ourselves that not having sinned we may be silent, he increases in boldness, and uses every effort to tempt and conquer us."

He who heard the general confessions of Blessed Leonard during the last years of his life, thus gave his attestation and deposition: "I hold it for certain that his brightest crown in heaven will be in reward for his chastity and purity of heart, having watched over them to guard them from the least danger; and most pure and spotless did he keep them."

Finally, he proved how greatly he loved chastity by the fervent zeal with which he preached against the contrary vice. Many dissolute persons, moved by his earnest manner, changed their vicious mode of life, and became chaste and exemplary, and wherever he gave a mission, great numbers were reclaimed from this sin. He exclaimed vehemently and with apostolic zeal against all the enemies of chastity, against the abuse of love, familiar conversations, lascivious and loose talking, reading immoral and profane books, immodest pictures, balls, and assemblies, and all that could be an occasion of offending against chastity. He declared himself an enemy of all these things, and told the people how they were to guard themselves against these temptations of the devil to lead away souls to shame and perdition. And it pleased God to make his zeal fruitful, for besides the numerous conversions to which we have already referred, in many places the theaters were closed, comedies prohibited, the carnival abandoned, and the most extraordinary change produced, all the effect of the hatred Blessed Leonard bore to the vice of impurity, and the means of occasioning it, and of the love he nourished in his breast for chastity.

CHAPTER XV

Of the Heroic Fortitude of Blessed Leonard

T is considered most important to possess the virtue of fortitude, for it gives strength to the soul to make men overcome every obstacle which may stand in the way of perfection, receiving with courage and composure every cross and contradiction as coming directly from God; therefore, we shall briefly detail its effect on the mind of Blessed Leonard, who possessed this virtue in a wonderful degree. It may be seen in the whole course of his life, which was full of such dangers, difficulties, and contradictions, as seldom fall to the lot of man. It was truly astonishing to see how he undertook great and arduous works for the glory of God and the salvation of his neighbor, without ever failing in courage and firmness, and without ever seeming weak in body or faint in heart; however arduous the undertaking might be, he began, followed it up, and brought it to perfection. The first occasion he had of showing his great courage was in establishing in his Retreat the observance of all our rules and constitutions, and his vigilance in enforcing the exact fulfilment of them. We have seen what he had to contend with in establishing the Retreat del Monte in Florence, what difficulties he overcame, how it was opposed by many, and how he bore with admirable patience and fortitude the animosity of his own countrymen as well as strangers, till he was forced to say, "They may abuse and even beat me, I shall willingly bear it, so that the rules and constitutions of our institute are kept up." For this object he made many journeys from Florence to Rome barefoot, never losing courage, whatever opposition or cross he might moot with. Wherever he found obstacles or difficulties, with dauntless courage he overcame them all, saying that he was ready and willing to suffer even more for the glory of God and the well-being of the institute, and would give his life for the same end were it necessary.

When he was superior of the Retreat, he showed himself so firm and unflinching in reproving with holy zeal and without human respect the transgressors in the least particular of the rules, and enjoining forcibly the exact observance of them. The virtue of fortitude is most requisite in fighting against sin and hell, for he who undertakes this holy war is exposed to the scorn of libertines, who hear themselves reproved, and to the persecution of the vicious, who find themselves confounded, and to the abuse of the hardened sinner, who fears no one. Whoever listened to the sermons of Blessed Leonard, might say that he never evinced timidity, and that he was most unflinching and regardless of human respect. All admired in him a wonderful strength of mind and courage in preaching against sin and sinners, without fear of giving offence to any one present.

Wherever he found scandal, he inveighed against it with all his power of language, admonishing sinners, notwithstanding the displeasure he caused, but he had the prudence and discretion not to mention names. If this was not sufficient, and if all he said from the pulpit did not put a stop to the scandal, he sent for, or called at the houses of those who caused it, and laying aside all reserve and human respect, with courage and apostolic freedom admonished and reminded them of their duties, and their danger of eternal damnation. It was not only to persons in the lower class of life, to whom in the opinion of the world a priest may speak with the greatest freedom, that he thus acted, but also to people of distinction, whether for their talents or high birth. Many, even the ministers of God, were astonished at his intrepidity, since he, fearlessly in public and private, with zeal for the honor of God and the salvation of souls, reproved all who deserved reproof.

A person well known in Rome, and a confidential friend of

Blessed Leonard, and who had done many good works at his suggestion, fell sick, and our holy father knew that he mortally hated his nephew, and had refused to see, or hear his name mentioned; he therefore went immediately to the dying man, and without wasting time in preamble, said, "My dear friend, I have loved you in life and whilst you were in health, much greater, however, is my love for you now that you are sick and at the point of death: for the love of your soul, then, I tell you that you must forgive your nephew." On hearing these words, the sick man, who had been deaf to the prayers of others, and to whom no one had spoken in such strong terms on the duty of reconciliation, was moved and touched with compunction, sent for his nephew, and with Christian charity embraced him, and became perfectly reconciled before his death, which took place soon after.

When he was giving a mission in a town near Rome, he was told that the women did not dress with becoming modesty, therefore he publicly admonished them, and desired that the young women especially should dress with modesty, coming closely veiled to church. Some young women who belonged to the upper class, flattered themselves that because the missionary lodged in the house of the archpriest, their uncle, and because they were people of some distinction in the place, he would have some consideration for them, and without taking heed of his admonitions, went to the church dressed as usual, with their shoulders bare, and placed themselves near the pulpit to hear the sermon. The good missionary perceived them, and at the end of his discourse reminded his hearers of the duty of remembering the wants of their neighbors, and earnestly recommended them to give abundant alms that evening, as many were in need. All remained attentive to hear how the collection was to be used, when with holy freedom and courage, he said, "Do you wish to know how the collection made after the sermon is to be used? For nothing less than to buy cloth to divide amongst certain young ladies who are here, having attended the sermon, but who have not sufficient clothing to cover their shoulders decently." These words caused all the young women to blush and feel ashamed, they covered themselves up as well as they could, and resolved to be more discreet for the future. They felt that the missionary was full of zeal for their conversion, and esteemed his extraordinary courage, setting at nought human respect in procuring their salvation.

Although all the places which were enlightened by Blessed Leonard are testimonies of the zeal and strength of mind with which he put an end to all disorders and sin, I shall confine myself to Rome, where he gave many missions, and was regarded as a man full of the Holy Spirit, especially when he preached in the Piazza Navona, to prepare the people for the jubilee. For fifteen successive days he appeared in the piazza, in which, besides the common people who crowded to hear him, many nobles, almost all the cardinals, and frequently the holy pontiff Benedict XIV, were present. Anyone but our hero would have lost courage and strength of mind in seeing himself exposed to the gaze of such a multitude, composed of people of every grade and condition, with the obligation of speaking to all, to convert, or at least to improve all. He, however, as an apostolic man, who thought only of the glory of God, inveighed with such wonderful force and energy against vice, that everyone felt he was filled with that spirit of which it is written, "Ubi spiritus Domini ibi libertas." In fact, with courage and firmness he inveighed against the sins of the people, the libertinism of the nobles, the injustice to the poor, and the excesses of the rich, speaking with so much vehemence and clearness, that each one, ecclesiastic and secular, noble or plebeian, rich or poor, applied what he said to himself. More than one person, on seeing the intrepidity with which the man of God reproved vice in people of every denomination, shrugged their shoulders, openly confessed their weakness, declared that they should not have the courage to speak in that way, and that such wonderful strength of mind was to be found only in Blessed Leonard.

He preached with even greater zeal and force against scandalous livers, against whom he had often to contend, as will appear from the following fact. In the year 1743 he was preaching in a town near Genoa, where a gentleman was living, to the scandal of the place, and displeasure of his relations, in concubinage, and no one had power to dissuade him from leading so scandalous a life, or to lead him to think of the consequences. Blessed Leonard in his sermons inveighed most strongly against this sin, and represented in the most earnest manner the dreadful punishment in store for those, who, not satisfied with sinning themselves, are the means, by the scandal they cause, of leading others to damnation. These threats and admonitions, however, made no impression on the hardened sinner, for the following evening, when Blessed Leonard came to preach in the Piazza, he appeared at the window with his concubine, under pretense of listening to the sermon, but in reality to make a display of his sin in the sight of all. When the zealous missionary perceived him, he was quite inflamed with holy indignation; the scandal being public, he publicly reproved it, and with such vehemence, that every word must have seemed like a thunderbolt to awaken the wretched man from the lethargy of sin. Not satisfied with this, when the sermon was ended, he went to the house, fearless of the danger to which he was exposed, of receiving some affront from the man who had been thus publicly reproved; he spoke to him with invincible courage, and used every argument which his zeal suggested to gain him, but without effect; and finding him obdurate, he turned away, warning him that his sin would be punished before long. His words were soon verified, for not many days after the unfortunate man was murdered by his own brother at the door of his palace. It was quite evident that this was sent as a punishment for his wickedness and hardness of heart; the place where he fell was covered with blood, which no washing or scraping could efface, but the stains remained for a long time visible to all as a sign of the just vengeance of God on those, who, instead of submitting to the admonitions of His servants, remain obstinate in their sin, and scoff at them.

In a still more wonderful manner did the strength of mind of Blessed Leonard shine when he undertook the mission in Corsica, for he had to deal with a people at war with his own nation, and divided by internal factions, and he was obliged to preach in the midst of armed men belonging to the different factions, as we have seen; exposed, even, to the danger of losing his life, but his courage and fortitude never once failed. Wherever he went throughout the island to give missions, a certain person, named Marco Aurelio, appeared, who called himself chancellor of the pretended king Theodore. This man, being held in high esteem by his partisans, endeavored to maintain and increase his own party; he followed Blessed Leonard wherever he went, and gave him cause to pray for greater courage when he began to preach, for he knew not why he was followed in this way.

During the missions given in Omessa, he had preached with extraordinary fervor against the evils of war and enmity, and Marco Aurelio sent to tell him that if he did not cease preaching in that way, that they should have a renewal in Corsica of the martyrdoms in Japan. Blessed Leonard, when he was informed of this, did not feel the least intimidated, but with the courage of a hero caused Marco to be brought into his presence, when the man who was considered so bold knew not what to say to the persuasive eloquence of the servant of God, who in an imperious tone of voice desired him to kneel down, which order he obeyed instantly; then Blessed Leonard said: "Hear me, you obstinate sinner, since you refuse to submit to grace, at least do this; recite every day a Pater noster to S. Vincent Ferrer." Then sending him away, he said: "Go, take yourself out of my sight." Marco Aurelio promised to say this short prayer, and went away much humbled. All present were astonished at the courage and boldness of our holy father in thus speaking to the man who was the leader of the factious party, and caused fear wherever he went.

A few days after this Blessed Leonard went to Corti, in the diocese of Aleria, one of the most considerable places in the island, where he began a mission. The governor of Bastia was informed that a letter was circulated in the name of the missionary, inviting all the heads of the factions, and the authorities, to meet in Corti on a certain day, to hold a conference concerning the peace of the island. It was indeed a most perilous undertaking, but they all obeyed the summons; and Blessed Leonard, armed with his wonted courage, ascended the platform, declared he was not the writer, and knew nothing of the letter circulated in his name, and then went on to say, "It is a fiendish plot, and whoever is the author may be sure that he will be held accountable for the sins committed." On hearing these words, the chiefs of the different parties assembled were quite astonished, and remained silent for a moment, when suddenly a simultaneous cry was heard, "Peace, peace." Marco Aurelio was amongst them, and although followed by a numerous band, came and knelt at the feet of Blessed Leonard, confessed that he was the writer of the letter, and in obedience to him went directly to the governor of Bastia, and having promised peace, obtained pardon.

Not less intrepidity did Blessed Leonard manifest in Caccia, where two families were living in mortal hatred and enmity; he preached so forcibly against this vice, that they resolved to be reconciled. The two contending parties came to the convent where Blessed Leonard was lodged. As one, however, refused to admit the adjustment of some mutual interest which the other proposed, they both took arms, one of them seized a gun, and was about to fire on his adversary, when the holy father, with admirable courage, rushed between them, not caring to lose his life if he saved a soul, and with prayers and exhortations at last succeeded in quelling the tumult and restoring peace. There are many examples of the heroic fortitude shown by Blessed Leonard in overcoming every difficulty which might be mentioned, were it not that it would make this history too long; sufficient has been said, however, to prove how heroically he was endowed with this virtue.

CHAPTER XV

On the Humility and Patience of Blessed Leonard

UMILITY being a virtue which consists in having a low esteem of ourselves, it follows that according to the greater or less knowledge we have of our worthlessness, so will be the corresponding degree of our humility; thus one who thinks meanly of himself is called humble, if he is willing that everyone should have the same opinion of him, he is more humble, and if he desires and seeks to be despised, he is called most humble. Blessed Leonard proved that he possessed the virtue of humility in these three degrees, so that not only had he the lowest esteem of himself, but also desired that others should have the same, and sincerely loved to be despised and abused by all. The low esteem he had of himself clearly appears in the "Resolutions" drawn up by him, which came from his heart, and were an index of his soul. He was never heard to utter a word which redounded to his own praise, and all that he said tended to his self-abasement. Although great and abundant fruit was gathered from his preaching, and still more from his virtuous example, and although he saw himself universally applauded and esteemed, he never became vain-glorious, but was confused and covered with blushes, attributing it to the simplicity of the people, who made these demonstrations of satisfaction because they knew not what he was. It often happened that in walking through the streets the people crowded to look at him, kiss his hand, and impede his progress, but he, quite abstracted, seemed unconscious of the cause, and so pursued his way.

Sometimes his companions asked him what he thought of this devotion of the people, and he would reply: "Brother, they are very simple; they do not know me; if they did they would not make these demonstrations." The low esteem he had of himself caused him to be most humble to everyone, and to count himself the worst of men was a usual and continual thing with him. He often in the convent knelt in the presence of the community, and confessed that he was a broken reed, and that whilst he was promoting the salvation of others, and inflaming them with the love of God, he remained cold and hard-hearted, and begged of them to pray to God to grant him grace, that in preaching to others, and leading them to heaven, he might not be a castaway, and lose his own soul. He spoke these words with so much feeling and weeping, that all believed they came from a heart truly humble, and from the mouth of one who esteemed himself worthless.

Wherever he went to give missions, the first thing he did after visiting the church, was to go to the parish priest to kiss his hand and ask his blessing. When he preached the sermon on devotion to our Blessed Lady, he publicly kissed the feet of all the priests present, and by this act of humility he obtained for many the grace to abandon their sins, and to be reconciled to their enemies. The bishops in some places seeing the edification and compunction of the people, rose from their thrones after the sermon, and imitating his example, kissed the feet of those persons with whom they had had disagreements. Not only did Blessed Leonard show himself humble toward his superiors, "but also to those inferior to him, asking their opinion, and following their advice. His answer to those, even simple laymen, who gave him advice, generally was this: "Yes, brother, you are right, I shall do what you recommend." And to one who wrote to him, saying that he hoped the success of the missions would not make him vain-glorious, he replied thus: "I thank you for the warning and good advice, which I much need."

On another occasion his companion having advised him to vary his sermons a little, he replied that he had no intention of doing so, for it would serve rather to entice the people than to profit them; but afterwards reflecting on this answer, the following day he knelt at the feet of the same companion, and asked pardon for having replied in that manner, beseeching him to take pity on him for having caused scandal in being so proud. He was aware that when the missions were ended he would be followed by the people on his departure, therefore he set off before daybreak without being perceived; and if he was obliged to pass through places where he was known, he drew his hood over his head, and walked very fast, and sometimes preferred going far out of his way to being met by any one whom he knew, for he feared the honors they would pay him more than the worldling would fear affronts and ill usage. When he gave missions in Port Maurice, his native place, his fellow citizens wished to have his portrait, as he appeared in the attitude of preaching, and it was taken unknown to him. When it was finished they brought it to him, and asked if he could tell who it resembled. On looking at the picture he became quite confused, and turning to them, said: "What have you done? may God forgive you." He wept, and seemed so distressed, that his friends were touched with compunction, and much edified, and said one to the other: "We believed we were doing something to please Father Leonard, and we have made him weep."

He was much displeased when he perceived that anyone, in devotion, had cut off a bit of his habit or cloak, and endeavored to lessen the high regard they had for him by saying something to make them despise him. When he was preaching in Arpino, a person who stood near dexterously cut off a piece of his habit, which when he perceived he said in a contemptuous tone, as disdaining the act, "You have gained much. Go away; you are rich indeed!" In the same town they changed his pilgrim's staff for another, and kept it as a relic. When he had ended his sermon he perceived on taking it that it was not his own, but had been changed, and he said, shrugging his shoulders, "Ah! I see the simplicity of these people; such a staff will be very useful when they gather their figs." In this way he endeavored to show the contempt in which he held himself, and his desire that others should feel the same.

He was always more willing to hear the confessions of the poor than the rich, and exhorted his companions to the same desire, giving this reason, that they ought to receive and hear the poor more readily, since the rich could suit their convenience whenever they pleased, being always able to find time and a confessor, but not so the poor. This love of self-abasement induced him to put an end to all communication with persons of distinction who had been his intimate friends; and if circumstances obliged him to meet them, he simply satisfied their wishes, and took leave of them as soon as possible. He used to say on this subject: "It is not for a religious who humbly professes to follow the teaching of the cross to be seen every day in the palaces of noblemen, and seem ambitious of corresponding with the great people in the world." Being asked by one of his community, why in some of his discourses he introduced extracts from books of sermons well known, and mentioned the names of the authors by which he exposed himself to the danger of being called a copyist, he replied, smiling: "And what does it matter if they do call me a copyist? I know that if I were to spend time and thought I should never succeed in expressing myself so well as the authors from which I have borrowed; why, then, do you wish that I should give them that which is not so well adapted for the good of their souls? This would give me concern, but I care not to be taken for an ignorant copyist."

He rejoiced whenever he was made contemptible in the esteem of men; and when anything occurred to humble him, he used to say: "Humble thyself, proud man." On one occasion when he went to the solitude dell' Incontro to perform his spiritual exercises, he gave a signal proof of his wonderful humility. I shall relate it in the words of the president of that sanctuary, who has left it thus written: "When I was president of the solitude dell'

Incontro, Father Leonard came to perform the exercises, along with Brother Diego; one morning they were both kneeling in the refectory, Father Leonard accusing himself of his faults, when I was seized with a sudden desire to try his spirit, and amongst other things said this: 'You seem to be a great man, Father Leonard, on account of your missions, and, because you have preached a few sermons all wish to have you, and proclaim you to be a great missionary. Ah! what pride you must have in your heart; rise then, Brother Diego, stand up and put your foot on his neck, and say, *Father Leonard, humble yourself.*' I had no sooner pronounced the words than I felt compunction, and said to myself 'What have I done?' However, I soon found that my words had been for his spiritual good, for he was quite composed, resigned, and in peace, and with a joyful countenance he turned to me, and said: 'May Almighty God reward you.'" This same president frequently exercised him in similar acts of humiliation, but he was never disturbed, and always thanked him with all his heart. He constantly desired that all things might tend to his self-abasement, and has left it thus written: "I desire to be despised and treated with contempt, abused and trodden under foot like dirt, and I pray to God that I may die in some obscure place where I am supposed to be a reprobate, and my body thrown into a ditch without honor." That he loved self-abasement appears from the fact that he obtained the promise from the two holy pontiffs Clement XII, and Benedict XIV, that he might never be raised to superiority in the order, contented to go always barefoot, dressed like a beggar, with a patched habit, and employed in the lowest office in the monastery, subject to all, and depending on the will and opinion of others, even when he was on a mission. During the holy year he went every Sunday to the palace by order of the Pope Benedict XIV, by whom he was received with honor and affection; his companion on returning with him after a secret conference, asked him what became of his humility when he was treated in this way by the vicar of Christ; he replied: "Listen, brother, whatever God does with a miserable creature such as I am, He does in His clemency and goodness. However, I should have rejoiced much if his Holiness had well mortified me, calling me a hypocrite, deceiver, and ruffian, and had driven me from his presence, forbidding me ever to approach the palace; and indeed every time I go there I am prepared to receive some great mortification, for I know too well that I deserve it, and shall deem myself truly happy if ever this comes to pass."

With the same sentiments he received every demonstration of veneration and esteem from the people in the places through which he passed, or wherever he lived, or was employed in giving missions. The esteem in which he was held was so great, not only by the common people, but by those of the highest rank, that wherever he went he was received and venerated as a saint. In Tuscany and elsewhere he was called an Apostle; in Corsica he was never called by any other name but that of the holy father; in Tuscany they praised him as an "Apostolic man," and an "Angel of the Lord." In the diocese of Lucca and Aquila, when he arrived at a town they rang the bells joyously, and the inhabitants, leaving their work, assembled to receive his blessing, and with them came the clergy, even when he was not going to give a mission there. In Rome he was followed by the people whenever he appeared, and the children ran to kiss his hands or his cloak, and became quiet and orderly whenever they saw him approaching.

In the holy year of 1750, when the chapter-general of the Franciscan order was held in the church of Araceli, all the religious of the order in Rome walked together in procession to S. Peter's, amongst them was Blessed Leonard. So great was the crowd assembled to behold him, that their progress was impeded, and it was with great difficulty they reached the Vatican. When they came out the crowd pressed round him, so that they were obliged to have a guard of soldiers to escort him to the capitol, and in the visits to the other basilicas it was deemed proper to leave him in the convent, to prevent disorders arising from the concourse of people. The esteem and veneration of the people for him reached such an extreme point, that he who succeeded in procuring a small piece of his habit, or anything belonging to him, was considered as supremely blessed. Whenever he appeared in public, they cut off pieces of his habit, and frequently managed to change his cloak for a new one. His girdle, crucifix, a wooden cross with points of iron, which he used to wear on his breast, his rosary, discipline, and everything he used, were all exchanged in turn; they even took the towel he used for his hands, the sandals he put on when he approached the altar, considering them as relics, and preserving them with devotion. Not only was it the simple and poor who held him in such veneration, but those also of the intellectual and higher classes, for when he gave a mission in Ferrara in 1746, the gentlemen of the place, to satisfy the devotion of the people, had his picture engraved and distributed; many copies were sent to places at a distance.

The Duke of Sant' Aignan, at that time the French ambassador in Rome, begged the crucifix which Blessed Leonard had worn on his missions, he also had his portrait taken by a first-rate artist, and carried both to his country as treasures. Her majesty, the Queen Mary Clementina of England,[2] a most virtuous and pious princess, desired to consult him on points of conscience, and to have his advice concerning the attainment of the high state of perfection to which he aspired. But overwhelmed as he was by these honors and testimonials of esteem, this meek and humble servant of God never became

---

[2] Editor's note: Maria Clementina Sobieska (1702-1735) the wife of James Francis Edward Stuart, styled James III of England by allies and the "old pretender" by official British history. His birth sparked the revolution that removed his father, James II from the throne in 1688. Though recognized by many rulers, she never formally ruled in England.

vain-glorious, or ceased to have a low opinion of himself; even amid these acclamations and the deep reverence paid to him, his only desire was to remain obscure, or to be treated with contempt, and despised.

The patience of Blessed Leonard may be said to equal his humility, for his self-abasement made him ready and willing to endure any calamity which might befall him. With what patience he exercised his apostolic ministry for so many years, we have already given sufficient evidence; it remains only to add that whatever he had to encounter, whether adverse or prosperous, he received it with the same joy and cheerfulness as coming from the hand of God.

His father, then a very old man, came to visit him at the convent, and although many years had passed since they had seen each other, the superior ordered him to be sent away at the end of three days; he obeyed without uttering a complaint, or showing the least sign of sorrow, although the order was inconsiderate, and he felt sure that he should never see his father again; and so it happened.

When he was going on one occasion to the Monte della Verna with the father superior of Prato, to the provincial chapter which was to be held there, they were overtaken by a heavy shower of rain. Just as they reached a village where they were not known, Blessed Leonard said, "Now that we have arrived at this place where we know not anyone likely to admit us into their house, dripping wet as we are, if they refuse to look at us, and if they send us away, shall we bear it patiently and willingly?" His companion replied, that he did not believe that such would be the case, but if it was, he should feel much displeased. Then the servant of God said, "If it should happen, as I anticipate, we ought to rejoice, for in this consists the perfection of 'Friars Minor,' as our holy father S. Francis taught Brother Leone." As he predicted so it happened, for on arriving late, and knocking at the door of a cottage, they were refused admittance, as the occupants were poor, and could not accommodate them. From thence they went to a large house, where they were received most rudely by a servant, who, however, gave them a truss of straw to dry themselves, and led them into a stable; but in a short time she returned, and told them in an angry tone to go away, for she could not allow them to remain without her master's leave; they were forced to leave their miserable shelter. The companion complained of the treatment they had received, but Blessed Leonard said quite joyously: "This is the time to merit; this is a favor from the beneficent hand of God, and shall we refuse to receive it? Come, let us go, He will provide for us." And thus it happened; for on leaving the stable they were met by a person who gave them a lodging for the night.

He was once in the infirmary in consequence of a wound in his foot, which kept him in bed. Being visited by a religious, he asked him how he felt; he replied joyfully: "Very well." "How can you be well," said the other, "when you are suffering so much from your foot, that you cannot move?" He replied: "I am doing the will of God, and he who does that holy will must be well." This great principle was so fixed in his heart, that he was never seen to be the least disturbed or impatient, even in the most unforeseen and unlucky accidents. In the exercise of his apostolic ministry he found many occasions of showing this virtue, for he often received treatment little pleasing to man, which he endured without ever losing the tranquil composure usual to him. In 1743, when he was giving a mission in Genoa, he received orders from Rome to go to Nizza di Provenza immediately. When he arrived there, although the people received him very well at first, and seemed disposed to promote the mission, and although they had requested that he might be sent there, still they were now quite opposed to him, and refused to give the missionaries an audience, and gave him to understand that they wished him to return from whence he came. His companions were quite astonished at this unexpected reception, and much troubled; but Blessed Leonard, with his usual composure, said to them: "Almighty God has now made the balance even; the applause we met with in Genoa might have made us vain-glorious, so here we are rejected. This opposition is sent to make us humble." Without feeling the least irritated he caused everything to be packed up that had been brought for the mission, and left the place, making it evident that he had humility sufficient to be abased, and patience to suffer in peace, and joy the opposition he had met with, and that he was adorned with every virtue, the possession of which constitutes holiness. We have hitherto treated of the various virtues of Blessed Leonard, it now remains to tell of the supernatural gifts bestowed upon him by God.

CHAPTER XVII

*On the Gift of Prophecy and Discernment of Spirits with Which Blessed
Leonard Was Endowed*

AMONGST the gifts and graces spoken of by S. Paul in the 12th chapter of the 1st Epistle to the Corinthians, as those which Almighty God grants to some, is that of prophecy and discerning spirits, and with this gift our holy Father was abundantly endowed. Many facts in proof of this might be adduced, but I shall briefly refer to a few. In the year 1750 Giustina Capodacque Parenti having come from Capistrella to Rome for the jubilee, on the morning of the 8th of November went to the church of S. Buonaventura to make her confession to Blessed Leonard. She was already known to him, and he enjoined her to visit the "Way of the Cross," and come to him after breakfast. Giustina replied, that it was impossible to do so, for her companions were waiting for her, and in haste to depart. Blessed Leonard replied: "Since you cannot come back today, come tomorrow she told him she could not come back for three days, when he continued: "My child, you must come to me today, or tomorrow, or never." Giustina declared that she would have time to return, for she was to stay in Rome for some weeks. Blessed Leonard ended by saying: "No, you cannot; I know that you are not to leave Rome so soon, but if you do not return today or tomorrow you will never be here again to see me, or anyone else." Giustina then left the church, and related what had occurred to her sisters, said that Father Leonard had terrified her, and she feared that something would happen to prevent her again visiting that church. In fact, two days after, although at the time of the prediction she was perfectly well, she was attacked by a severe fever, which obliged her to keep her bed for many days, and as soon as she was sufficiently recovered, she was ordered by the doctors to return home without delay, which she did, and never again visited the church of S. Buonaventura, as Blessed Leonard had predicted.

Angela Savelli of Poggiomirteto, after remaining three years in the convent of S. Chiara, in Roccantica, for education, returned home, where Blessed Leonard, who was giving a mission in 1741, found her, and exhorted her to return to the same convent for three months, to perform all the spiritual exercises, and think seriously of her soul, as by these means she would learn the will of God regarding her state of life. The young girl obeyed, and was taken back to the convent by her mother, to remain for three months, and then return home. When the time came for her to leave the convent she was taken ill, but when the doctor came he found her free from fever; however, a few days after she became worse, and at noon on the same day, to the wonder of all who had heard of the advice given by Blessed Leonard, she passed from this world peacefully, and in dispositions of singular devotion and piety.

Maria Francesca Strafforello was placed in the convent of Port Maurice, her native place, for education, and Blessed Leonard being there on a mission in 1743, gave at the same time the religious exercises in the convent, where he had many conversations with her. Amongst other things which he exhorted her to do, one was to put on the religious habit, to observe the rule strictly, to be diligent in the acquisition of every virtue, and to prepare herself for eternity, for before she was twenty years of age an accident would happen to cause her death. A few days after the young girl assumed the religious habit, and took the name of Sister Anna Violante, and always remembering what the missionary had told her, lived in continual fear, and when she attained her nineteenth year, she began with much devotion to prepare for death. Amongst other things she provided herself with a skull, which she kept in her cell, and placing it before her eyes, employed herself in continual meditation, waiting the summons of her God. One day she was suddenly seized with inflammation, and in the belief that death was approaching, she became more than ever fervent in preparing for the great change, and related to the nuns for the first time what Blessed Leonard had predicted some years before. However, she recovered from this attack, but a short time after her foot became inflamed, in consequence of one of her toenails growing into the flesh. They sent for a surgeon, who found it necessary to perform a painful operation, which threw her into convulsions, and she became delirious. No remedy could be found, and at the end of three days she died, aged nineteen years and seven months, to the great grief and astonishment of the sisters who deposed to these facts.

In the same convent, and on the same occasion of the spiritual exercises being given, Anna Gandolfi, a native of Port Maurice, consulted Blessed Leonard regarding spiritual things, and imparted to him her desire to embrace the religious life. The father heard all she had to say, and then replied: "You will never be a nun;" and as she seemed displeased at this reply, and declared her determination, from which no one had ever attempted to turn her, he added: "Yes, my child you have now the desire to be clothed in the religious habit, but I tell you for all that you will never be a nun." Blessed Leonard left Port Maurice, and Anna went on persevering in her resolution for two years, at the end of which she desired to be received into the community. A chapter was held, and she was accepted; everything was prepared for the sacred function, which was to take place in a few days. In the meantime, the young girl expressed a desire to quit the convent to take leave of her relatives, declaring that she would soon return to the cloister, and assume the habit she so much desired; however, the pleasure of the world soon allured her, she thought no more of becoming a nun, married a gentleman of Sanremo, and died soon after in the bloom of youth, thus verifying the prediction of Blessed

Leonard.

There lived in the convent of S. Catherine of San Severino, one Angela Rosalia Servanzi, a penitent of Blessed Leonard. She was in perfect health, when one day he told her to prepare for eternity, as her death was near; and so it happened. When he was giving a mission in Frascati, Anna Antonia di Niccola came to make her general confession to him. When he had heard it he said to her: "You are about to give birth to a son; however, he will not be for you, but for Paradise." And so it was, for in the course of time a son was born to her, who died before he was seven months old. Not less extraordinary was his penetration in discerning the thoughts of his penitents, as will appear from the following facts.

Whilst he was giving missions in Aquila, in 1748, a man came to the house he occupied, with whom he had traveled some time before in going to the same place; and after some spiritual conversation begged him to hear his confession. The man of God received him with charity, bid him take courage, and exhorted him to make a good confession, for this holy inspiration had come from God. The penitent began his confession; seven months had passed since he had frequented the sacraments; having unburdened his conscience, or seemed to have done so, he concluded by saying those were all the sins he could call to his remembrance, when Father Leonard said to him: "No, my son, think a little better, make a more diligent examination, and you will find something more to confess." The man began to reflect more seriously on his past life, and then said that he remembered nothing else. Then the confessor went on to say: "But do you not remember that in a certain month and on a certain day you committed a mortal sin?" The penitent was astonished to hear his sin thus minutely recorded, which he had forgotten; and accusing himself, received absolution; he afterwards related what had happened to many persons, and after the death of Blessed Leonard gave his evidence juridically, for the glory of God and His servant.

When he was giving a mission in Ancona, Father Sanzi, prior of the Camaldolese, came to hear him preach, and in listening to his sermons, felt some doubts arise, which he determined to make known to the missionary. When the sermon was ended, and Blessed Leonard came down from the pulpit, he drew the father prior on one side, and, to his great astonishment, told him of the doubts that troubled his mind, and very soon put them to flight.

In the convent of Levanto there was a young religious who desired to confess to Blessed Leonard. He went accordingly to the convent, and heard the confessions of the nuns. The young woman above mentioned went in her turn, made her confession, and seemed quite contented, but on going over the examination of conscience again she felt scruples, and was much troubled. After having heard all the confessions of the community, Blessed Leonard sent for her, and desired her to make her confession again, and sent her away much consoled, and filled with wonder.

He was preaching on one occasion in the Campagna, near Rome, and amongst many who came to confess to him, was one who some years before had secretly committed a murder, which he had never had courage to confess. Many times he knelt at the feet of his confessor, and was about to confess this great sin, when the devil tempted him with various suggestions, and prevented him, and he added sin to sin by making many sacrilegious confessions and communions.

Blessed Leonard arrived in the town to give a mission, and the unfortunate man, tormented with remorse of conscience in listening to the sermons, became utterly miserable. He determined, however, to confess his crime, and disclose his sin to the missionary. Accordingly, he went to the man of God, began his confession, accusing himself of various sins, but when he was about to reveal the murder he was again tempted by the devil, and had not courage to accuse himself, and so ended his confession. The good father encouraged him, and told him to go on, for he was there to hear and absolve him from all sin; but the wretched man, yielding to the diabolical suggestions, replied that he had confessed all that troubled his conscience. On hearing this, Blessed Leonard said to him: "Since you have not courage to confess your sin, I will prompt you." He went on to say; "My brother, you have a garden, in which some years ago, in a certain month, and on a certain day, a man came in the dark to steal your artichokes. You were keeping guard over your garden, and had collected some stones together, and threw one of them at his head, and killed him on the spot. Finding that you had murdered him, you dug a hole under a fig-tree, and buried his body. This deed, although it was not seen by man, is written on high, and you have never had the courage to confess it; do so now, that you may receive pardon from Almighty God, who has mercifully waited for you so long." It may be imagined what the wretched man felt when he heard what had been done so many years before, thus minutely recorded, with all the circumstances, which could only be known to God; but he felt assured, although almost out of his senses, that the Lord Almighty had, for the good of his soul, revealed it to His servant. He quickly made a good confession, and some years afterwards, meeting with two monks of the same order as Blessed Leonard, he related to them the facts, and declared his deep obligation to him for being the means of saving his soul.

In 1748, having ended the missions in Arpino with great profit to the people, the nuns established there wished to hear him preach, and to obtain advice concerning their spiritual well-being, and the means of attaining perfection. They requested him, therefore, to visit their convent, and one of the community, who was advanced in years, came the first to consult him respecting her soul, without the intention of confessing, and told him she had nothing on her conscience. He listened for some time, and at last interrupted her, saying: "My daughter, I have no time to lose, you have something to confess, for when you were very young you committed a certain sin, which you have always forgotten to mention in your confessions. Is it not so? Now make your confession, and I am ready to give you absolution." The nun on hearing this remembered the fault she had committed, which, however, she had never confessed from forgetfulness, she was at first lost in amazement, but as soon as she had recovered, she returned thanks to God for having sent a man who had penetrated her conscience, and after the death of Blessed Leonard attested the fact juridically.

Many others have also declared that Blessed Leonard in hearing their confessions was so gifted with discretion and discernment, that he frequently reminded them of sins they had not courage to confess, or had entirely forgotten. It would be too long to mention all the instances, therefore I shall proceed to give an account of the other graces and gifts which God was pleased to bestow on His servant.

CHAPTER XVIII

Of Other Supernatural Gifts Bestowed by God on Blessed Leonard

OUR holy father does not appear to have possessed the gift of tongues, or to have been able to make himself understood by people of various nations, nor was this essential to him, since he never left Italy to preach to other people. However, Almighty God gave so much force to his voice, that he made many wonderful conversions, softening the hearts of the most hardened and obdurate sinners. Sufficient evidence is given of this in the first part of this history, in giving an account of his missions, as also the authentic testimony of those in authority, which is found at the end of his life, written by F. Raffaele of Rome, a religious in the same convent of S. Buonaventura, a contemporary of Blessed Leonard, and dedicated to the holy pontiff Benedict XIV, published in Rome in 1754.

This true testimonial assures us of his virtue and holiness, and cardinal Guadagni, at that time the pope's vicar, thus writes: "The word of God came with such force from his lips, that all who heard him were touched with compunction." Monsignore Don Ferdinando Romualdo Giuccioli, archbishop of Ravenna, expressed himself in the following terms: "The power of his voice, and the fame of his virtue, together made a wonderful impression on all hearts. In short, if he had not, as we have said, the gift of tongues, he worked miracles by the power and sweetness of his preaching; we may justly say that God "dedit voci suae vocem virtutis," and that the voice of Blessed Leonard was "Vox Domini in virtute, vox Domini in magnificentia, vox Domini confrigentis cedros." His voice was always sonorous and penetrating, and was heard at a great distance, and sometimes he seemed to have the power of making himself understood, when preaching in Italian, by those who knew not a word of the language. Whilst he was giving the mission in Assisi, at the German Conservatorio in that town, there was a young girl named Maria Cebidaure Adleri, who was placed there for her education, and afterwards became a nun in the convent of the Assumption at San Giusto. She had come from Germany a short time before the mission, and knowing nothing of the Italian language, refused to attend the sermons; however the confessor obliged her to go, when, to her great astonishment she felt that she understood the sermon quite well, and when she returned home, repeated the greater part of it in her own language most clearly and distinctly.

It pleased God also to give him power over the elements. When it threatened rain, he desired it would keep off until the sacred function was finished, that the people who came from a distance to attend the mission might not be prevented attending it. In 1744 he was giving missions in Vioreggio, in the diocese of Lucca, and as the church was not large enough to contain the number of people who came from the places in the neighborhood, he was obliged to preach in the Piazza. One day when the people were assembled expecting the sermon, it became suddenly dark, and the rain fell in torrents, and all ran to seek shelter, so that it became impossible for him to preach in the open air, or for the country people to return home. Blessed Leonard, in compassion towards them, and being desirous that they should hear the word of God, opened the window of the room in which he was, and made the sign of the cross in the air. To the astonishment of all, the rain instantly ceased, the clouds dispersed, and the sun shone brightly and clear, so that he was able to preach in the Piazza, and all returned home, praising and magnifying God in His servant. In another place, whilst he was preaching, a fearful thunderstorm came on, which terrified the audience, and torrents of rain began to fall; he desired them to say a Pater and Ave, and immediately the storm abated, and the rain ceased. This happened also in Monticelli, in the diocese of Tivoli, in Port Maurice, his native place, and elsewhere.

He had dominion also over the devil, as we shall see from the following fact. In 1742, when he was giving the mission in Piperno, a platform was raised near the high altar, on which he was to preach; it was constructed of boards, supported by poles tied together; and one of the confraternity of the Saccone knelt at his side, holding a crucifix. One day Tiburzio Zaccaglione was performing this office, out of devotion; he noticed that when Blessed Leonard had half finished his sermon he stopped, and stamping with his feet, said these words: "What, have you not done yet, beast?" Tiburzio was astonished, and knew not what he meant, but hearing a whispering in the crowd assembled below, he enquired into the cause, and found that all the ropes which bound the poles together were taken away, they knew not how, or by whom, and they feared the platform would fall with the missionary, and all who stood upon it; this would naturally have been the case, but Blessed Leonard, although he was aware of it, continued his sermon, pacing up and down on the platform as usual, as if nothing had happened. In fact, the people, seeing the cords cut in pieces, became alarmed, but the platform remained firm in its place without falling, as they expected. They could only suppose that the cutting of the ropes was the work of the devil, to interrupt the sacred function, and that Almighty God had interposed, and miraculously preserved them from the assaults of the enemy of mankind. All were agreed in this opinion, for no person had been seen to cut the ropes, and they were confirmed in it when Tiburzio told them of the words uttered by Blessed Leonard when he had paused in his sermon, which words he could not then understand. He and all assembled were persuaded that when he spoke and stamped with his feet, the devil was at work cutting the ropes, and to confound him, he obtained the miraculous interposition of God.

When he gave a mission in Porto di Fermo, Don Giovanni,

parish priest of Tochiano, saw Blessed Leonard raised two feet from the ground whilst he was praying before a crucifix, and from that time he held him in such high esteem, that he regarded him as a most holy man, and a servant of God. He was also seen by a priest at Montecchio, when he was preaching in the piazza, walking across the platform, without touching it with his feet, and standing for some time raised a foot above it. Tho same priest also declared that he seated himself on the highest step of the platform to listen to the sermon, to assure himself of this fact.

The Preposto of Dulcedo, a learned and good man, on one occasion went to Port Maurice to visit Blessed Leonard, who was giving a mission there; and he declares that on entering the house, and opening the door of the room in which he was very quietly, he beheld him surrounded by bright rays of light; lost in wonder and fear he closed the door, and went away without speaking to him, reserving what he had to say for another occasion. Maria Teresa Mindes, fell sick in Florence, and desired that Blessed Leonard might be sent for to hear her confession; her servant, Antonio Burresi, went for him, as his wife, who is still living, can testify. He went to the monastery and asked for Blessed Leonard, saying that his mistress was ill and desired to confess to him; he was told that he had left Florence for Rome some days before, and returned to inform his mistress of this fact, who at first was much distressed and disappointed, but soon became resigned to the will of God. About a quarter of an hour after she had received this intelligence, she saw Blessed Leonard admitted into her room by the same Antonio, who remained waiting outside the door, to show the holy father out of the house; presently he heard his mistress call him, and ran quickly to her bedside, when she reproved him for having falsely reported that Blessed Leonard was not in Rome, for that she had just seen him in her room, and that he himself had conducted him there. Antonio replied that he had certainly been told so at the monastery, but for all that, he had to his great astonishment seen him there, and had opened the door to admit him into her room, but that he had not seen him come out, though he had never left the hall, and that he knew not whether he had come out, or where he was, but supposed that he was in her room hearing her confession. The lady was amazed on hearing this, and caused an inquiry to be made, and a search through Florence, but he had not been seen by anyone else either there or in the neighborhood; she therefore returned thanks to God for the grace and consolation she had received in so wonderful and miraculous a way.

In January, 1742, Blessed Leonard was sent to give a mission in Bocchignano, and was lodged in the house of Signor Xavier Guadagni, who gave up to the missioners a large hall, part of which was divided into small rooms; he was taken to that destined for him, and Signor Guadagni shut the door after him, and went to speak to the arch-priest of the place, leaving Blessed Leonard in his room. Meanwhile his companions went to church to prepare all that was necessary for beginning the mission, and Signor Guadagni remembering that he had left some papers in a box in one of the rooms, went for them. Feeling sure that no one was in the room, he opened the door without hesitation, and to his astonishment found Blessed Leonard kneeling on the bed in prayer, surrounded by flowers and beautiful fruit; he was so affected at the sight, that he closed the door without making any noise, and returned to relate what he had seen to the arch-priest, who was equally astonished. Their wonder increased when they reflected that a very short time before they had left him, in the room assigned to him, and that he must have passed invisibly through the hall where they were standing to go into the room where they now found him. They were lost in wonder at so extraordinary an occurrence, and returning again, looked through a hole in the door, and there beheld the holy father in the same posture, surrounded by flowers and fruit. In the meantime his companions returned from the church to tell him that everything was prepared for beginning the mission, and Blessed Leonard appeared in readiness to go and preach his first sermon; but before he went out he desired Guadagni to remove two pictures from the room appropriated for him, as they were not quite appropriate, and he was quickly obeyed. As soon as Blessed Leonard left the house, Guadagni feeling most desirous to behold the unusual sight of fruit and flowers in the depth of winter, made his way in all haste to the room, but all had disappeared, nothing remained but the most fragrant odor.

To this miracle many more might be added, but sufficient has been detailed to prove that Almighty God endowed Blessed Leonard with many supernatural gifts; and as he preached for the honor and glory of God, so He was pleased to confirm his preaching by wonderful signs and miracles. It may be said of him, as it was of the first apostles: "But they going forth, preached everywhere: the Lord working withal, and confirming the words with signs that followed." Mark 16:20.

CHAPTER XIX

Various Cures Wrought by Blessed Leonard During His Life

PIETRO Bitti, a Roman, had a thorn in one of his thumbs, which inflamed his hand, and finding no doctor to extract it, he went to Blessed Leonard in the monastery of S. Buonaventura, and asked him to prescribe something. The holy Father blessed him with the little image of the Madonna which he carried about with him, when immediately his hand was cured, and he never again suffered from the same cause.

Rosa Pecci, of Mantelica, was suffering from an internal disorder, and feeling a great repugnance to be examined by a doctor, went to make her confession to Blessed Leonard, and disclosed to him her distress, when he assured her that there would be no necessity even to describe her sufferings to anyone. And so it happened, for in a few days she was cured of the malady without medical aid, and was ever after free from it. In the Island of Corsica, it happened one day that a girl of eighteen, who was working in the fields, fell asleep with her mouth open; a serpent crept in; and awaking in terror, she had not the presence of mind to pull it out; it consequently entered her stomach, and there remained for some months, causing her the greatest pain and torture; she was always obliged to carry a piece of bread with her, and be constantly eating, to feed the serpent; she suffered dreadfully night and day, without being able to sleep, and very soon was reduced to a mere shadow, and excited the compassion of all who beheld her. After having tried every means to destroy it without success, she was taken by her father and brother to Rostino, in the diocese of Mariana, where Blessed Leonard was giving a mission. They reached the place about noon, after many days' journey, when they found he had just arrived; at the church door, when he was going to say mass, he found the poor girl lying, overcome by fatigue and the excessive heat, for it was July. Blessed Leonard desired one of his companions to ask what was the matter with her, whilst he went to the sacristy and vested himself. The companion gave his blessing to the unfortunate girl, and she went into the church to mass, even there she was obliged to be constantly eating bread to appease the serpent, which never ceased gnawing and torturing her. As soon as mass was ended she was taken to the sacristy, and prostrating herself on the floor at his feet, she implored Blessed Leonard with tears to help her. He listened to the facts, and seeing the poor girl so reduced and suffering, was touched with compassion, and drew from his sleeve his little image of the Madonna, and saying three Aves, gave her benediction with it. Instantly the serpent was quiet, and the poor girl free from pain; she left Rostino with her relations to return home, and before they had proceeded far, she vomited forth the serpent dead and in pieces. The fame of this miraculous cure was spread through the island, and added considerably to the esteem and veneration of the people for Blessed Leonard, so that he was known everywhere by the name of the "holy Father Leonard."

When he was giving a mission in Orezza, also in Corsica, a girl was brought to him who had been dumb for some time, to the great distress of her parents, especially her mother, who never ceased lamenting and weeping over the misfortune of her child. They were induced to bring her to Blessed Leonard, who blessed her with his image of the Madonna, and then celebrated the holy sacrifice, at which she attended with her parents. They returned home, and she went to bed at the usual hour; in the middle of the night she awoke, and began to speak distinctly. The sound of her voice awakened the mother, who got up and enquired who was speaking in the room, the girl replied: "It is I, who have received the gift of speech from the good missionary." Her parents rejoiced exceedingly, and in the morning went with her to church, where they returned thanks to God for the benefit received; and all the people hearing the poor girl, who had been dumb for years, speak distinctly, gave praise to God, and marveled at the wonders worked by His servant.

In Toffia, in the abbacy of Farfa, he blessed with his Image of the Madonna, the son of Signor Antonio Calandra, who was lame in one leg, which he always had bound with ligatures, when he instantly found himself cured, and his limb perfectly straight. In another place in the same neighborhood, named Monte Santa Maria, a woman touched the eyes of her blind child with a piece of the habit of Blessed Leonard, and instantly his sight was restored.

Luigi Sabbatini, of Todi, after a long illness became dropsical, and his body was so swollen that he excited the compassion of all who beheld him. The doctors wished to draw off the water, but on considering the case, they found an operation would be useless, and that he was not in a state to bear it. He remained in this pitiable condition for a year, when Blessed Leonard came to the town to give a mission. One evening after the sermon the missionary was returning home, when he met Luigi, and moved with compassion said to him: "Be very devout to the holy mother of God," and making the sign of the cross on his forehead and breast, he left him. The sick man returned home and went to bed, when he suddenly began to sweat profusely, the water oozed from every pore in his skin, and in the morning he found himself not in the least swollen, free from pain, and in perfect health, and he continued so as long as he lived, without having recourse to medicine or natural remedies.

Whilst Blessed Leonard was giving the missions in Massa Lombarda, in the diocese of Imola, he was requested to visit the wife of Gabriele Zeroni, who had been ill for five years, and never left her bed. Scarcely had the servant of God entered the house, and was seen by the patient, than she raised herself up and declared that she felt quite well. In the same place he was sent for to visit the wife of Dr. Achille Gabioni, who was suffering from dropsy, and restored her to perfect health. When he left Massa Lombarda to go to Argenta, he was followed by many of the people, who entreated him to go into the house of a woman who had been ill for some time, and desired his blessing; he entered the room where she lay, gave her his blessing, and desired her to get up, and instantly she arose from her bed quite cured, to the wonder of all present.

In the year 1739, when he was giving a mission in Ancona, he was sent for to hear the confessions of the nuns in the convent of S. Palazia, amongst whom was one named Sister Maria Rosalbella Pamocchi, who had not risen from her bed for three years, suffering acute pain in her side, which sometimes took away her breath, and having had recourse to every remedy that art could suggest, without any avail, her disorder was considered, humanly speaking, incurable. On the morning Blessed Leonard went to the convent to hear confessions, as soon as she beheld him she was quite free from pain, but as soon as he left the room it returned. He went after breakfast to the confessional, and sending for the mother-superior, desired her to tell Sister Maria Rosalbella, that S. Vincent Ferrer had obtained for her the blessing of health, and that she was to get up and come to the confessional. The mother-superior, who was aware of the state she was in, was astonished at this command, but the high esteem in which she held the missionary induced her to obey him quickly; she went to the cell of the sick sister, whom she found had risen in perfect health, dressed herself, and was ready to go to the confessional; she then made her confession to Blessed Leonard, who assured her that she would never again suffer from the same malady. However, some years after this she was taken ill, and became swollen from head to foot, and not finding any remedy, had recourse again to Blessed Leonard, who was then giving a mission in Monte Filatrano, in the diocese of Osimo; she wrote to him describing her sufferings, and at the moment when she reckoned that he would receive her letter, the swelling abated, and she lived for years in perfect health.

When he was on the point of leaving Mantelica, Francesca Benigni, a blind woman, was brought by her husband and son into the street through which he was passing, and all three threw themselves at his feet, entreating him to restore the sight of a poor blind woman, that she might gain the means of living. The prayer of the poor people reached his ears, he stopped, and telling them to have faith and say an Ave Maria, he gave them his little image of the Madonna to kiss, and went on his way. In a moment the poor woman felt her sight return, and walking steadily without a guide, she went into the church of the Trinita to return thanks to our Blessed Lady, and from that time until her death she had the perfect use of her sight.

Having finished the missions in Castel Nuovo in Farfa, the arch-priest Don Giacinto Nobile, desired, in devotion, to accompany him to Poggio Mirteto, and passing by Bocchignano, his native place, he invited him to stay at his house. Blessed Leonard accepted the invitation, and on entering the house Vittoria, the wife of Silvestro Nobile, advanced to meet him with her little son in her arms, who was so deformed that he was a most pitiable object; besides other defects, he had a hunch on his back, and another on his breast. The poor mother cast herself at the feet of Blessed Leonard weeping, and entreated him to touch her child, and with his blessing to cure him of his deformity. Moved with compassion for the child and the mother, who declared that she would never cease to thank God if he would obtain this blessing, he turned to the bystanders, and said to them: "You see what faith she has;" gave his blessing to the child, and assured his mother he would soon be cured. And so it was, for the following morning Vittoria awoke, and found her child perfectly straight and healthy, free from all those defects which caused him to be looked upon as a monster; and he remained so as long as he lived, to the great joy of his relatives, and especially the arch-priest his uncle, who was present, and deposed the facts to the glory of God.

When he was passing through Colle, in the diocese of Rieti, he was asked to preach, and on his way to the church he was stopped by a man who entreated him to come to the aid of Giuseppe Federici, who had been confined to his bed for some time with rheumatic fever, which caused him severe pain, and prevented his sleeping. Blessed Leonard desired them to bring him to the church to hear the sermon, which they did, and placed him on a seat. When the sermon was ended they carried him to the sacristy, where the minister of God signed him with the sign of the cross, and instantly he was free from pain, and returned home walking without any assistance, resumed his work as a laborer in the fields, and never had a return of the disorder as long as he lived.

Pietro Difolco, a woolen draper, came from Arpino to Rome to buy wool, but on his arrival he was seized with gout in his hands and feet, so that he was unable to negotiate his business. As time passed he became impatient, and one day made an effort to walk out, though in great pain, supporting himself with a crutch, when he met Blessed Leonard passing through the piazza with his companion. Pietro came forward to kiss his hand, but he could only move slowly, and would not have succeeded if Blessed Leonard had not stopped to speak to some person. Seeing him standing he took hold of his cloak, which he perceiving, inquired what was the matter. Pietro replied, that he was suffering intense pain from the gout in his feet and hands, and entreated his aid. Hearing this, Blessed Leonard made the sign of the cross on his hands and feet, and instantly he was free from pain, was able that same day to attend to his business, and never again had an attack of gout, as he deposed on oath.

When he was giving a mission in Arpino, he was returning one evening from the church, and found Giacinta Quaglieri Fiortetta, who told him she had brought her son, a child about three years old, called Gaetano, to receive his blessing. Both his legs were deformed, and his feet so crippled, he could not stand upright or walk a step. The afflicted mother entreated the missionary to have mercy on her child, who, unable to work, would be obliged to beg his bread. Blessed Leonard was moved to compassion on seeing the poor little deformed creature, and making over him the sign of the cross, said to the mother: "Go; your son is healed of his infirmity." Giacinta returned home quite consoled, hoping that from the words spoken by the servant of God she might be so blessed, and put her child to bed. The following morning, to her great joy and astonishment, she found him quite well, his legs perfectly straight, and he was able to walk; and after he was dressed he ran out of the house, and in a little while she saw him playing with the children in the street, to their great wonder, for they had always seen him carried in his mother's arms. Carlo Morelli, also of Arpino, after having for some time suffered from leprosy, was at last cured by means of medicine; his hands, however, remained swollen and spotted. Not knowing how to get rid of the evil, he was recommended to wash his hands in the water which months before had been used by Blessed Leonard, and which had been kept as a relic. He was induced to bathe his hands several times with it, and the swelling soon abated, and the spots disappeared, so that no one could ever suppose that he had been afflicted with that dreadful disease.

Father Sebastiano da Zinoni, priest of the order of the reformed Franciscans of Turin, when he was in Florence in the convent dell Monte, obtained, out of devotion, a piece of bread loft by Blessed Leonard at dinner, and preserved it with great care. On the 23rd of June, 1751, he was in the plain of Pistoia, and was sent for to visit Joseph Capecchio, whom he found lying in bed, and suffering great agony in a high fever; his death was expected every moment Father Sebastiano, touched with compassion, gave a cup of water, with a small portion of the bread before mentioned, to the sick man, who instantly rose up in his bed in perfect health, and gave alms in wine to the Father, who was on a begging mission from the monastery. Two days after Joseph Capecchio met Father Sebastiano in Pistoia, and said to him: "May you be blessed, Father! for Almighty God sent you with that holy bread, which has been to me as the manna of Paradise, for I had scarcely taken it when my fever abated, and I no longer felt the slightest pain, and I am now as strong as if I had never been ill."

The same F. Sebastiano was sent one evening by the Prior of S. Rocca, in Pistoia, to confess a man who was at the point of death, to whom, after having administered the sacraments, he gave a portion of the bread which he kept as a relic of Blessed Leonard, and the following morning the man rose from his bed perfectly well. Maria Mazzei, of Poggia, was cured in the same miraculous manner. She was lying sick of a fever, and recovered as soon as she had eaten a piece of the bread. To many others Almighty God restored health at the prayer of His servant whilst he was on earth. It would take too long to relate all the instances, and I shall proceed to relate the miracles wrought after his death.

CHAPTER XX

On the Various Cures Effected Through the Merits of Blessed Leonard in Answer to Those Who Invoked His Assistance.

THE virtues and gifts with which Blessed Leonard was endowed caused him to be held in such high esteem and veneration by the people, that they called him the Apostolic man, the Apostle of our times, a man filled with the Holy Spirit, and the holy Father. This veneration was found not only in the common and simple people, but also in most learned ecclesiastics and people in the highest grade, as well as in most eminent cardinals, and many bishops, whose dioceses he enlightened by his missions. This great esteem caused many to come to the convent of S. Buonaventura, to touch his body as soon as they heard of his death, and to obtain some relic of him. Many also gave him the title of Saint, and very soon after his death images were made of him, which, with the things he had worn or used, were in great request, even in remote parts of the country, and were preserved with singular devotion.

As a proof of the veneration in which he was held in Rome, his funeral was conducted with the greatest solemnity in the church of the Rotunda, and a secular priest pronounced the funeral oration, which was afterwards published. It began thus: "The apostolic man was held in the highest veneration by men, because he was believed to be a man of God, and filled with the Holy Spirit," etc. The Genoese also desired to give testimony of their veneration for our holy Father, and published, as soon as his death was announced, a print dedicated to the Pope, which was composed of a shield, with a ship representing the Church, which destroys all heresies, and within it the three theological virtues, with a corresponding inscription in praise of this great man.

Almighty God confirmed the universal veneration for His servant by working many miracles after his death, in restoring to health those who had recourse to his intercession, some of which we shall relate. Maddelena of Rocchetta, in the diocese of Spoleti, the wife of Giacomo Arcari, had an infant four months old, named Agostino, who from his birth had been covered with sores, so that the skin adhered to the cloths with which his mother covered him; his head, moreover, was one horrible sore, and he excited the compassion of all who beheld him. Ten days after the death of Blessed Leonard, Maddelena dreamt that he appeared to her, that she kissed his hand, and entreated him to heal her son, and he seemed to grant her prayer. Full of joy and faith she went the same day to the church of S. Buonaventura, carrying her child in her arms, to place him on the tomb of the blessed servant of God. On entering the church she found it so crowded that it was with the greatest difficulty she could approach the screen of the chancel, before the high altar, where the tomb of Blessed Leonard was; but she took courage, and putting her child through the grate, entreated a man who stood within to place him on the tomb, as she was unable to do so herself, in consequence of the crowd. The man complied with her request, and the child had scarcely been there while you could say a *Pater Noster*, when he was seen to smile, and appear quite joyous, and very soon he was brought back to his mother perfectly well, not a sore was to be seen in any part of his body, and his head, which had been so disfigured, was covered with hair.

Anna Maria Calandrelli, after having twice miscarried, heard that another woman similarly afflicted had happily given birth to a child after wearing a piece of the habit of Blessed Leonard whilst he was living; she prayed to God that if ever she was again pregnant she might, through his intercession, bring the infant she expected safely into the world. A few months after this she was again with child, and suffering much from pain and fever, she was in great fear. One night, towards the end of November, 1751, a few days after the death of Blessed Leonard, the intelligence of which had not reached Arpino, where she lived, in her sleep she felt a hand on her head, and on awaking found herself free from pain, and by the light of the lamp which was burning in the room she perceived Blessed Leonard, whom she recognized, having often attended his missions; he said to her, "You will recover; place my habit on your back, and fear not." Having said these words, he disappeared, and she composed herself to sleep again; but in a few minutes awoke, and saw, for the second time in the same place, Blessed Leonard, who repeated the same words, desired her to hear mass every day, and disappeared. The following day she inquired of everyone she knew in Arpino where she could procure a piece of Blessed Leonard's habit, and having succeeded in obtaining it, she wore it constantly with devotion and faith. The effect was most evident, since if by chance she forgot to put it on, the pains returned. When her time came she was in pain for eight days, and then gave birth to a son, to whom in gratitude she gave the name of Leonard.

Giuseppe Orsolino, of Genoa, a mason, in devotion to Blessed Leonard always wore a piece of his habit, and when he heard of his death, said every day three Paters, Aves, and Glorias, because he believed him to be a holy man. About a week after his death, he was employed in placing a ladder across a street in Genoa, in order to prop up a wall which was falling. He was advised by a friend, Stefano Brenati, who was passing through the street, to take care, for there was danger of his being crushed beneath the wall, which was sixty feet high. Giuseppe replied, that he had no fear, for he wore a piece of Blessed Leonard's habit, and he would save him by his intercession from being hurt. Stefano went on his way, and in a little while the wall gave way, the ladder was broken in pieces, and Giuseppe fell from the height, but in his fall he invoked the aid of Blessed Leonard, who, in his habit of a Franciscan monk, came to his assistance, took him by the hand, and drew him out from the ruins. Giuseppe went to the hospital of Pamattone, where they bound up a wound in his head. It was feared he was injured internally, and this fear was increased the following day, by his feeling violent pains in every part of his body, so that he was not able to move. He again recommended himself to the prayers of Blessed Leonard, who appeared to him in the night when he was sleeping, and told him that he might return to his work. In the morning he awoke and found himself perfectly well, rose from his bed, and returned home; he afterwards juridically deposed to the miracle.

Sister Maria Fortunata, di Gesú, a nun in the convent of Moricone, in Sabina, suffered for some time from a terrible illness, which caused her very often to fall suddenly to the ground, to the great distress of the sisters. She was induced to invoke the assistance of Blessed Leonard to release her from so severe and dangerous an illness. One night the holy father appeared to her in a dream, and reproved her for not having followed the instructions he had given her when she made her general confession to him, assured her, however, that she would not suffer any more from that illness, but that she would have a constant headache. And so it happened, for she was forever free from the fits to which she had been subject, but constantly suffered violent pain in her head, as the holy servant of God had predicted.

Don Bernardino Talcioni, of Belmonte, in the diocese of Rieti, a priest aged sixty-three years, was attacked by a severe fit of rheumatism, which kept him in bed for two days, and he suffered the greatest pain whenever he tried to move. One night he thought he saw, as he afterwards attested juridically, Blessed Leonard with his little image of the Madonna, and in the morning when he awoke he beheld him visibly at the side of his bed seated on a footstool, and dressed in a beautiful robe. Thus sitting he spoke, and assured him that he would soon be free from pain, and added, that Niccola, his niece, had greatly benefitted in a place where she had gone to take the air for her health's sake; he then added, "Eviva la croce,"[3] and disappeared. The sick man felt himself at that moment perfectly cured of his rheumatism, and called out quite joyfully, "I am quite well and free from pain." He got up, and went to offer the Holy Sacrifice, returning thanks to God and His servant.

Maddalena Romagnoli Sciarbonieri, of Zagarola, at that time living in Rome, was afflicted for some months with an illness which caused her excessive pain, for which she had tried every remedy that art could invent; she was constantly confined to her bed, and when the paroxysms came on, she groaned and screamed so fearfully, that the people passing in the streets stopped with wonder, and asked the cause of the noise. After having suffered in this way for some time, she had recourse to the intercession of Blessed Leonard, and on the 22nd of May, 1752, she was taken by her husband in a carriage to the church of S. Buenaventura; she was carried by two persons, for she was unable to walk, to the tomb of Blessed Leonard, where, with her arms stretched out, and prostrate with her face to the ground, she began to weep, and after having prayed earnestly for some time, she concluded her prayer with these words: "Father Leonard, I will not go away and leave your tomb until you have granted my petition." The moment she uttered these words, she raised herself, to the astonishment of all present, and walked through the church, visited all the altars, and then returned home, full of joy and gratitude, declaring that she felt quite well. She remained in this state of perfect health for three days, when she was again attacked with the same disorder; and raving more than ever, she bewailed her misfortune. They induced her to bless herself with a small quantity of oil from the lamp in the

---

[3] "Long live the cross."

church of the "Madonna del Divino Amore," but her sufferings still continued, and she endured for thirty days such martyrdom, that she could not sleep, even with the aid of opium. On the morning of the 4th of July, the pains became so violent that it was thought she could not survive; she again had recourse to Blessed Leonard, and raising her voice, said with great faith: "Father Leonard, I entreat your assistance, pray give me a token of it." She then took a small fragment of his habit in water, and soon after fell asleep, and those who were attending on her left the room; this was about ten o'clock in the morning. A short time after, she was half awake, or dozing, when she saw Blessed Leonard appear, take the stuff, and dip it in the oil before mentioned, and having desired her to be very devout to the Holy Virgin, he made the sign of the cross over her, replaced the piece of habit where he found it, and making a genuflection before the image of the Blessed Virgin, which was in the room, disappeared. She became perfectly well from that moment, and calling to her attendants, who were in the adjoining room, related to them what had occurred, and afterwards attested it juridically.

Maria, the daughter of Giovanni Tubelli, of Gerano, a young woman about twenty-five years of age, having by accident taken poison, was for twenty-four hours tortured with severe internal pains; and although they had administered an antidote, and she had vomited up part of the poison, she suffered intense pain from laceration in the intestines. The doctors decided that it was impossible she could survive, and she received the last sacraments from the archpriest, Don Domenico Perelli, and Don Francesco Pozzi, who expected her death every moment. At four o'clock on the morning of the 2nd of August, it occurred to the archpriest to give the dying woman a portion of the habit of Blessed Leonard, which he had in his house; he went for it, and returning quickly, asked her if she had ever heard of this holy man; she having replied in the affirmative by an inclination of her head, the archpriest continued: "Very well; I have brought you a bit of his habit; have faith; and if you receive grace and favor you must make your deposition, which shall be sent to Rome." Having said this, he cut off a very small portion of the cloth, said three Aves to the Blessed Virgin, and one Pater and Ave to Blessed Leonard, put it in a little water, and gave it to the sick woman, when she swallowed it; she remained for about the time it would take to say the creed twice quite immoveable, with her eyes wide open, as if she were in an ecstasy, and then turning to the archpriest, she said quite briskly: "I am cured; I no longer feel the least pain; go and thank God for me, and take some repose." However, they were unwilling to leave her so soon, and desired her to return thanks, whilst they conversed together, but she entreated them to leave her, and they were obliged to go to keep her quiet, but before they went they said three Paters and three Aves to the Holy Trinity, the Litany of the Blessed Virgin, and one Pater and Ave to Blessed Leonard, to return thanks for this miraculous cure. The following day, the young woman told the archpriest that during the time she was immoveable, as if in ecstasy, with her eyes open, she saw Blessed Leonard, who, after having told her that she was cured by the will of God, having exhorted her to obey the Divine Will in all things, and to be very devout to the Blessed Virgin Mary, disappeared. Four days after this the court of Subiaco went to Gerano to take the deposition of the young woman, and to ascertain who had given her the poison, and to analyze what she had vomited, but in vain; it had been thrown away; however, they gave her an antidote, when she vomited more of the poison, which had remained in her stomach after the cure was effected without giving her the least pain or inconvenience, so that there could be no doubt of the miracle, which was attested by the doctor in attendance, Giambattista Gentilezza, the two priests, and Maria Tubelli herself.

Angola, the wife of Andrea Micheletti, of Terra di Nerola, in Sabina, had a daughter named Maria Antonia, who fell sick of the smallpox, which left a weakness in her back and knees, so that she was bent double, and could scarcely walk. On the Feast of the Purification, the 2nd of February, 1777, Angela had recourse to the intercession of Blessed Leonard, who appeared in the evening, and she repeated her prayer, entreating him either to cure her daughter, or take her to heaven, desiring rather that she should die than to see her so pitiable an object. The following day, to her great joy and wonder, she found her daughter perfectly well, and took her to mass to return thanks; she never had a return of the malady as long as she lived.

At Posticciola, in Sabina, the priest Don Domenico, a native of Borgo San Pietro, after a long illness was attacked by a complaint in his throat, which brought him to the point of death. He recommended himself to Blessed Leonard, who the same night appeared to him, made the sign of the cross on his brow and throat; he awoke soon after, and found himself perfectly well and free from pain.

Angelo Manni, priest of Terni, also attested that after having suffered from a severe illness for some months, arising from an abscess in his side, fever, and other evils, he had recourse to Blessed Leonard. The doctors had pronounced his case hopeless, for they had tried every remedy without avail; one day the pain was so great that he became quite delirious, and his groans and screams were heard through the house; his friends gave him a towel which had been used by Blessed Leonard, and he in devotion applied it to his side, and threw himself with his face on a bed, with his feet resting on the floor. Whilst he lay in this position, he felt a hand on his forehead, and heard a voice telling him to arise. He instantly stood up, and declared he was quite free from pain, and walked about the house quite joyfully, saying: "I am restored to perfect health; Father Leonard has relieved me from all pain he also attested that he never again suffered from the same malady. Lastly, we shall relate what we have heard from a learned and pious priest, that Blessed Leonard appeared to one of his penitents, whose name does not appear, accompanied by a great number of souls, saved through his means, saying: "Behold how God in His goodness acts towards us, for through His grace did I preach; through Him did I receive strength, power, voice, and everything, and He has rewarded me, as if they had been my own."

CHAPTER XXI

Other Miraculous Cures Wrought by Blessed Leonard after His Death

ARIA MADDALENA PALLARI, of Pergola, whilst she was in Rome suffered for some time from a swelling in her leg, which made her very lame, and she was not able to walk without the greatest pain and inconvenience. After suffering in this manner for eight years, she went to the tomb of Blessed Leonard, and when she was praying there the swelling suddenly abated, the pain ceased, she recovered the use of her leg, and returned home quite well.

In Torri, in the Abbacy of San Salvatore Maggiore, the wife of Antonio Lepori was afflicted with a severe illness, and it was thought she must soon die. After having applied every remedy without avail, she was induced to wear a piece of the habit of Blessed Leonard, when she was instantly freed from pain. A short time after, she mislaid the relic, and the pains returned; but finding it again she applied it a second time, and instantly she was freed from pain as before. After this experience she always wore it, and remained perfectly well as long as she lived.

Giuseppe Raffi, of Fara, a tailor by trade, in striking a dog with a tool hurt his hand severely; the wound became black, and turned to a gangrene; mortification ensued, and the doctors decided that the hand must be amputated. In great fear and trouble Giuseppe had recourse to the aid of Blessed Leonard, and had so much faith in his intercession, that he was induced to touch his hand with a piece of his habit, and instantly he was cured.

Sister Chiara Francesca Tuani, a nun in the convent of S. Chiara in Sarzana, where she had been educated, suffered much from an abscess in her left foot; the sore had festered, and although it had been lanced and burnt with caustic, it did not heal, and she was unable to walk. The abbess, seeing the evil increase, so that the bone of her foot was visible, deemed it necessary to try some other remedy, but nothing they did was of any avail, and at length they had recourse to the intercession of Blessed Leonard, and at the same time applied to the sore a piece of his handkerchief. Having done this she slept quietly that night, which she had not done for some time, and in the morning the sore was perfectly healed.

Maria Giovanni, wife of Signor Paolo Panizza, living in Masserano, in the diocese of Vercelli, for eight years suffered from a nervous affection, which caused her great pain; and after trying many remedies, and consulting many doctors, it was decided to be chronic, and incurable. In short, for four months, she was never free from pain, and was reduced to a perfect skeleton. One day a monk came to her house, who gave her a piece of Blessed Leonard's habit, and a morsel of the bread left by him at table; she ate a little of the bread, and hung the piece of cloth round her neck, when she instantly felt a shock in her system, and from that moment recovered her health, and was free from pain as long as she lived.

In the town of Aquila, a little girl three years old, niece of the priest, and also of Don Venanzio de Bernardis, was seized with fever, and on the fifth day she was reduced to the last extreme; her parent and uncle wept, thinking her dead. Whilst the child remained in this state, silent and immoveable, her uncle implored the assistance of Blessed Leonard, promising that if he heard his prayer, he would make a public attestation of the cure. He therefore took a relic of the man of God, which he had in the house, said three Paters and three Aves, made the sign of the cross over the dying child, who the same moment opened her eyes, spoke distinctly, and asked for something to eat; she then rose up and walked across the room, to the astonishment of all present; her uncle felt her pulse, and found her quite free from fever and perfectly well, and she continued so, as Don Venanzio afterwards attested juridically.

Donna Costante Maria Salvatore, a nun of the convent of the Annunciation in Mantelica, of the order of S. Benedict, in 1744 was struck on the head by a heavy weight, and in consequence a tumor formed the size of an egg, which, in the course of time, disappeared. A few months afterwards she was again struck on the head in opening a window, which came with sudden force against her. She suffered intense pain, and frequently her mind was seriously affected, and she went about the convent at times quite like an idiot, and at length became perfectly deaf, was not able to walk without crutches, and could retain nothing on her stomach; the pain was sometimes so violent, that it was thought she could not survive from day to day. Some years after this, she again had a severe blow on the head, which caused a fainting fit, and she was carried to her bed, to which she was confined for a long time; and her malady increased so rapidly, that her death was daily expected. Meanwhile the intelligence of the death of Blessed Leonard reached Mantelica, and the nuns implored his intercession, and having sent to Rome for a piece of his habit, they applied it to her ears, for the agony she endured was such as to deprive her of the sense of hearing, and she lay apparently unconscious of what was passing around her. Scarcely had they applied the relic when she felt, as she afterwards deposed, something like myriads of ants creeping round her head, and after sneezing violently, she found herself quite free from pain, arose and went into the choir along with the community; they were all filled with wonder, and praised God for the mercy and favor vouchsafed to their sister. She never had a return of the disorder.

Marcantonio Minna, of Pofi, in the diocese of Veroli, was sick of a malignant fever, and after having tried every remedy without avail, was given up by the doctor, received the sacraments, and seemed at the point of death. One of his relatives bound a piece of the habit of Blessed Leonard to his arm, imploring his assistance, when immediately he became well, to the astonishment of the doctor, who attested the fact.

Violante Maidé, in Rome, had a gangrene in her leg, which had so corroded her flesh, that there was a hole large enough to contain a roll, she was given up by the surgeons, who considered the case incurable. Reduced to this state, she had recourse to the intercession of Blessed Leonard, entreated him to hear her, and promised that if her prayer was granted, she would give her deposition juridically, and bring a silver leg to his tomb as a votive offering. She then applied a bit of his habit to the wound, when instantly the pain ceased, and in a short time she was entirely cured, and fulfilled her promise.

Don Carlo Maria Carpano Busti, of Villicino, in the diocese of Milan, for the space of ten years was troubled in the spring, especially in traveling, with a severe complaint in his throat, for which he had consulted many doctors without alleviation; having heard of the holiness of Blessed Leonard, and the favors granted to him by Almighty God through his merits, he determined to have recourse to him. One evening of February, 1756, he was suffering more than usual, and being employed in reading the life of the holy Father, began to feel a devotion to him, and so much faith in his intercession, that he knelt down and entreated his aid; he had scarcely concluded his prayer when he felt perfectly cured, and never suffered again from the disorder as long as he lived.

Catherine Carozina, of Genoa, for twelve years was tormented by severe suffering, which sometimes deprived her of her senses for many hours, and frequently she had been at the point of death, and the doctors by whom she was attended had tried every remedy in vain. In January, 1752, her malady had increased rapidly, and in addition to it, she had violent pains in her head, and sometimes vomited blood; her case was decided to be quite hopeless. Catterina on learning this had recourse to the intercession of Blessed Leonard, and having obtained a piece of his habit, applied it with firm faith, and instantly found herself free from all pain, and arose from her bed to return thanks to Almighty God and His servant, and she afterwards gave her deposition juridically.

Sister Maria Bocella, a nun in the convent of San Niccolo Novella, in Lucca, after having had epileptic fits for some time, for which no human remedy was found of any avail, on the night of the 21st of October, 1769, was attacked by a violent fever, and reduced to the last extremity. In her distress she turned with faith to Blessed Leonard, and entreated him to help her, reminding him of the promise he had made her before his death, that if he was received into Paradise he would aid her. In the morning she found herself quite well, and healed of her malady. This miraculous cure is referred to by Catterina in two sonnets which she composed; in the first, she describes her illness; and in the second, relates how she was released from it; the sonnet concludes with these words:

> "Ne seppi allor, che avenne di me stessa
> So ben che grazia ricevei compita
> Sorgendo sana allo spuntar d' Aurora."[4]

Giuseppe, a child of seven years old, the son of Benedetto Gai, a Roman, was affected with a tumor in his right arm, the size of a large apple, which caused him severe pain, and after suffering for some months, he was obliged to undergo an operation; the tumor was lanced, and a quantity of matter was drawn from it. For a long time after this the sore remained open, and nothing that was applied had the effect of healing it. In short, the father had consulted many doctors, and applied every

---

[4] "I know the moment it happened/I know the grace I received/I was restored to health in the morning."

remedy that art could suggest, without any avail, and at last sought the aid of Blessed Leonard. The poor child had been in this state for two years; consumed, moreover, with a burning fever, which sometimes made him delirious. One evening when he was suffering more than usual, his father exhorted him to have faith, and say a *Pater, Ave,* and *Gloria* to Blessed Leonard, and touching him with a relic and his image, he placed both under his pillow, and in the morning found him quite well, the sore in his arm healed; the child got up and dressed himself, without the least sensation of pain, and never had a return of the malady.

Elisabetta Notarantonio Morelli, of Arpino, was cruelly tormented by a pain in her knee, which prevented her from walking without support, and she could not move without pain; in February, 1752, her sufferings increased, and she was induced to invoke the aid of Blessed Leonard, since every human remedy had failed; she applied a piece of cloth which he had worn over his chest to her knees, and instantly the pain ceased, and she who a few moments before was groaning in agony, was now quite joyous, and walked about the house to the astonishment of everyone, especially the doctor, who, with her, attested juridically to the truth of the miracle.

Atanasio of Ormea, a lay brother in the convent of S. Buonaventura, was afflicted for a whole year with an affection of the heart, which ended in dropsy, and his case was pronounced incurable. He was advised to have recourse to the intercession of Blessed Leonard; accordingly he swallowed a piece of his habit, and applied his image to his loins, when in a few moments he was restored to perfect health.

Signora Eugenia Visconti de' Cesari, of Tivoli, was suffering the pains of childbirth, and had not strength to bring forth the infant she bore in her womb; she became delirious, and her mother and the midwife who was assisting her, feared she would die. In their distress they had recourse to the intercession of

Blessed Leonard, and the midwife taking his image, uttered these words: "Father Leonard, if you are a saint in heaven, aid us, and bring to light of day this poor little creature, that it may receive holy baptism." Having said this, she applied the image, and two infants were born three months before their time; the first which came forth was living, but the other on examination proved to be dead. The living child was instantly baptized, and in their sorrow for the dead one, they again sought the aid of Blessed Leonard. The midwife placed his image on the body, and said, "Father Leonard, since you have worked one miracle, aid us once more, and make it plain to us whether this infant is living or dead." She had scarcely uttered the words when the child opened its eyes, and they baptized it. Half an hour after this both the infants expired, and all present returned thanks to God, for having, through the means of His servant, saved their souls.

Anna Vittoria Marchetti, who was placed, for education, in the convent of the Quattro Coronati, in Rome, for the space of three years was a great sufferer from several disorders, and amongst them a fever, which lasted two or three months; and when she was free from it, she never recovered her strength, but as the doctors declared, she seemed even worse after the fever had left her. On the 15th of October, 1751, she was attacked so severely, that the remedies they applied had no effect in easing her; she had a violent pain in her head, an affection of the chest, frequent fainting-fits, sleepless nights, loss of appetite, convulsions of the muscles and nerves, so that she became quite epileptic. The medicines they gave her had no effect, but on the contrary aggravated her sufferings; she was so reduced that she could not rise from her bed without the aid of crutches, and even with two persons to assist her, she sometimes fell. The doctors declared her to be hopelessly paralytic; she lay motionless, and so emaciated, that everyone who saw her was touched with compassion; she looked like a skeleton. Eight months had now passed since she was reduced to this pitiable state, when on the morning of the feast of the ascension, which that year fell on the 11th of May, the sacristan, sister Maria Serafina Pettuccioli, having written an account of her sufferings to Father Martino, of the monastery of S. Buonaventura, who was at that time their confessor extraordinary, he exhorted her to have recourse to Blessed Leonard. Sister Maria told the sick girl what was prescribed for her, and then left the room; Anna Vittoria immediately made an act of faith, took the image of Blessed Leonard, which was placed near her bed, and applied it to her leg, when instantly she felt herself entirely cured. Presently one of the nuns entered her room, and she asked for her clothes, put them on, and got out of bed without assistance, and declared she was entirely free from pain, her strength also returned at the same moment, and she recovered her flesh, and fresh bright complexion. As soon as she was dressed, she ran through the dormitory and downstairs, where the nuns and children were assembled, and joyfully related what had happened to her, and afterwards made her confessor acquainted with the facts. They were all filled with wonder on hearing of this miraculous cure, having just before seen her at the point of death, and looking almost like a corpse, and now she came before them in perfect health, and robust, as if she never had been ill. The following day Francesco Raniero Parazzini, the medical attendant of the convent, came to visit her, who, when he beheld her, was thunderstruck, and in order to feel more certain of the miracle, he ordered that no medicine should be given her, and that she should return to her former mode of life. This was done, but she continued in perfect health, and the nuns and the physician juridically testified to the miracle.

Sinforosa Betti, of Leprignano, the wife of Alessandro Pezza, in January, 1787, was returning home from Civitella through a wood, when she accidentally fell amongst the briars, and tore the skin off her leg; and although it was most painful, and the blood flowed, she continued her journey. On arriving at home she was occupied with other things, and took no thought of the accident until her leg became inflamed and swollen; there was a great discharge of blood and matter, which corroded the skin. Four or five days after, in putting on her shoes by mistake, she put the left shoe, which had been, steeped in the blood and matter which flowed from the sore, on the right foot, and caused a similar wound to break out in the right leg. It increased by degrees until it extended from her knee to her foot, and became so offensive that no one could bear to come near her. For some time she applied no remedy, but her sufferings increasing she consulted a surgeon, who pronounced her case incurable. However, to alleviate the pain, and correct the acrimony of the blood, he prescribed some decoctions of herbs, and other medicines, which were of no avail. In July, 1788, she went to Rome, where she consulted another surgeon, who also pronounced her case incurable, and although he ordered her some ointment to mitigate the pain, it was of no use. At last she applied dock leaves, but this failed; nothing was found of the least avail; the evil increased every day and was terrible to behold. At the end of September, 1789, she was to return to Leprignano with her companion Felice Perini, and on the 19th she went to the church of S. Buonaventura, to ask the prayers of Blessed Leonard. As she went along she kept constantly saying, "My Saint, cure my leg." This was her only prayer; for as she said, the pain prevented her even saying a *Pater noster*. Whilst she was thus praying, the pain by degrees ceased in both legs, and she felt a great irritation in the skin, a sign of the cure effected, and on her return home she walked without the least difficulty. She slept soundly all night, and the following day returned to Leprignano, her native place. As soon as she reached home she took off her shoes, and found both her legs entirely cured, the linen with which they were swathed and the dock leaves fell off, quite dry; she saw to her great amazement and joy that all the sores were healed, as well as the swelling and inflammation, and the skin perfectly smooth and healthy. She called her husband quickly, who was quite astonished, as also were the neighbors, and all praised the Lord, for having, through the merits of His servant, worked so great a miracle.

These two last most wonderful miracles were proposed and examined according to the usual most rigid rules in the holy Congregation of Rites by the Pontiff Pius VI, and published by the decree of Approbation, on the 2nd of August, 1795, when the holy pontiff went to the monastery of S. Buenaventura, and caused the same proclamation to be made in the room from whence Blessed Leonard ascended to heaven, leaving us so bright an example to imitate, and a firm faith that we may obtain through his intercession graces and favors from heaven. If we consider all his apostolical labors, his heroic virtues, described to the best of our abilities in the present volume, we may truly say as did Monsignore Pieragostini, bishop of San Severino, when in 1740 he gave a mission in his diocese. This worthy prelate, in a sermon he preached on the devotion to the Blessed Virgin, took the occasion to speak in praise of Blessed Leonard, and after having declared that he was a man sent from heaven to extirpate vice and plant virtue, and that, according to the signification of his name, he was a lion, who, with his roaring, made hell tremble, and raised souls who were dead in their sins, and that he was also the oil of spikenard, for with the odor of his virtues lie regenerated the Church: he concluded by repeating the following lines:

"Praeco Leonardus. Leo profert ore salutem.
Nardus virtutem replet odore domum."